INFORMATICS
AND TEACHER TRAINING

IFIP Working Conference on
Informatics and Teacher Training
Birmingham, U.K., 16-20 July, 1984

organised by
Working Group 3.1 of
IFIP Technical Committee 3, Education
International Federation for Information Processing

Programme Committee
J. D. Tinsley (UK), P. Bollerslev (Denmark), U. Bosler (FRG),
F. B. Lovis (Editor, UK) B. Samways (UK),
E. D. Tagg (Editor, UK), T. van Weert (The Netherlands)

Organising Committee
B. Samways, M. Puddephat, P. Russell,
J. D. Tinsley, E. Vincent, C. Watkins (all UK)

NORTH-HOLLAND
AMSTERDAM ● NEW YORK ● OXFORD

INFORMATICS
AND TEACHER TRAINING

Proceedings of the IFIP WG 3.1 Working Conference on
Informatics and Teacher Training
Birmingham, U.K., 16-20 July, 1984

edited by

F. B. LOVIS
Faculty of Mathematics
The Open University, U.K.

and

E. D. TAGG
Formerly Senior Lecturer in Mathematics
University of Lancaster, U.K.

1984

NORTH-HOLLAND
AMSTERDAM ● NEW YORK ● OXFORD

ISBN: 0 444 87639 1

Published by:
ELSEVIER SCIENCE PUBLISHERS B.V.
P.O. Box 1991
1000 BZ Amsterdam
The Netherlands

Sole distributors for the U.S.A. and Canada:
ELSEVIER SCIENCE PUBLISHING COMPANY, INC.
52 Vanderbilt Avenue
New York, N.Y. 10017
U.S.A.

Library of Congress Cataloging in Publication Data

IFIP WG 3.1 Working Conference on Informatics and
    Teacher Training (1984 : Birmingham, West Midlands,
    England)
    Informatics and teacher training.

    "Organised by Working Group 3.1 of IFIP Technical
Committee 3, Education, International Federation for
Information Processing"--
    1. Electronic data processing--Study and teaching--
Congresses. 2. Electronic data processing--Teacher
training--Congresses. I. Lovis, F. B. (Frank B.)
II. Tagg, E. D., 1913-   . III. International
Federation for Information Processing. Working Group 3.1.
IV. Title.
QA76.27.I337 1984   001.64'07   84-21040
ISBN 0-444-87639-1

PRINTED IN THE NETHERLANDS

PREFACE

Technical Committee 3 (TC 3) of the International Federation for Information Processing (IFIP) oversees the activities of five Working Groups, one of which, WG 3.1, is concerned very much with the field of teacher training.

WG 3.1 organised a working conference which took place at Birmingham Polytechnic, UK, from 16th to 20th July 1984. The theme was 'Informatics and Teacher Training'. A total of 24 papers was presented and the contents of a number of subsequent discussion sessions were carefully recorded. These papers and discussion reports form the main part of the contents of these proceedings.

The task of organising the logistics of this Conference was undertaken by a committee under the Chairmanship of Brian Samways, Director of Birmingham Educational Computing Centre. The Birmingham Polytechnic proved to be an ideal site for the conference and the arrangements for accomodation were excellent. We are most grateful to Brian Samways and his team for the hard work which made our stay so pleasant and, in particular to the secretaries, Mrs. Sally Mills, Ms. Sue Tittley and Mrs. Maureen Walker, who worked so hard and willingly during the whole conference.

As Chairman of WG 3.1, I finally express my heartfelt thanks to the two Editors of this book, who worked as hard as anyone to enable us to have these proceedings published in good time to make a significant contribution to the field of 'Informatics and Teacher Training'.

In conclusion, this book is in essence a bank of ideas : you are invited to use them as you will.

Peter Bollerslev
Chairman WG 3.1

EDITORIAL

The papers and the discussions of each group of papers are arranged in the order in which they were presented. There is one collective report on the activities of the various discussion groups and this, together with the report on the one plenary session, will be found after the last paper.

After the suppression of the inevitable, but slight, early hiccups, the text processing system provided for our use by the host institution, the City of Birmingham Polytechnic, proved invaluable and greatly lightened our labours. We are most grateful to all those who helped to make this possible and also to the speedy and efficient rapporteurs.

Above all, though, our thanks are due to the two ladies who supplied unfailing, eager secretarial assistance — Mrs. Sally Mills and Ms. Sue Tittley.

Frank Lovis
Donovan Tagg
Editors

TABLE OF CONTENTS

OPENING SESSION

Councillor J. Eames, Chairman of the City of Birmingham Education Committee, in formally welcoming members of the conference to the City, looked forward to seeing the conclusions of the conference. Birmingham took a pride in being a technically advanced city and in its innovative roll in computer education. It was expected that advances would be accelerated when more money became available.

Mr. Graham Shaylor, City Planning Officer, also welcomed members to Birmingham as the officer responsible for advising the City on measures to deal with its severe unemployment and recession problems. He looked to IFIP to contribute to the solution of some of the problems through assisting in the use of new technology in training programmes for young people and for the redundant to help them towards self-employment or change of occupation. Birmingham was making its contribution in setting up high technology at Aston University, in encouraging conventions and large conferences at the National Exhibition Centre and in organising schemes for the training of young people and the redundant.

Mr. Peter Bollerslev, Chairman of IFIP WG 3.1, welcomed members of the conference on behalf of IFIP. He outlined the work that the Working Group had done since its formation in 1967. From the early 70s it had recognised Teacher Training as a key issue, first of all in Secondary Schools and more recently also in Elementary Schools. He expected that all would be much wiser at the end of a meeting of such a highly qualified group anmd emphasised that this was a working conference.

At the reception kindly provided by the Lord Mayor and Lady Mayoress, the Lord Mayor gave his welcome to the conference and expressed his pleasure that Birmingham was able to act as host to the working conference following previous conferences in Bulgraria, Paris and West Germany. Birmingham had been much involved in pioneering the development of Teacher Training in Informatics through the close partnership between the Education Department, the University of Birmingham, Westhill and Newman Colleges and the Polytechnic where the conference is being held.

Mr. P. Bollerslev thanked the Lord Mayor and Lady Mayoress for their hospitality and for the honour they had done the conference by their presence.

OPENING ADDRESS

TEACHER TRAINING IN ENGLAND, WALES AND NORTHERN IRELAND

Richard Fothergill
Director, Microelectronics Education Programme

On behalf of the Microelectronics Education Programme in this Country, may I welcome you to Britain and this conference. MEP is a Programme, sponsored by the Departments of Education of England, Northern Ireland and Wales, which has within its remit a responsibility for teacher training in microelectronics for primary and secondary schools, and I am sure you will be hearing a considerable amount, both good and bad, about its activities during this conference. My brief, this afternoon, is to give a rapid survey of the various approaches to the teacher training problem that we have adopted during the last three and a half years since the Programme began.

Before I start, just a few statistics that will give you an idea of the scale of the problem. The territory the Programme covers, which omits Scotland which has its own Programme, is divided among 109 Local Education Authorities, each with their responsibility for the curriculum in their schools and for in-service training of its teachers, and all very independent-minded, I must add. There are over 400,000 teachers in the primary and secondary schools, and our figures show that about 100,000 of them, that is about a quarter, have been on our courses or used our materials at some time. We have an annual budget of around £4.5 million per year, and almost 40% of this is devoted to teacher training.

Now, how have we approached the problem? The answer is in a variety of ways which I will try and spell out to you in the time left to me. Among the major impacts on our activities have been the hardware schemes for school initiated by the Department of Trade and Industry. That for secondary schools was the first, the offer being half the purchase price of one or two computer systems, which was taken up by nearly all of them. At our insistence, a teacher training programme was a condition of the scheme, each school having to send two teachers for training. This was undertaken on a taught course of at least four days and made use of a range of materials, which we prepared centrally and which we taught the tutors and advisers provided by the Authorities to use. I ought to add that some Local Education Authorities required longer courses from their teachers, and quite rightly added their own materials as well. With the Primary scheme that followed, a very much larger number of schools were able to choose one of three computer systems, again at the half price arrangement. This offer has not completed its run, but it looks likely that well over 90% of the Primary schools will take advantage of it. In this case too, training for two teachers was a requirement, but instead of a totally tutored course, a substantial pack of self study materials was provided, followed by about two days of tutoring. Again, several Authorities required more time than this.

Both these courses were really only designed as basic introductions to the computer. Indeed, the circumstances prevented them from being more. At the beginning, there is a major requirement for such simple computer literacy, and it was this general awareness which featured prominently in the early days of our more substantial in-service operation. Let me start by a brief description of this.

We have divided the field of work of the Programme into four domains, rather artificial but a practical necessity. These are electronics and control technology; the computer, which incorporates computer studies, computer based learning across the curriculum; communication and information studies, which includes business studies, as well as the more obvious work on information retrieval and databases. To organise the training, we appointed a national co-ordinator for each domain, and each of these was assisted by regional co-ordinators in all fourteen of the regions into which the Authorities helped us to divide the country. Between them, that is the national co-ordinator and his team of regional co-ordinators, and with the assistance of a working advisory group of wide expertise, an analysis of the needs for in-service training was undertaken. This exercise resulted in the development of a range of modules which could be offered separately or collectively as courses. Three layers of courses were defined, awareness, intermediate and advanced, all basically available as short courses as necessary. As for the clientele, this was defined as trainers in the local authorities - each of our regions has an average of nine authorities in it - although from the beginning, many of our courses were attended by practising school teachers. The training from our side is done by our regional co-ordinators, but often there are many other practitioners in the field adding their expertise as well. The teachers and trainers on the courses come with Local Authority support and mostly at their expense as well, so there is considerable commitment and investment from the authorities in this system. At the end of their course, it is hoped that the teachers and trainers go back to their authorities and schools and train up other teachers, on the cascade principle. In many cases, this is working very successfully, but in others the cascade stops very soon after it starts, and this is a pity. After all, as every good teacher knows, the best way of learning is to teach others, and the trainers should benefit greatly from its operation.

One of the important features of these courses, based as I have indicated, on a centrally designed set of modules, has been the encouragement given to regions to add their own materials and sections, so that they reflect the interests and special features that are needed in that part of the country. Apart from the practical value of this, that is the inclusion of items that meet the real needs of the local teachers, such an approach introduces new ideas and materials to the courses, and these are brought back with experience of their value to the update meetings of the co-ordinators in each domain. These meetings occur regularly, about four or five times a year, and the co-ordinators work together on new materials and devices, new approaches to their teaching, identification of new needs, and reflect back to each other their experiences around the country and the reactions of their clients. From this constant feedback, the courses have been amended, enlivened and hopefully are more closely attuned to the real needs of the teachers they service.

Over the two and half years they have been running, certain trends have become clear. Courses are getting longer, particularly in computer studies, and we are now preparing for long courses of 150 hours or more. For each of our courses modules, written materials, software and other items have been produced in more permanent forms, and these are getting increasingly linked to new devices and materials that are emerging from the many curriculum development projects that the Programme sponsors.

Since the government-sponsored primary scheme was announced, the need for work in this sector has become urgent. Feeding off the work of our cascade system would be insufficient and inadequate, and so we have initiated a national primary project. Once more, the target is the 700 or so trainers of primary teachers in our colleges and local authorities. Courses are being held all round the country, slightly amended to reflect local interests, experience and needs. At the end of each course, the trainers take away packs of materials and software, which they can and do use on their own courses for their teachers. We have only six months experience of this so far, but the feedback is proving very positive indeed.

In the field of Special Education, that is the schools for children with special learning needs, we started with a series of courses which built up awareness and concentrated also on helping with aids to communication for the physically handicapped. These are also supported by our information centres for special education.

Central courses of this type have finished, and we have now moved into those that deal with curriculum definition and the specification of materials, courses which are similar to those in intermediate and advanced levels in our cascade system. Interestingly, this is a natural development from the needs of the teachers, particularly with the bulk of the general introductory work being done by the information centres.

Those then are the substantial, tutored courses that form our in-service training activities. However, in parallel to these, we have been preparing materials for trainers who will be training teachers of business studies in schools and further education. Now that the electronic office is becoming increasingly commonplace, there is a great deal of retraining required for these teachers and a package has been developed in association with the appropriate examination board. Another very substantial package has also been produced in association with another major organisation, the Open University. It has produced a series of five packs, each a self-standing module but with distinct links to the others. While there are variations in detail, each of these distance learning packs contains a study text, reader, project book, software, or device. The general titles for each module are Awareness, Educational Software,

Microelectronics, Microcomputers and Micros in Action in the Classroom. I referred earlier to a device, because the Open University has developed a special instrument, called Desmond, to assist teachers studying the microelectronics module with their understanding of the technology.

One of the major problems facing us in the preparation of these packages, and indeed the ones that accompany the tutored modules that I described earlier, has been to fit the practical work to the computer to which the teachers had access. Through the government schemes, we have narrowed this to just the three in the primary and secondary schemes, but this still means three versions of the software. The Open University packages introduced a further complication for themselves, because the educational software module was dependent in part on the use of LOGO. Unfortunately, there was no version available for one of the most popular machines, in spite of promises, and it is only now that it is appearing. The best laid plans for materials often run into these unforeseen troubles.

Materials for in-service training do not always take the form of courses, as such. Much can be learned from books, videos, tape-slides and so on, and the programme has been diligent in preparing a wide selection. Some 30 videos, for example, are now available and being used, and in books, we have been supporting the preparation of case studies and readers. I am particularly pleased with the latter series, five already in print, three more on their way through the printers and others in preparation, as they present a wide spectrum of views and attitudes to the value of the computer in different subject areas like English, Geography and Biology. Teacher who read them generally seem to find at least one writer with whom they can feel total empathy. Our latest venture is to produce a series entitled 'Reports from the classroom', written by good journalists, and giving a broader perspective than just the teachers' views. As these emerge later this year, I hope they will find a complementary place alongside the case studies and readers, together providing a rich description of the best way to get the most out of the computer in the classroom.

Of course, you may say that those publications are hardly in-service training as you would describe it. However, I would argue that all means that help teachers understand the activities that are facilitated by the new technologies and become sensitive to them are helpful and could be covered by that term. Another way of improving the value of all the modular material that we have had written, and also making the books and videos more helpful is the development of supported self-study. We have just commissioned the preparation of linking texts which will help a small group of teachers, working together in a school, get closer to the values behind these materials, through group study. They should be on trial very shortly now.

There is another area of in-service training that needs to be referred to, and that is through the development of curriculum materials. One critic, decrying some of our projects, described them as an 'expensive form of in-service training'. Not so expensive really, but those projects that have failed to result in useful materials have proved valuable in training the developers. In our successful projects, the vast majority I must add, there is a considerable amount of valuable learning taking place among the teachers involved. We have over 200 projects happening now, some 90 of them substantial. In some people's view, this is some of the most valuable in-service training that we are doing, particularly when the participants in some of our projects move into other groups sponsored by different organisations like the local authorities. It has always been true that good in-service training is associated with curriculum development. One of our other strategies to pass the benefits onwards is to associate a regional co-ordinator with a curriculum development project, as a link person. In the best cases, the co-ordinators are being helpful to the developers, gaining an insight into the decision-making as the development proceeds, and preparing ways of presenting the finished materials to teachers on their courses later. In the meantime, they will be sharing their knowledge of these developments with their fellow co-ordinators at the updating meetings that I referred to at the beginning of this talk.

Up to now, I have only discussed our approach to in-service training. We concentrated on that first, because it was going to have the fastest impact on the contemporary classroom, but there is obvious concern about pre-service training, the preparation of new teachers. So far, we have only nibbled at the edges of this issue, offering four briefing courses of a week or so each for representatives from colleges. Naturally they have access to most of the in-service materials, and are using many of them. There is also some joint development work in the preparation of our longer courses, but for the most part the leading Colleges have been preparing their own approaches, in many cases based on the definition of modules that we prepared for our in-service courses. Our co-ordinators too, many of whom are attached to Colleges where pre-service training takes place, are often used as points of expertise.

And so we have come full circle. I hope you have gained the impression of a wide range of approaches to the problem of teacher training. Some accompany hardware, to help teachers get started. The most substantial attack is through the tutored courses at different levels of difficulty and over a wide spectrum of subject areas. Backing this up are distance learning packages for those who would prefer this approach, or who cannot attend courses conveniently. In addition, there is a range of supplementary materials and books trying to give depth and a perspective to the studies. Finally, there is the curriculum development activity.

Teacher training is a major imperative to meet the challenge of information technology. It is a never-ending task, for after you have been round once, the technology has moved on and there is more to be learned. In this Instant Coffee age, the hardware may change rapidly, but teachers' attitudes take much longer. The future demands endless retraining, and that is why our groups of co-ordinators, constantly updated, and with their continually upgraded materials, will have to maintain their work for a very long time to come.

KEYNOTE ADDRESS

David Tinsley
Education Officer, Birmingham Education Department.

It is a privilege to have the opportunity to deliver the keynote address at this important international working conference. I have been a member of Working Group 3.1 for over fifteen years and can vouch for the benefits which can flow from such an association. In particular, the development of computer education in Birmingham owes much of its intellectual quality, organisational arrangements and practical good sense to the influence of the International Federation for Information Processing. This Conference has now given Birmingham the opportunity to say thank you to friends and colleagues from across the world who have contributed so much to our work, particularly in the field of teacher education.

The theme of our working conference is informatics and teacher training, a topic about which IFIP has been concerned since the establishment of this Working Group. At first, the need was for a forum and an information source for the few enthusiastic pioneers in secondary schools who had seen the potential of the computer in the educational process. Sufficient interest was aroused within IFIP member countries that by 1970 a key World Conference on Computer Education was held in Amsterdam during which this Working Group played both an organisational and a developmental role. A series of booklets was planned on the theme of Computer Education for Teachers in Secondary Schools which were published over succeeding years following detailed and intensive consultation within the group:

> "An Outline Guide to Computing Concepts"
> "Aims and Objectives in Teacher Training"
> "The Use of the Computer in Teaching and Learning
> (with Working Group 3.3)"
> "Elements of Information and Information Processing"
> "Analysis and Algorithms"

These booklets had wide circulation within IFIP member organisations and enabled those who were becoming responsible for the development of informatics education in their own countries to refer to a professional base line which helped to qualify any local bureaucratic, structural or financial constraints. In particular, the Working Group joined with the Organisation for Economic Co-operation and Development in Paris to help formulate governmental policies and visited Spain and Atlanta, Georgia to assist with the preparation of local strategies for curriculum development.

Let me try to illustrate this influence by two examples in this city. The introduction in 1974 of an on-line computing service to schools based on the Open University student computing service was a direct result of

the advice of IFIP to use the computer as an illustrative tool rather
than to dwell on the latest manifestation of the circuit makers' art.
Secondly, contact with the Minnesota Educational Computing Centre (MECC)
in St. Paul had shown us the way forward in the provision of computing
services for schools and colleges. Its methods and systems were
reflected in the contributions to IFIP of its key teacher educator,
Professor David Johnson, who I am pleased to say is joining us for part
of this Working Conference as is the Director of Curriculum Development
at MECC, Dr. Pollak.

The most significant strategy for teacher education in informatics in
Birmingham has been, however, the creation of a team of peripatetic
resource teachers working from the Educational Computing Centre at
Bordesley. This team has been able to work alongside teachers who have
had no previous experience of teaching informatics and has been the
channel through which new teachers of the subject can gain access to
curriculum materials, appropriate software and advice on hardware
systems. The specification of the tasks of such a team of specialist
advisory teachers had already been drawn up by Working Group WG3.1 at its
Atlanta, Georgia meeting which led to the publication of the booklet
"Aims and Objectives in Teacher Training".

The first Director of the Birmingham Centre, Eric Vincent, has now
retired but is acting as Bursar to this conference and the current
Director, Brian Samways, is Chairman of the Local Organising Committee.
I would like to pay particular tribute to the work of these two
colleagues in the preparations for this international event.

The 1970's saw a dramatic growth in the development of secondary school
computing and IFIP responded by creating a wider forum for discussion
between experts of the content and practice of educational computing.
The World Conferences at Marseilles in 1975 and in Lausanne in 1981
showed how interest and resources had expanded in most countries. But
the most important aspects of curriculum content and professional
practice could not adequately be debated in such large gatherings. The
Working Conference, however, gives an opportunity for detailed debate
between invited experts from IFIP member countries. Through the
publication of invited papers and reports of the discussion on these
papers IFIP can provide the opportunity for a wider international
audience to partake in the intellectual stimulus we are to enjoy for the
rest of this week.

Three Working Conference have already been organised by this Working
Group. They were

    "Informatics and Mathematics; Impacts and Relationships"
        Varna, Bulgaria, 1977

    "Microcomputers in Secondary Education"
        Sevres, France, 1980

    "Informatics in Elementary Education"
        Kiel, Germany, 1983

In Bulgaria we explored the relationship between informatics and mathematics. For many years, teachers of mathematics had taken responsibility for teaching about the computer as if the subjects were synonymous. The 1976 Working Conference helped to clarify the differences and the similarities and showed what elements of the discipline of mathematics were essential to a proper understanding of computing and where the computer could help support the learning of mathematics.

The Paris working conference was arranged at a time when microcomputers were heralding a significant reduction in the cost of practical work in computing but were also showing how lessons learnt in support of more expensive main frame and network systems could easily be forgotten if the price of inferior facilities was the main attraction.

Finally last year in Malente, Germany, we were able to consider the progress made in developing the use of computers in primary education. The papers and discussion showed that judgements could now be made on some aspects of new curriculum practice but the conference concluded that much further study was required before an acceptable overall philosophy could emerge.

So why have we chosen the theme of teacher training for this particular conference when so much has already been done by the Working Group? Simply because we regard teacher education as the fundamental issue in the development of informatics at both primary and secondary level and we believe that we must continue regularly to review our theories and practice in this important field.

During the week ahead we will be hearing about the teacher training systems of various countries and will have the opportunity to find out what each other is doing. The papers provide the basic information but the discussion will bring out the main problems and opportunities we are all facing. By publishing our activities we will aim to achieve a wide dissemination of ideas and experience so as to reduce the time lag between new developments and their general implementation. In particular we shall be concerned with the problems of how software is developed and evaluated, so that other colleagues in other places can benefit from the collective expertise of our working conference.

My responsibility, however, must be to set your themes for the conference and to point out those particular elements which have arisen in my own career which might prove helpful as a stimulus to debate. I have therefore listed five phrases which illustrate on our local experience of teacher training Birmingham:

> "Teachers need time"
> "Concepts not hardware"
> "Not invented here"
> "Who teaches the teachers of teachers?"
> "Students know more than teachers"

<u>Teachers need time</u> to become sufficiently familiar with information
processing before they can feel confident enough to conduct a class.
Unfortunately there are insufficient opportunities for teachers to stand
back from the routine of their professional activities to prepare
adequately for the adoption of a new and rapidly developing curriculum.
In the rush to bring our schools "up to date" by the installation of the
latest product from the computer manufacturer, we often forget that the
philosophy and practice of teaching informatics are still being formed
and that teachers lack the background which is normal in more traditional
subject areas.

Perhaps in time we will be able to rely on the standard training sequence
for potential teachers of informatics, namely pre-service courses which
consider both content and methodology. But the novelty of informatics is
such that many pre-service training agencies have yet to incorporate the
subject within their graduate or post graduate studies. Until that is
done, teachers will have to rely on their own initiatives and on the many
in-service courses which are are being organised to support the expansion
of informatics courses within the school curriculum.

<u>Concepts not hardware</u> is a theme which IFIP has continually addressed
within the Working Group which has organised this conference. It is
interesting to compare the topics of today with the outline guides of
1970. The continuous and rapid changes which have taken place in
computer systems should not mask the few basic concepts which still
underpin the justification for including a study of informatics within
the standard curriculum. A study of the algorithm, an understanding of
of automation and a sympathy for the effect of new technology on the
lives of individuals and whole communities - all are matters which can
lay claim to a key place in the education of the whole person.

We heard from Professor Jaques Hebenstreit in 1973 that we were in danger
of producing a generation of "FORTRAN idiots". A later concern was that
we might become "BASIC idiots" instead. The main concept of the computer
program as a mechanical interpretation of the algorithm became lost in a
preoccupation with coding systems and the computer you could get rather
than the one you wanted. Fortunately the "top down" languages of the
1980's have enabled teachers to concentrate on the development of problem
solving techniques in their students rather than on skill in making do
with what you have got in the latest home computer.

The same difficulty arises with the use of video screens for the delivery
of teaching materials rather than books, pictures, slides or tapes. We
must be on our guard lest we accept a lower quality teaching product from
the computer than that which calls upon more traditional publishing
skills. We may find that interactive video does provide a generally
useful tool for education but until more experience is gained within
ordinary classroom practice on robust and reliable equipment, we are
right to be cautious of people making claims for new technologies.

The <u>not invented here</u> syndrome is a particular worry in this regard.
Whilst it is an exciting challenge to teachers to develop their own
teaching material and for groups of teachers to prepare new courses

within workshops, there are dangers if the local leaders of these groups have no access to the work of pioneers who have passed through their early love affair with the computer and have started to reflect on whether computer based education really does create a better environment for learning. Within our Working Group we have addressed some of these fundamental themes: what is the relationship between algorithms, computer programming and the learning of mathematics?; are data and information synonymous?; what are the elements of good design in a computer based learning system?

It is, I would maintain, a crucial responsibility of those of us who can benefit from a workshop such as this to take back and promulgate good practice and to persuade those with governmental and financial responsibility that not only do teachers need time but so also do the teachers of teachers and the <u>teachers</u> of <u>teachers</u> of <u>teachers</u>. This is where a professional body such as IFIP can point the way and provide an independent forum for the debate of uncomfortable ideas. The outcome should be greater co-operation over the dissemination of proven technique rather than the calm acceptance of advertisers' claims. Local professional associations can also do much to promote a healthy scepticism of current curriculum arrangements and can alert all concerned with teaching to the danger of being overwhelmed by a rapidly changing technology.

Finally I would propose that we must ensure that teachers do not prevent students from learning. It is evident that <u>students often know more than their teachers</u> about advances in new technology. They have fresh minds which can adapt rapidly to the advent of new tools and techniques. Perhaps teachers now have the chance to break through with individualised learning and become true conductors of learning. class. We must not, however, underestimate the difficulty which the majority of teachers will face if such a change comes about. To relax and work alongside students who may know more than you requires great confidence and skill. For some teachers this is too democratic a process and unacceptable as a system of education.

But during this week we will hear about the discoveries which children make through their exploration of the LOGO environment. We will exchange information about the management of teacher training and the development of individualised learning systems. We will also hear about the evaluation of new teaching materials and see demonstrations of the latest software creations from the authors of computer based materials. I trust that my scepticism will help you to remain critical and that we can all benefit from professional debate on the merits of our current practice. Through such exchange comes real progress.

Ladies and gentlemen, I wish you well for a successful conference.

SESSION 1

Chairman: Donovan Tagg

INFORMATICS AND TEACHER TRAINING
F.B. Lovis and E.D. Tagg (editors)
Elsevier Science Publishers B.V. (North-Holland)
© IFIP, 1984

IN-SERVICE TEACHER TRAINING IN INFORMATICS
(For Teachers in Lower Secondary Education)

Tom J. van Weert

Department of Mathematics
Institute for Teacher Education
'Ubbo Emmius'
Groningen, The Netherlands.

Organisation for
Post-Academic Education
in Informatics
Amsterdam, The Netherlands.

Abstract

The organisation for post-academic education in informatics
(PAE in informatics) has developed a model syllabus for
post-academic courses in informatics for teachers, comprising
a model syllabus for pupils as an integral part. In this
paper part of both model syllabuses will be presented: a
model syllabus (literacy in informatics) for all pupils (in
the age range from 12 to 14 years) and a model syllabus for
in-service courses in informatics for teachers in lower
secondary education who want to teach informatics as a
discipline. The institute for teacher education 'Ubbo
Emmius' has developed a literacy course in informatics for
all teachers along the lines set out in the model syllabus
(literacy in informatics) for all pupils. This course will
also be discussed in this paper.

1. INTRODUCTION

The Dutch universities cooperate with one another in organizations that provide
post-academic courses in certain subjects. One such organization for Post-Academic
Education in Informatics (PAE in Informatics) on the one hand provides
post-academic courses for professionals in the field of informatics and on the
other hand in-service courses in informatics for teachers. A model syllabus was
developed for these post-academic courses for teachers (who want to teach
informatics as a discipline) comprising a model syllabus for pupils as an integral
part. This model syllabus for pupils (in the age range from about 12 to about 14
years) is aimed at literacy in informatics for all pupils and covers four subject
areas: Informatics and Society, Use of Application Systems, Problem Analysis and
Programming and the fourth, Principles of Software and Machine Architecture. The
syllabus favours a didactical method whereby pupils gain their own experience as
end-users of very sheltered application or algorithmic environments.
The model syllabus for post-academic in-service courses presupposes teachers who
want to join those courses to be literate in informatics. To bridge the gap for
teachers without any experience in informatics the department of mathematics of
Ubbo Emmius has developed a literacy course in informatics for all teachers along
the lines set out in the model syllabus 'Literacy in informatics for all pupils'.
In this paper the PAE in Informatics model syllabuses and the Ubbo Emmius literacy
course for all teachers are described.

2. LITERACY IN INFORMATICS FOR ALL PUPILS [PAOI 83] [NGI 83]

The model syllabus 'Literacy in Informatics' is defined on the basis of the
hypothesis that:
- the learning content is intended to reach all pupils
- for part of the pupils this literacy in informatics will be the only thing
  taught about informatics, while other pupils will use this literacy as a basis

for further studies; the learning content therefore has to be reasonably self-contained, but also has to provide a good basis for other courses in informatics
- knowledge and skills concerning informatics are rapidly changing; it is therefore desirable to impart invariant knowledge to the pupils and have them develop invariant skills, i.e. knowledge and skills that are not dependent on a particular machine or particular software

The central issue in the syllabus is to bring about insight which enables the pupils to develop a reasoned and balanced attitude towards informatics and which enables them furthermore to react appropriately to situations in which contact with automated systems takes place.

Four important means to achieve this goal are:
1. The gaining of experience in man-machine interactions, where such interactions take place as end-user of application software and (only in as far as cannot be avoided) as end-user of operating system software.
2. The gaining of experience with situations where informatics is or is not able to provide for the needs of the individual or society. In reference to these experiences much weight should be laid on reasons for and consequences of these situations.
3. The development of good models of thinking which enable the pupils to think adequately about their experience of automated systems. The development of these models relies heavily on the systematic use of 'black boxes' (i.e. elements of which the pupil does not know the internal functioning).
4. The gaining of some experience with algorithmic thinking and modular struct- ures. This experience should be broad in that it gives the pupils an overview, and should be gained through problem solving. This will be possible with the aid of software and hardware that enables the pupils to solve problems in a very sheltered (i.e. user friendly) application or algorithmic environment.
The above implies that a central point in the teaching of literacy in informatics is that the pupils gain their own experience. Learning content, learning material and teacher activities have to enable the pupils to gain insight and to develop a 'reasoned and balanced attitude' towards informatics.

The learning content can be separated into four main subject areas:
A. **Informatics and society**
B. **Use of application systems**
C. **Problem analysis and programming**
D. **Principles of software and machine architecture**

2.1 LEARNING CONTENT

The most important problem in filling in the learning content is the fact that this content has to be suitable for all pupils in an age range from about 12 to about 14 years. The learning material should not demotivate a pupil by lack of structure or degree of difficulty.

A. **Informatics and society**

The following aspects are of importance:
- the gathering of data
- the protection and integrity of data
- changing methods of work
- changing employment
- quality of work
- influence on individuals and their cooperation
- influence on organizations
- influence of simulation
These aspects should be treated while teaching the learning content of **B: Use of application systems**. In this treatment reasons for, consequences of, enhancement

and limitation of opportunities because of the computer related formalisation (including the algorithmic approach) should play a role. These should not only be seen in today's perspective but also be related to past and future.

B. Use of application systems

The title of this subject area is not chosen at random. It reflects the active gaining of experience which is aimed at here. The classroom treatment of this subject area should have a strong relation with subject area **A: Informatics and society**.

On the one hand an overview should be given to the application areas given below, on the other hand pupils should work actively with available application systems as much as possible.
Application areas suitable for treatment are:
- text processing
    e.g. club journal, club correspondence, professional text processing
- information systems
    . retrieval systems like videotex, library systems, reservation systems, hospital systems
    . administrative systems like school administration, social security or wage payment systems, banking systems
- simulation systems
    e.g. population growth, agricultural production
- process control
    e.g. traffic light systems, robotics
- applications in education
    . learning with the aid of informatics
    . learning by means of informatics (Computer Assisted Instruction, Computer Managed Instruction)

For each type of application some examples were given. Some of these are closely related to the everyday environment of the pupil. Others involve stepping out of this environment.
Finding a motivating form does not seem to present problems. Not only are very concrete 'do it yourself' experiences possible, but also excursions e.g. to an automated design department, a library with an automated index, or a computer managed farm.

C. Problem analysis and programming

The aim here is to let the pupil gain some experience with:
- algorithmic thinking
- modular structure
- strategies for problem solution and systematic refinement of algorithms
- programming in a sheltered application or algorithmic environment

The applications summed up in **B. Use of application systems** should play a role in problem analysis and programming, especially in concretely demonstrating the finding of solutions for complex unstructured problems and in enabling pupils to 'program' solutions for simple application oriented problems in a sheltered application or algorithmic environment. But other more or less isolated problems can also be treated in the classroom.
From the above it follows that the pupil should be confronted with very diverse sheltered application environments (e.g. very user friendly implementations of applications suitable for the pupils). The teaching material should be suitable and motivating for boys and for girls, for pupils oriented towards the exact sciences and for pupils who are not, for pupils from different cultural backgrounds, etc..

When trying to find a good and correct translation of the abstract notions mentioned above to concrete learning material one should look for examples which will not dominate too much or alienate some pupils. Therefore, it seems wise to try and find examples outside arithmetic (e.g. numeric algorithms) and the manipulation of texts. One could for instance find examples in the area of graphical applications. A possible way to organize the learning material could be first to have the pupil design a few basic algorithms (or to have him make changes in existing algorithms) and second to have the pupil construct higher algorithms from the first ones. These algorithms could then be translated to programs, to be run in a sheltered application or algorithmic environment.

D. Principles of software and machine architecture

- The fundamental notion is that of <u>process</u>, described in a <u>program</u> and executed by a <u>processor</u>
- Storage/memory
- The different levels on which one can communicate with a machine (the total of hardware and software)
- Data communication
- Micro-electronics

The aim here is to provide the pupil with functional models which enable him or her to understand the experiences gained in the interaction with the 'machine'. It is very important to stress the idea that all results of computers are brought about as a result of data and values put into the computer by human beings. Insight into the structure of a system requires the pupils to learn and work with black boxes.

2.2 PRESENTATION OF THE LEARNING CONTENT

- At all times the teacher should be aware of the fact that the learning content is meant to reach <u>all</u> pupils.
- The presentation of the learning content should be directed towards the pupils gaining their own experience in a human-machine interaction: learning by doing.
- This process of gaining experience of their own can be influenced by group processes; the teacher should try to stop these processes from frustrating the

- While letting the pupils gain their own experience the teacher has to stop the chance material or the chance examples from dominating the learning process; the aim is to supply the pupil with general and invariant notions which will lead the pupil towards developing models of thinking and the gaining of an independent attitude.
- Because of the importance of bringing about insight which will lead to a reasoned and balanced attitude, several didactic models can be used; learning material from the subject areas **A** to **D** could be suitably presented in a concentric way around 'nodes' in the lessons; the nodes being taken from **B. Use of application systems.**
- The didactic model has to be made concrete in practice. One essential element is, however, the close relation to reality, to the everyday environment of the pupils, in particular when new concepts are to be learned.

3. A LITERACY COURSE IN INFORMATICS FOR ALL TEACHERS [UE 83]

A characteristic of the course is the role of the participants as end-users of application software. The course covers two subject areas: text processing and use of databanks (a further subject area: use of "spread sheet" - application software is to be added). The course is modelled after the literacy course in informatics for all pupils (see section 2) and no specific background is assumed.

3.1 DIDACTIC ISSUES.

- Insight.
  The teaching material should encourage the course participants (by means of hand simulation) to think first about what they will do in practical work later.

- Invariant knowledge.
  The participants are encouraged to think about the application software they use in an intermediate, Dutch user language in which the essential elements of the application environment are incorporated in an invariant way i.e. not dependent on the particular application software used (see appendix A).
- Informatics and society.
  In connection with the experiences of the participants with computer use in concrete, everyday examples, several social aspects are treated and evaluated; it is hoped that in this way participants will develop a reasoned and balanced attitude towards informatics.
- Problem analysis and programming.
  Participants solve problems with the application software and develop algorithms in the intermediate user language (with the help of pseudo-code control structures); these algorithms are then translated to the actual user language of the particular application software.
- Principles of software and machine architecture.
  Participants are supplied with functional models to help explain what happens when the application software is loaded and used in the computer system.

3.2 DESIGN ISSUES

- Multiplier effect.
  The course material is so complete that the course can be run by teachers who themselves have just completed it.
- Software and hardware independence.
  In using an intermediate user language that incorporates the essential elements of an application environment, the course material has been made highly software and hardware independent (although, of course, a minimum performance level is assumed). For the most part, information about the details of the particular software and hardware used have been assembled in a separate appendix to the course material. Participants solve their problems in the intermediate user language and then translate their solutions into the level of the actual software (and hardware) using the contents of this appendix.
- Standard software and hardware.
  In the course, standard software and hardware are used, i.e. professional application software under CP/M on a Z-80 based machine.
  This ensures continuity, while development time has been reduced dramatically. On the other hand the application environments are not so sheltered (user friendly) as one might wish.

3.3 APPLICATION CONTENT

Text processing: basic text processing operations, adaption of a standard letter (an invitation from a class teacher to parents), production of a mailing letter (an invitation for an in-service course sent to participants).

Databanks: stock control, house broker information system, Inland Revenue check on house broker data (combination of data files).

3.4 EVALUATION

During the school year 1983/1984 the course was run for student groups (students in chemistry, economics, mathematics and physics), in in-service training (for teachers of various backgrounds) and as a training course for teaching staff (staff from as varying a background as exact sciences, languages, humanities, educational sciences and arts). The way in which the social aspects were treated turned out to be unsatisfactory. In their eagerness to use the application system, course participants were not easily persuaded to take an interest in social aspects. Possibilities are being explored to have participants experience social effects in a more personal way, e.g. they are confronted with private data supplied by themselves but used in an unauthorized way or the situation is

simulated where part of the participants' teaching job is threatened by the introduction of information technology.
As far as text processing is concerned the course material has proved to be very easily adaptable to other text processing software (editors).

4. IN-SERVICE COURSES IN INFORMATICS [PAOI 83]

The model PAE in the Informatics syllabus for in-service courses in informatics consists of two parts: courses for teachers in lower secondary education, described in this paper and courses for teachers in upper secondary education, described in [Kris 84]. Courses are meant for teachers who want to teach informatics as a discipline.

Course 1 : Application Software.

The aim of this course is to let teachers acquaint themselves with various examples of application software which can or cannot be used in the classroom.
The following are treated:
- the use of the application software in a professional environment
- possibilities for treatment (with reduced complexity) in the classroom
- possibilities and limitations for teachers to design and support application software.

Application areas treated are: text processing, information systems, simulation of physical and administrative systems and applications in education. The completion of this course will take an average of 70 working hours.

Course 2 : Programming.

The aim of this course is to give teachers a first introduction to systematic design of algorithms and simple data structures, including the realization of these algorithms in a higher level programming language. The course consists of a theoretical and a practical part. The following subjects are treated:
- general notions: algorithm, object, program, programming language, translator, interpreter
- notation of algorithms and objects
- simple data types and their characteristic operations
- top-down design of algorithms, where problem analysis and design strategy receive special attention
- some typical algorithms using simple data structures
- the realization of algorithms in one actual higher level programming language.

The systematic analysis of problems and the systematic design of algorithms receive more attention than the peculiarities of the programming language used. The completion of this course will take an average of 140 working hours.

Course 3 : Introduction to Machine Architecture.

The aim of this course is to give teachers an introduction to the architecture of programmed systems (computer systems), by means of a hierarchic model where each level is characterized by some communicating processes. In this introductory course the following levels will be treated: the level of the micro-electronic components, conventional machine level, assembly language level, operating system level, translator and interpreter level. The treatment will be neither exhaustive nor systematic, but exploratory. This explorative treatment is meant to introduce the notions: process, object, process description, algorithm, processor, inter process communication, interface and protocol. The completion of this course will take an average of 70 working hours.

Course 4 : Working Group Information Technology and Society.

The aim of this course is to bring about insight into the place in society and consequences for society of information technology (micro-electronics, informatics, tele-communication). This insight should enable course participants to develop a reasoned and balanced attitude towards information technology.

Subjects treated are:
- information and society.
  Information processing, information technology, the "Third Wave" [Toff 80], the "Information Society".
- automatic information processing and process control; consequences of various applications of information technology.
- the consequences of information technology in everyday life, work and study, organisations (including educational organisations), democratic and social structures, international relations.
- information technology as an industry: its organization, functions, importance, social responsibilities.

The completion of this course will take an average of 70 working hours.

Course 5 : Didactics of Informatics.

Didactics of informatics should be aimed at the implementation of the central aims of informatics education as stated in section 2 of this paper.
The course content includes:
- Teacher activities, like selection of learning materials, sequencing of learning materials, use of learning materials, interaction with pupils.
- Pupil activities, like use of learning materials, interaction between pupils, self-feedback.

Practical didactical work should be an integral part of the course: training, group assignments, games simulating class situations, etc.. In this practical work the following aspects play a role:
- evaluation of available learning material (including software and hardware)
- development of a set of learning materials for a (small) number of consecutive (laboratory) lessons.

A consideration of literature concerning the didactics of informatics should also be part of the course.

The course builds on the didactical abilities of acting teachers and its completion will take an average of 70 working hours.

The course contents relate to the four main subjects areas **A**, **B**, **C** and **D** (as described in section 2 of this paper) in the following way:

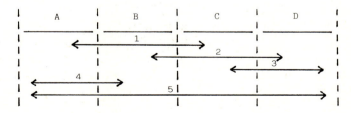

Figure 1

The order in which the courses should be taken is illustrated below:

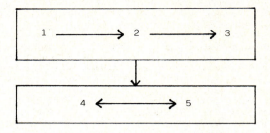

Figure 2

APPENDIX A.

Text processing.

The text processing commands are partitioned into eight groups:

> 0. Starting/ending text processing
> 1. Moving the text window over the text
> 2. Moving the cursor over the text
> 3. Character processing
> 4. String processing
> 5. Line processing
> 6. Block processing
> 7. Data file handling.

Description		Command (in Dutch)
0-1	Start the text processing system	TVW START
0-2	Close down the text processing system	TVW STOP
1-1	Text window up	VENSTER OP
1-2	Text window down	VENSTER NEER
2-1	Cursor up	OP
2-2	Cursor down	NEER
2-3	Cursor left	LINKS
2-4	Cursor right	RECHTS
3-1	Find a character	ZOEK (CH)
3-2	Delete a character	WIS KARAKTER
3-3	Insert a character	VOEGIN (CH)
3-4	Replace a character	ZOEK (CH1) VERVANG DOOR (CH2)
4-1	Find a string	ZOEK ($)
4-2	Delete a string of n characters	WIS KARAKTER(n)
4-3	Insert a string	VOEGIN ($)
4-4	Replace a string	ZOEK ($1) VERVANG DOOR ($2)
5-1	Break a line	BREEK REGEL
5-2	Join lines	VERENIG REGELS
5-3	Delete a line	WIS REGEL

Description		Command (in Dutch)
6-1.1	Mark block begin	MARKEER BLOK BEGIN
.2	Mark block end	MARKEER BLOK EINDE
.3	Unmark block begin	DEMARKEER BLOK BEGIN
.4	Unmark block end	DEMARKEER BLOK EINDE
6-2	Erase marked block	WIS BLOK
6-3	Copy marked block	KOPIEER BLOK
6-4	Move marked block	VERPLAATS BLOK
7-1	Open new data file	MAAK (B)
7-2	Get data file	HAAL (B)
7-3	Print data file	PRINT (B)
7-4	Rename data file	HERNOEM (B1→B2)
7-5	Save data file	BEWAAR (B)
7-6	Copy data file	KOPIEER (B1→B2)
7-7	Kill data file	WIS (B)
7-8	Show file directory	KATALOGUS

References

[KRIS 84]   Kristel, Theo, In-Service Teacher Training in Informatics (for Teachers in Upper Secondary Education). (in this volume)

[NGI 83]   Learning about Information Technology: What, How and What With? (Dutch Computer Society/Organization for Commerce and Industry, Haarlem, 1983)
Leren over informatietechnologie: wat, hoe en waarmee? (Werkgroep informaticaonderwijs van het Nederlands Genootschap voor Informatica en de Nederlandsche Maatschappij voor Nijverheid en Handel, Haarlem, 1983)

[PAOI 83]   A Structure for In-Service Education in Informatics (Organization for Post-Academic Education in Informatics, Amsterdam, 1983)
Structuurplan Nascholing VO (PAO-Informatica, Amsterdam, 1983)

[Toff 80]   Toffler, Alvin, The Third Wave, Bantam Books, 1980.

[UE 83]   Ubbo Emmius Teaching Materials, Literacy in Informatics (Burgerinformatica), Tom J. van Weert / Wilko J.J. Kuiper / Marc Beugels, Ubbo Emmius, The Netherlands, 1983.

INFORMATICS AND TEACHER TRAINING
F.B. Lovis and E.D. Tagg (editors)
Elsevier Science Publishers B.V. (North-Holland)
© IFIP, 1984

IN-SERVICE TEACHER TRAINING IN INFORMATICS
(FOR TEACHERS IN UPPER SECONDARY EDUCATION)

Theo Kristel

Department of Mathematics and Informatics,
Institute for Teacher Training "Interstudie",
Nijmegen, The Netherlands

This paper is a sequel to the paper of Mr. T.J. van Weert,
presented at this conference. It describes a Dutch proposal
for a curriculum in informatics for children in the upper part
of secondary education, and a curriculum for teachers who need
to be trained to teach this school curriculum. The main emphases in both curricula are learning to use programming methodology and acquiring insights in the fundamental concepts of machine architecture.

1. INTRODUCTION

A model syllabus for the lower part of secondary education, developed by the Dutch
organisation "PAE in informatics", has been described in the paper of Mr. T.J. van
Weert. This model syllabus includes both a school curriculum and a teacher curriculum. The same organisation has also developed a model syllabus for the upper part
of secondary education (1) based on the same thinking: first one should know which
subjects pupils have to be taught, and how they have to be taught, before a
teacher curriculum can be devised.
The teacher curriculum is not a very revolutionary proposal when judged by its
contents. It is the link with classroom activities that gives the curriculum its
flavour. This explains why the larger part of this paper is dedicated to a description of a school curriculum in order to arrive at a better understanding of
the philosophy of the teacher curriculum. 1)

2. THE SCHOOL CURRICULUM

2.1. General remarks

According to the proposals, a defining description of an informatics curriculum
for both the lower part and the upper part of secondary education can be divided
into four subject areas:

> (A) Informatics and society
>
> (B) Use of application systems
>
> (C) Problem analysis and programming
>
> (D) Principles of machine architecture

The subject areas (A) and (B) have a central position in the lower part of secondary education, as can be inferred from the paper of Mr. T.J. van Weert(13). The
emphases have shifted in the upper part of secondary education. Now the subject
areas (C) and (D) play the important roles, and they provide the context to discuss aspects of the subject areas (A) and (B).

The rationale for this particular choice is based on two boundary conditions for
upper education characteristic for the Dutch (and other) School system.

- The upper part of secondary education is general education, which means that the subject matter to be taught is supposed to help the pupil wherever possible when functioning in society on his own.

- The upper part of secondary education is also the gateway to various forms of higher education, so that the subject matter to be taught is supposed to prepare the pupil wherever possible for further study.

The organisation "PAE in informatics" thinks to have made the most judicious choice meeting the boundary conditions by choosing (C) and (D) as the principal subject areas.

2.2. The subject area "Problem analysis and programming"

The general objective underlying this subject area can be stated as follows:

The development of an attitude and corresponding skills to be able to
- recognize which problems can be solved by means of an algorithmic approach
- develop algorithmic solutions for appropriate problems in a systematic way
- code an algorithmic solution by means of an available programming language into the form of computer program.

A number of key remarks pertaining specifically to the teaching guided by this objective, will now be made.

(a) Wherever possible the problems are derived from applications of informatics, and are posed in as realistic a context as possible . The reason for this is twofold. First, the spirit of the curriculum of the lower part of secondary education is continued this way. Second, these problems are the gateway to subject matter relating to subject areas (A) and (B). For example, it is possible to treat a real case of an application system in relation to such a problem. As a consequence of this point of view many algorithmic application environments, defining among other things problem related primitives, will have to be developed for the pupils to work in.

(b) The tripartite division of the general objective corresponds to distinguishable classroom activities, separated by reasonably well defined "interfaces". For instance, the first stage of orientation with regard to the problem situation ((2), (3)) could end with an informal description of the input and output of the algorithm to be developed, with the main ideas of the strategy to arrive at the solution, and with the description of some key variables which seem important on the basis of the chosen strategy.

(c) After a problem analysis, as described under (b), it will generally be clear whether the problem can be solved by a (small group of) pupil(s), or whether the work has to be divided over a number of (small groups of) pupils. In the second case the teacher will guide the class into the definition of a well-defined interface, which afterwards will be synthesized bottom-up by (small groups of) pupils. In both cases, each (small group of) pupil(s) has to solve a problem small enough to use the method of top-down analysis as a strategy, if necessary. The crucial methodological principle of abstraction, in the sense of "intentionally abandoning details" (4), is the leading thread during this stage.

(d) The coding of the algorithm into a programming language is often a necessary stage, because the language used to formulate the problem solving strategy is not necessarily a real programming language. Some reasons for this may be:

- the locally available programming language does not support ordinary control structures such as choice and repetition
- the number of details to take into account when using a real programming language may very well divert the attention from the problem to

be solved to the programming language to be used
- not many current programming languages support top-down programming
  (by means of a refinement concept) and/or bottom-up programming (by
  means of a packet (or package) or module concept) as a problem solving strategy 2)

The actual use of a programming language supporting bottom-up programming has the
added advantage that algorithmic application environments, as referred to under
(a), are easily implementable.

2.3. The subject area "Principles of machine architecture"

The general objective underlying this subject area can be stated as follows:

> The acquisition of some insights and corresponding elementary
> knowledge with regard to the most important levels determining
> the architecture of programmed systems.

Some terminological clarification may be justified. "Machine" and "programmed system" mean the same : the interacting union of hardware and software. "Architecture" means the view of one or more different humans on the workings (of the programmed system), as opposed to (though related to) technical realisation or economical considerations (8). Slightly different descriptions of architecture are not
unusual ((9), (10)). However, in a didactical sense, machine architecture is the
subject of making models of programmed systems according to the level the pupil
needs to know about them.

A number of key remarks, pertaining specifically to the teaching guided by this
objective, will now be made.

(a) An important set of levels describing currently available computer systems is
    the set indicated by

    - low levels such as semiconductor components, switching circuits,
      micro-architecture, and conventional machine level
    - medium levels such as assembly language, operating system, and (com-
      pilers and interpreters for) higher level languages
    - upper levels such as application software and database management
      systems

    So this seems to be a major area to scout. It is suggested in the proposals
    not to spend very much time in the low levels.

(b) Another set of levels is the one describing the hierarchical structure of
    database management systems (11). Also, one can think of the set of levels de-
    fined by the ISO reference model (12) describing computer networks. A lot can
    be learned about the structured way in which marine architecture is looked at
    these days just by wandering about some simplified specific instances of
    database management systems and computer networks.

(c) Still other sets of levels can be found in industrial systems requiring process
    control or robot manipulation. Also, individual models pupils develop themsel-
    ves are worth looking at. For, within a specific context, the principal issue
    always is: which black boxes are opened (to show other sets of black boxes)
    and which black boxes remain closed.

(d) On purpose, the previous remarks contain a mixture of somewhat unrelated exam-
    ples in the company of vague words like "to scout", "wandering about", and
    "looking at individual models". For this is the spirit of a lot of the
    teaching according to the proposal. The reason for this didactical choice is
    the following. To acquire some insights (and hence some elementary knowledge)
    it is necessary to be able to abstract from the various forms in which hardwa-
    re and software expose themselves. Such abstractions can be formulated by
    means of a set of basic concepts describing architecture levels (8):

    - process (specification)

- (process) algorithm
- processor
- interface (between processes)
- protocol (corresponding to an interface)

But it takes a long time, and many specific and different examples (and counter-examples), to lead pupils towards these basic concepts in such a way that they stay somewhat anchored in their minds. And that is what the roaming around the world of machine architecture is all about. For this reason the proposals state that it is unnecessary, not even a good idea, to go through all levels described under (a) extensively: the scouting, leading to some important concepts, is all that is proposed with respect to machine architecture.

3. THE TEACHER CURRICULUM

The teacher curriculum has been decided upon within boundary conditions derived from the specific circumstances of in-service training. The principal boundary condition is derived from the fact that an average teacher is not able to spend more than 10 hours studying in one week, while a training programme of 3 years is considered the maximum one can ask from a teacher while in service. If one calculates 14 effective weeks per semester, the total training programme is bounded by the amount of 840 hours of study. Clearly, the training programme is a minimum programme, that has to be supplemented after the training programme by the teacher.

Further, it is a reasonable requirement that a teacher who works in the upper part of secondary education possesses at least the same knowledge and skills as a teacher who works in the lower part of secondary education. Referring to the paper of Mr. T.J. van Weert for the description of this part of the training programme, this means that 420 hours of study have been accounted for.

During the training programme for the lower part of secondary education the teacher acquires most of the knowledge and skills that have been described in the school curriculum for the upper part of secondary education. The remaining 420 hours is meant mainly to increase the teacher's level of understanding of the school curriculum in such a way that the teacher is able to reflect upon the school curriculum with the aim of optimizing his didactical approach. Also, the teacher has to be introduced to at least one subject from general informatics that is not found in the school curriculum, so as to have a start for independent study, which in turn makes the teacher more competent to choose his own subject matter.

Now the school curriculum proposal will be described.

(1) A second course in programming, requiring 140 hours of study.

The skill of top-down analysis of problem solving strategies, already present, is supplemented with the skill of bottom-up synthesis of program layers. Further topics in this course are : recursive algorithms (including backtracking algorithms), program correctness, implementations of abstract data structures (specifically lists and trees). The course includes intensive practical work, wherever possible tailored to the classroom situation of the teachers.

(2) A second course in machine architecture, requiring to 70 hours of study.

Because of the boundary conditions of in-service training, the first course in machine architecture has not been adequate for the teacher to be able to implement the didactical method described under 2.3. Therefore, this course is a necessary supplement. Topics in this course are: more extensive treatment of the medium levels of classical machine architecture with special attention to differences between microcomputers and mainframes, database management systems, application software, networks. Furthermore, the way this course is taught must mirror the didactical strategy to be used in the teaching of this part of the school curriculum, for obvious reasons.

(3) A second course in application systems, requiring 70 hours of study

The idea behind this course is to give the teacher a background in real (problems and their solutions occurring in) application software systems, including the social and managerial aspects. This course is related to the school curriculum as a background for 2.2 : the teacher is better equipped to select real and interesting programming projects, to design (whenever necessary) an algorithmic application environment, and to put the project into perspective by treating a real case of system implementation related to this project. Application categories mentioned in the proposals are: information systems, telecommunications, educational applications, office automation, and industrial process control. Further, it is suggested that about one half of the course is dedicated to real cases, while the other half is divided between a general treatment of applications and the actual design of some algorithmic application environments.

(4) A course in a subject from general informatics, requiring 140 hours of study

It has already been explained why a course like this is proposed. Examples of such courses are: file organisation and databases, theory of automata and formal languages, introduction to compiler construction, introduction to operating systems. However, there has to be a common philosophy behind these different course options : applying the already mastered fundamental principles of informatics to a new subject of generally accepted importance.

A last remark pertains to the order of the courses in the training programme.(1) and (2) should come first, but in which order is unimportant. After this, (3) and (4) follow in precisely this order.

NOTES

1) The interpretation of these curriculum proposals in the form of this paper is the sole responsibility of the author.

2) Contrary to common beliefs, PASCAL does not support top-down programming because procedures have to be defined before they can be applied. The language COMAL-80 (5), developed in Denmark by B. Christensen and others, does support top-down programming. The language ELAN ((6), (7)), developed in Germany by C.H.A. Koster and others, does support both top-down programming and bottom-up programming. Within the framework of secondary education ADA should not be considered.

REFERENCES

(1)   (Dutch) Programmacommissie PAO Informatica voor leraren, Structuurplan na-scholing VO (Voorbereidingscommissie PAO in de Informatica, Plantage Muider-gracht 6, 1018 TV Amsterdam).

(2)   (English) Polya, G., How to solve it (Princeton university, Princeton, 1957).

(3)   (English) Wickelgren, W.A., How to solve problems (Freeman, San Francisco, 1974).

(4)   (Dutch) Koster, C.H.A., en Kristel, Th., Programmeren in de bovenbouw van het VO, Euclides 9 (1983/1984) 397-410.

(5)   (English) METANIC COMAL-80 User's manual, (METANIC, Virum, 1981).

(6)   (German) Hommel, G., Jäckel, J., Jähnichen, S., Kleine, K., Koch, W., und Koster, K., ELAN - Sprachbeschreibung (Akademische Verlagsgesellschaft, Wiesbaden, 1979).

(7)   (German) Hommel, G., Jähnichen, S., und Koster, C.H.A., Methodisches programmieren (Walter de Gruyter, Berlin, 1983).

(8)   (English) Lawson, jr., H., Understanding computer systems (Lawson, Linköping, 1979).

(9) (English) Tomek, I., Introduction to computer organisation (Pitman, London, 1981).

(10) (English) Tanenbaum, A.S., Structured computer organization (Prentice - Hall, Englewood Cliffs, 1976).

(11) (English) Date, C.J., An introduction to database systems, third edition (Addison - Wesley, Reading, 1981).

(12) (English) Tanenbaum, A.S., Computer networks (Prentice - Hall, Englewood Cliffs, 1981).

(13) (English) van Weert, T.J., In service teacher training in informatics (for teachers in lower secondary education), in Informatics and Teacher training, Proceedings of the IFIP working conference, North Holland, 1984.

INFORMATICS AND TEACHER TRAINING
F.B. Lovis and E.D. Tagg (editors)
Elsevier Science Publishers B.V. (North-Holland)
© IFIP, 1984

INFORMATICS AND TEACHER TRAINING IN ICELAND

Yngvi Pétursson
The University College of Education
Reykjavik
Iceland

This paper is in four parts. First is a description of in-service courses for teachers in compulsory education (ages 7-16) held in the summer 1978-83 and for teachers in the upper secondary school (ages 16-20). The second part describes the program at the University College of Education, but this course is only a part of Mathematics. The third part describes Informatics in the teacher program at the University of Iceland but the University mainly graduates teachers for the upper secondary schools. The final part discusses future programs in Informatics.

1. INSERVICE COURSES FOR TEACHERS

1.1 COMPULSORY EDUCATION

The University College of Education has organized several training courses for in-service teachers held in the summertime 1978-1983. A great majority of teachers attending the first courses were teachers of Mathematics and Science (ages 13-16), but in later courses teachers of different age groups (ages 6-15) have attended the courses. These courses have all been introductory courses and were held in the summertime over a period of one week (40 hours) and each course has been limited to 20 participants (2720 teachers have tenure in primary schools in Iceland).

In 1984 110 in-service teachers have been offered an introductory course (5 courses). But this means that we have offered 6% of teachers in compulsory education an introductory course in Informatics and 2/3 of that training has taken place this year.

Here is a summary of the contents of these courses, 1978-83.

a) August 1978
    Programming (60%)
    - Flowcharts and algorithms
    - Introduction to BASIC
    - Data processing and computer hardware
    - Computer development in Iceland
    Possibilities in the primary school (40%)
    - Discussion about development of computer-aided programs in education, especially in Denmark
    - Examination of books used in primary schools in Denmark and Great Britain
    - Some programs from Basic Computer Games and Creative Computing were run
    - Some upper secondary school teachers discussed their experience

b) June 1979
    Same description as the course from August 1978, but also
    including
    - a lecture on logic circuits
    - a visit to one of the grammar schools in Reykjavík and to
      local authorities in one of Reykjavíks suburbs to examine
      their computer equipment and programs

c) August 1981
    Programming (70%)
    - Running prepared programs
    - Flowcharts and algorithms
    - Introduction to BASIC
    Lectures and discussions (30%)
    - Computer development
    - Computer hardware
    - Use of computers in our society and their impact on people

d) August 1983
    Programming (50%)
    - Flowcharts and algorithms
    - Introduction to BASIC
    Lectures and some discussions about different topics (30%)
    - Hardware, software and artificial intelligence
    - The Infomation Society and data base systems
    - The impact of computers on people, employment problems and
      privacy issues
    Examples about computers use (20%)
    - Introduction to Wordstar
    - Introduction to Superpilot
    - Examination of educational programs

1.2 UPPER SECONDARY SCHOOLS

Secondary school teachers of Informatics have varying educational
backgrounds. Most of them are teachers of Mathematics who have
attended some courses in Computer Science, mainly introductory
courses in BASIC programming. Some teachers are from the
commercial field but only a few teachers have specialized in
Computer Science. Courses for in-service secondary teachers have
been held in the summertime and organized by the Society of Science
and Mathematics Teachers in Secondary Schools, with support from
the University of Iceland. A summary of the courses follows.

a) August 1973
    Programming in FORTRAN II and laboratory exercises.
    20 hours, 20 participants.

b) August 1974
    Programming in APL and laboratory exercises.
    30 hours, 20 participants.

c) August 1978
    Numerical Analysis.
    Solution of nonlinear equations with iteration. Interpolation
    and approximation and similar methods in differentiation,
    integration and solving differential equations. Matrices and
    systems of linear equations. Programs in FORTRAN were written
    to solve problems.
    40 hours, 15 participants.

d) August 1979
   Electronics.
   Measurement of resistance. Diodes, rectifiers, operational
   amplifiers and AC-bridges. Digital and analog data conversions.
   Microcomputers.
   60 hours including 40 laboratory exercises, 20 participants.

e) August 1980
   Computer hardware and software. Introduction to BASIC and
   laboratory exercises.
   60 hours, 60 participants.

f) August 1982
   Karel the robot. Programming in PASCAL. Strings, linked lists,
   stacks, trees, graphs and queues.
   60 hours, 20 participants.

g) June 1983
   Word processing and data processing.
   Introduction to PAPERCLIP, a word processing program for Commodore computers. Lectures on computer development, computer-
   aided programs in education, computer graphics, personal computers and wordprocessing computers. Introduction to Visicalc.
   20 hours, 50 participants.

h) June 1983
   Statistics.
   Elementary statistics. Regression and variance analysis.
   Exploratory data analysis. Statistical quality control.
   Programming exercises in BASIC.
   40 hours, 20 participants.

2. INFORMATICS AT THE UNIVERSITY COLLEGE OF EDUCATION

The compulsory section of the curriculum has not contained any hands on
experience. The main reason for this is that the University College
of Education has not received funds to buy necessary computer equipment in spite of repeated requests. But this situation seems to be
changing because the Ministry of Education has shown increasing
interest in this field. In January 1982 the Ministry of Education
established a working group to map out the situation and make
recommendations for further planning. The group has handed in a
report with proposals covering a wide area including educational
programs, in-service and pre-service. In continuation of this work,
the Ministry is preparing a curriculum in computer education for
primary schools, secondary schools and teachers educational
institutions. This work is so well under way that the curriculum is
expected to be available for the school system in autumn 1984.
Additionally the Ministry has laid down a tender brief for the
purchase of microcomputers for schools. The purchase decision will
take place in the spring of 1984.

The Mathematics Department of the University College of Education
owns a Commodore PET computer and the Department has organized three
courses in Informatics, an introductory course (30 lectures), a
programming course (30 lectures) and a course in wordprocessing (10
lectures). These three courses are part of an elective subject in
Mathematics and only a small portion (15%) of the students choose
them. Here is a description in some detail of these courses in order
to give some idea about them.

A.   AN INTRODUCTORY COURSE IN INFORMATICS

    A.1.   Hardware (15%)
        A.1.1.   Introduction to computers.
             Give examples of different computers both in size
             and capacity; measurement   instruments controlled
             by microprocessors, programmable calculators,
             microcomputers, minicomputers and mainframes.
        A.1.2.   The computer system.
             Discuss the basic concepts,   computer, data, a
             program and organization of computer systems,
             components such as CPU (control section, memory
             and arithmetic-logic-unit), input devices, output
             devices and secondary storage devices. Give a
             thorough description of what happens when the
             following program is run
             READ A
             READ B
             LET C ← A + B
             WRITE C
             END
             Write the instruction LET C ← A + B in machine
             language and use it to describe concepts like
             memory (RAM-ROM), register, arithmetic-logic-unit.
             Secondary storage devices i.e. magnetic disks and
             magnetic tape. Discuss different storage types
             considering retrieval of data, cost, magnitude of
             data possible to store and best suitable solution
             of different problems.
        A.1.3.   Technical points in data processing.
             Discuss the binary, decimal and hexadecimal number
             systems and how to convert a number from one
             system to another. Show how to add and multiply
             binary numbers. Explain how data is stored, both
             as numbers and characters in ASCII code. Discuss
             the concepts bit, byte, word and K. Introduce
             logical circuits and gates. Explain how those
             circuits work which are necessary for addition of
             two numbers, i.e. exclusive OR-AND. Make a table
             of addition of binary numbers and construct a
             circuit for adding 1-2 bit binary numbers using
             lightbulbs to simulate the addition.
    A.2.   Software   (70%)
        A.2.1.   Operating systems
             A.2.1.1.   Introduce the operating system on the
                       Commodore PET, which the students are to
                       work with. Teach necessary commands to
                       run prepared programs, write own programs,
                       run, test and correct them and at last
                       to save and load programs from secondary
                       storage devices.
             A.2.1.2.   Discuss the most common operating systems
                       on the market, e.g. CP/M, MS/DOS, UNIX
                       and point out the characteristics of the
                       systems and where they are used.
        A.2.2.   Program languages
             A.2.2.1.   Show a spectrum of programming languages
                       by giving examples of programs written
                       in various program languages, e.g.
                       machine language, assembly language,
                       ALGOL, APL, BASIC, COBOL, FORTRAN, LISP,

LOGO, PASCAL, PROLOG, RPG.

A.2.2.2. Emphasize that computers only understand machine language and compilers and interpreters are therefore necessary to translate from a high level language to machine language.

A.2.2.3. State the purpose of each language, its advantage and disadvantage. Classify the languages into groups of business, technical and mixed languages.

A.2.3. Flowcharts

A.2.3.1. Introduce flowcharts with examples from daily life and use them to explain the shape of the boxes used.

A.2.3.2. Write an algorithm e.g. to calculate postage for letters of different weight and then change it into a flowchart.

A.2.3.3. Show an algorithm written in Icelandic, convert it into a flowchart and then write a corresponding program. Give examples showing connections between program modules.

A.2.4. Programming
Introduce simple programming in BASIC, including
- getting programs from secondary storage devices
- running programs
- listing programs on screen and printer
- editing programs
- debugging and testing programs
- writing programs with simple input, processing and output
- writing programs with if-then-else and decisions
- writing programs with loops
- writing programs in modules
- writing programs with lists and strings

A.2.5. Program implementation and maintenance
Use flowcharts to give examples of writing a spaghetti program and a well structured program. Emphasize good documentation including a description of the system, program and running instructions. From the start programs are structured as much as possible and long variable names used.

A.3. The Information Processing Society   (15%)

A.3.1. The history of computers

A.3.1.1. Give a historical summary of development in data processing. Mention the main periods in the development and characteristics of each period, i.e. machines and problems. Compare size, processing speed and cost.

A.3.1.2. Discuss the environment of each machine, technical and social reasons for the development.

A.3.1.3. Discussion of computer development in Iceland.

A.3.2. Information

A.3.2.1. The information technology
Discuss the information industry and data communication, how to gather, value and update information.

                    A.3.2.2. The ability to use information
                              Give examples of information use
                              - collecting information,e.g. automatic
                                collection by digital instruments
                              - information processing
                              - information storage,e.g. data banks
                              - retrieval of information
          A.3.3. Impact of computers on people and organizations
                    A.3.3.1. Discuss common changes in jobs.
                    A.3.3.2. Discuss employment, both potential
                              benefits and dangers.
          A.3.4. Computers of tomorrow
                    A.3.4.1. Discuss problems facing society with the
                              utilization of data banks.
                    A.3.4.2. Consider the potential threat to freedom
                              and privacy policies by registration of
                              information.
                    A.3.4.3. Discuss technology in near future.
                    A.3.4.4. Discuss the impact of computers in
                              school.

B. PROGRAMMING

    B.1. Programming in BASIC
          Programming is more advanced in this course than in the
          introductory course. Use of computer graphics.
    B.2. File organization
          B.2.1. Discuss files, records, fields and secondary
                  storage devices. Introduce sequential, direct
                  and indexed sequential files. Discuss use of data
                  bases and their organization and how they differ
                  from ordinary file organization.
          B.2.2. Program in BASIC by using sequential and relative
                  files.
    B.3. Software design
          Give an example of designing a certain program package.
          Consider the following points
          - defining the need
          - system analysis
          - system design
          - programming analysis
          - program preparation
          - implementation and maintenance
    B.4. Artificial intelligence
          B.4.1. Discuss use of huge data banks in a certain process.
          B.4.2. Discuss the following question
                  Is the computer restrictive or can it think ?
          B.4.3. Give some examples of projects in the field of
                  artificial intelligence.

C. WORDPROCESSING

Introduce the wordprocessing program Wordstar and explain its
function and use in
- saving and loading document files
- on-screen formatting
- editing
- printing a file
- block handling

Students in this course have already attended a short introductory course including wordprocessing (see chapter 4) and therefore the main stress is on actual work in a wordprocessing system.

3. INFORMATICS IN THE TEACHER PROGRAM AT THE UNIVERSITY OF ICELAND

The University of Iceland mainly graduates teachers for upper secondary schools. The teacher qualification program is a one year course. Usually this program is taken after graduation in a specialized field. Some secondary teachers of Informatics have graduated with a degree of B.S. in Computer Science from the University but the objective of that study is not primarly to graduate teachers.

There is one elective course (60 hours) in the teacher training program at the University about computers and informatics. This introductory course introduces the program languages LOGO, BASIC, PROLOG and SUPERPILOT. The languages are compared and examples are given of different ways in using computers in school. Discussion of the possible impact of computerization on the school, people and jobs. Wordprocessing is taught.

4. FUTURE PROGRAMS

In July 1983 the Ministry of Education established a working group to make proposals for Informatics curriculum in the teacher education.

The group suggests that the University should add a one year program in the field of Informatics to the teacher program. The program should start with introductory courses (10-20%). About 30-40% should be common with the first courses in the Departments of Computer Science and Economics. 50% of the program should be courses specialized for teachers and they should include
a) Computers and Informatics in our Society
b) Ways to use computers in school
c) Programming languages
d) Designing educational packages

The future situation in the University College of Education is promising thanks to a generous gift last December from IBM in Iceland. The equipment gives possibilities for introductory courses for every pre-service student and further education, as well as research in the area of teaching. The first introductory course for all students was started in spring 1984. This course is based on the proposals made by the working group of January 1982. The course includes lectures on computer literacy, impact of computers on education in school, informatics and data base systems. In laboratory hours LOGO and Wordstar are introduced and programs from different subject areas are examined. The group suggests that the University College of Education should organize a half year additional program for primary school teachers. This program should include
a) Changing role of school in the Information Society
b) Hardware and software
c) Designing educational packages
d) Impact of computers on schoolwork
e) The characteristics of the Information Society

The working group made the following suggestions concerning courses
for in-service secondary school teachers
a) In-service teachers could attend introductory courses held in
   the summertime
b) These courses should be 40 hours, about a certain theme in
   computerization of schools, e.g. wordprocessing, educational
   packages, use of computers in various subjects, impact of
   computerization and computer languages (BASIC, LOGO, COMAL,
   PASCAL, ADA)

It is the working group's opinion that it is necessary to set up
programs for primary school teachers different from those for secondary school teachers. They propose to organize a sequence of courses
starting with introductory courses and ending with advanced courses.
These courses should include
a) Introductory course
b) Computer-aided education
c) Simple programming
d) Teaching about computers
e) Computers and better teaching methods

Finally, the group stresses the importance of giving in-service
teachers the opportunity to attend courses in the additional
programs at the University and the University College of Education
during the school year, by giving them advancement in their profession
in accordance with the number of courses they attend.

INFORMATICS AND TEACHER TRAINING
F.B. Lovis and E.D. Tagg (editors)
Elsevier Science Publishers B.V. (North-Holland)
© IFIP, 1984

TEACHER TRAINING, INFORMATICS
AND THE SOCIAL SCIENCES

Lars Runo Johansen

Lecturer and adviser for the
Danish Ministry of Education

In this paper, I describe Danish teacher training especially
in the social science based subjects. After this follows a
discussion of the introduction of informatics in Danish
teacher training, where I try to identify specific ethical,
political and economic arguments. Next, I analyse
informatics as a study object in the perspective of teacher
training: informatics is seen in connection with social,
cultural, economic and political structures and processes
in society. Informatics as a tool in social science based
subjects is then discussed, and I try, with examples, to
identify some problems in the concept of knowledge and
educational theory and practice. Finally, I discuss how to
develop informatics literacy for all teacher students.

DANISH TEACHER TRAINING

There are 25 teacher training colleges distributed throughout the country. At
these colleges, teachers are educated for the Folkeskole (Primary and Lower
Secondary School), for vocationally oriented youth education, and for voluntary
adult education. The education lasts 3½ or 4 years, according to the student's
own choice. The admission requirements are mostly Studentereksamen (Upper
Secondary Leaving Examination) or HF – eksamen (Higher Preparatory Examination).
The yearly intake of students is regulated, and for 1984 it is approximately
1800. The total number of teachers in the working force educated at teacher
training colleges is about 70,000. The contents of the education are common
core subjects: education, psychology, didactics, social studies, teaching
routine, Danish and Christian studies. In addition, the student must choose
three of the basic educational subjects: creative art, singing/music, physical
education or needlework. Two general school subjects at advanced level, among
these civics/contemporary studies, and a special study in the field of education,
must also be chosen.

Social studies is a compulsory subject in Danish teacher training, having 112
lessons. The aim is that the students acquire knowledge of fundamental economic,
social and political conditions, especially in Denmark, and acquire the ability
to evaluate how a teacher and a citizen influences and is influenced by changing
social conditions. The subject puts special focus on the conditions of living,
among these the conditions of the children and the young adolescents, and also
a focus on the relations between the educational system, work and society. As
such, social studies is a general professional subject in Danish teacher training.

Civics – or contemporary studies – is a main subject studied at an advanced
level, corresponding with civics in primary and secondary school and in
vocationally oriented youth education. In the comprehensive school system, civics
is placed with 3 lessons per week in the 8, 9 and 10 forms. Civics has – as
other main subjects in teacher training – 364 lessons, and roughly 8-10% of the

students choose this main subject. The aim is that the students acquire social
science based knowledge of modern problems at the local, national and global
level, and acquire the educational theory and practice and didactical
qualifications to teach in this area.

Work experience is a course in Danish teacher training, introduced as civics in
connection with the comprehensive school reform in 1975. Roughly 5% of the
students choose work experience, and in the comprehensive school system
approximately 10% of the pupils choose work experience. The aim of work
experience is that the students acquire broader qualifications in teaching labour
market conditions and the occupational school system following the comprehensive
school. Work experience as a course in Danish teacher training is studied in
56-112 lessons. In the comprehensive school system, work experience is placed
with 2-3 lessons per week in the 8, 9 and 10 forms.

THE INTRODUCTION OF INFORMATICS IN DANISH TEACHER TRAINING

In Danish teacher training, it is ultimately a case for democratic political
decision-making to decide, if and to what extent, how and with what aims,
informatics should be placed in Danish teacher training and other sections of
the educational system. Such a decision has not yet been taken. Below, I try
to identify some problems and arguments.

Ethical and philosophical arguments

Technology is more than just new techniques. By technology, I understand
the capacity to choose, install, utilise and perfect techniques with the aim of
gaining specific results. Among these new technologies is informatics.
Technology today has become a coherent technical and social system, both
conditioning and threatening the survival of mankind. Information processing is
a qualitative new kind of knowledge engineering. Rapid development of information
processing systems does not necessarily mean parallel qualitative growth in
fulfilling basic human needs. The computer contains a closed and reduced picture
and reflection of reality. The artificial intelligence of the computer differs
qualitatively from common sense knowledge and language used in interpersonal
relations outside the world of experts. If a so-called information society is
under development, we must analyse the impact of computer experiences, which
differ from various experiences known so far. If this premise is accepted, the
main task for the entire educational system related to introducing informatics
is to build a bridge between the patterns of value systems handed down from our
history, knowledge of conditions of life today, and strategies of actions
proportional thereto. Following this argument, informatics must be demystified,
and at the same time it must be analysed in relation to the problem-complex
regarding relations between mankind – work – nature and society. Technology is
part of this problem-complex.

Political arguments

Politics concerns the conflicts related to the establishing and the distribution
of material and immaterial values valid for society. In a democratic political
system, such as the Danish, extensive and qualified participation of the
population in the political process is of paramount importance, if conflicts are
to be solved through dialogue and with minimal use of violence. One of the
problems in connection with informatics concerns the power connected with
controlling the production and engineering of knowledge. The new techniques of
information processing create a possible very efficient basis for consciousness-
production and control. If this argument is accepted, informatics is related
both to new educational techniques and concepts, and to possible fundamental
changes in the social and political structures and processes in a democratic
society. Viewed from this perspective, data-hackers are perhaps pioneers of

counter-knowledge and power, although until now unorganized. The implications for the educational system of this series of points of view, should be two-fold. First, more stress must be laid on a democratic political education, both as an aim and as a process of participation. The opposite of a politically adapted human being, is a human being who does not see given conditions as a matter of course: a politically creative and acting human being, whom you cannot manipulate. Next, therefore, in relation to informatics, it is necessary that the educational system as such, among this teacher training, prepares children, young ones and adults for using, managing and evaluating information processing systems.

Economic arguments

Seen in a global context, a qualified and balanced economic growth is a necessity. However, economic growth in itself does not solve the problems related to the conditions of unequal exchange in the dominating economic world order of today. This implies a problem regarding the economic power structures and processes, which lie behind the unjust distribution of wealth. Now, one of the motive powers behind the rapid development of information technologies is purely economic. Informatics is one way of rationalizing administrative and manufacturing processes; informatics may also create qualitative growth in these processes. Viewed from this perspective, informatics is an economic tool. But a purely economic thinking implies a risk of one-dimensional thinking. Firstly, human beings should not be submitted to new technology, e.g. informatics, and should not be an appendage to any machine. Secondly, any tool is double edged. If one wants a new and more just economy both national and global, it is necessary to avoid monopolisation and a kind of informatics imperialism. In this context, the problems of patents and copyright on software, connected with the capacity to develop software, are of importance. Thirdly, the above mentioned arguments apply to informatics used in the educational system as well. Economics is an incentive behind informatics, which challenges the integrity of different cultural and social structures.

My conclusion, after having discussed various ethical, political and economic arguments related to informatics, is that informatics, both as a tool and as a study object, should systematically be introduced into the educational system in Denmark.

INFORMATICS AS A STUDY OBJECT

In this part, I first and foremost describe how informatics has already been introduced as a study object in the social science based subjects in Danish teacher training, and at the end raise some problems related to the concept of knowledge and the theory and practice in computer based learning.

In social studies, civics (contemporary studies), and in work experience, information technology is represented as a study object. It appears to a different extent and in various depths of arrangement, dependent on the different aims and contents of the subjects. From the reports to the teacher training section of the Danish Ministry of Education, coming from the 25 teacher training colleges, reports which I have to evaluate and adopt, I can state, that information technology is usually discussed, but not systematically. Very often, it is connected with new technology as such, as I earlier defined this concept, thus also including in the discussion for example new biochemical and biological technologies.

To give an impression of these reports, I will name some of the topics from them:

- new technology, economic growth and productivity

- computer technology, working hours and unemployment

- new technologies and their effects on work environment

- computer technology and its application in various industries, the locating of working places and distance work

- computer technology and possible effects on traditional women's work

- the development and application of new technologies: who decides?

- different labour market technology agreements: aims and effects

- computer technology, the shaping of state and commercial registers: a remedy for efficiency and/or a new centralized control system?

- new communication - technologies and computer games and the commercialising of the leisure time of the population

- communication and computer technologies and the future of family life, the development of a new socialisation process?

- the educational theory and practice and didactics of informatics.

The approaches often differ as regards the ambitions related to description, analysis, explanation, evaluation and strategic thinking. Besides, in the above mentioned subjects, the teacher and the students must approach the topics using different and alternative theories of social science, and different perceptions of society. Thus, the discussions lead forward to the relations between the new technologies, e.g. informatics, its conditions and incentives, and the changing structures and processes in the economic, the social, cultural, and the political ideological systems, on a local, a national and a global level.

Concluding, I want to focus on the concept of knowledge in connection with a possible computerisation of information. In the social sciences, we both handle quantitative, hard data, and qualitative, soft data. The capabilities of the computer may - at least at the present stage - to some extent exclude the development through social research of soft information, and accelerate the production of information accessible for transformation into hard data. The trends in electronic publishing and the national and global formation of data bases presuppose and support this development. So, the tool - the computer - used uncritically, may tend to be the master in social and perhaps also other sciences, and not just a very powerful tool. Thus we must deepen our discussions on methodology.

Finally, before dealing with the computer as a tool in teacher education, I shall shortly dwell on some possible implications of computer based education or computer assisted instruction in educational theory and practice, because this problem belongs more to this section of my paper. One question to raise is: what kind of educational aims (dannelsesideal in Danish) lies behind CBE or CAI, if these are at all deliberate? On which basis of educational aims is the rapid development of computer software in progress? What effects may traditional CBE and CAI have on the basic educational aims of a given educational system, e.g. the Danish one, built on a foundation of certain opinions and visions of man and society? Does the new LOGO system really create a student/pupil centred and controlled computer based education, or just a more sophisticated traditional one, based on well known rational-normative educational methods and aims? Actual research into these problems is necessary, and it needs interdisciplinary cooperation to be effective.

INFORMATICS AS A TOOL

Informatics as a tool in the social science based subjects in Danish teacher training is under rapid development. Most of the teachers at the teacher training colleges have no specific and systematic qualifications in the handling of computers. Or should I say had? Because, for a few years I have, as an adviser for the Danish Ministry of Education, been planning and organising in-service training for my colleagues (and at the same time for myself) in close cooperation with various university institutes, private corporations and experts. The enthusiasm of the teachers is great, so is the need, but the money for in-service training is little.

I work with the following list of areas where computers may yield creative assistance to the educational process in teacher training:

- Simulation programs, e.g. economic model simulation, on national and factory and family level, programs on production and consumption of natural resources, and others.

- Processing of primary information, e.g. handling of questionnaires which involves both the construction of a questionnaire, the collecting of information, the feeding of the computer and the information processing.

- Processing of secondary data, i.e. setting questions and getting answers from information sources placed in data bases and transformed from these into subsets useable on microcomputers. A field where we are developing interesting materials.

- A remedy for finding information and documentation, a field not directly accessible today because the teacher training colleges are not on-line to library, and other scientific data bases.

- Computer based education and computer assisted instruction, in the sense not covered by the above mentioned areas.

For the last few years, the microcomputer has been used, in various connections, practically in social science based subjects. For example:

- Processing of questionnaires in relation to an investigation into the recruitment and social - economic living conditions of vocational apprentices (College of Tender, 1981).

- Processing of questionnaires concerning the young ones' choice of education after the compulsory school system (College of Haderslev, 1982).

- Processing of questionnaires related to an investigation into political attitudes among the young (College of Aalborg, 1983).

- Economic and other simulation programs, constructed by the economic institutes at the University of Copenhagen, financial institutions and corporations, and teachers of social science (the teacher training college of Copenhagen, and others).

- Processing of secondary data from the Danish National Institute of Social Research, University and private investigation Institutes, political opinion research, and others - all data gathered at the Danish Data Archives at the University of Odense. The main objective of the DDA is to establish, maintain, and run a data bank for machine readable social science data. For almost a year now, a colleague and I, in cooperation with DDA

and private hardware corporations, have made designs for and actually
transformed social research bases into microcomputer useable programs.
(The teacher training college of Copenhagen, since 1983). Programs as
such will be in the non-profit educational market in the spring of 1984,
after being finally developed and tested by social science teacher
colleagues.

Finally, besides putting focus on information technology as a study object, and
besides the growing use of the computer as a tool, it is an established rule to
involve guest teachers from, and to go on study tours to, factories, offices and
institutions, where different information technologies are applied to
administrative, manufacturing or research processes. For example, computer
corporations, electronic plants, biological laboratories, social research
institutes, news agencies, and educational institutions, where informatics is
systematically part of the education. These activities, are also ways of avoiding
ending up in an ivory tower: the teachers and the students observe informatics
brought into practice and have conversations with employees handling these new
technologies, both in production and reproduction spheres of life. I find this
very fruitful, because prejudices are often held in connection with informatics,
which are difficult to break down, and they generally form an unfruitful basis
for consistent and rational thinking and action.

INFORMATICS LITERACY FOR ALL STUDENTS AND TEACHERS

I have described, analysed and raised some problems and arguments related to
informatics, especially in social science based subjects in Danish teacher
training. In my opinion, it is essential, that any subject in teacher training
evaluates the many facets of informatics, using the theories, methods and basic
concepts - i.e. the scientific structures-of the concerned subject. Informatics
is not a special or specialist area for mathematicians or social scientists,
although these may have a special responsibility for the further development of
informatics. Stressing this, I want to add that informatics, though important,
is only a small corner of the complex of problems challenging mankind in a
national and global context: starvation, shortage of drinking water, pollution,
destruction of the natural environment and the exhausting of natural resources,
and all kinds of economic, social and political repression, the threat of atomic
and chemical warfare - to name some other problems. Informatics, its
development and its use, is also to be evaluated in this connection. So, speaking
about informatics literacy, i.e. the ability to read and write - use and make
useable - informatics, is double-edged. The decision of contents in informatics
literacy must be based explicitly on certain values, not only regarding
informatics as such, but informatics viewed and evaluated in relation to the
opinions and visions of man and society, and their relations.

I ask you to have this in mind, when reading and evaluating the key areas of a
curriculum, which in my opinion ought to be compulsory for all student teachers
as a basis of informatics literacy, which ought to be developed in further steps,
organised in the various subjects of teacher education, and perhaps especially
in mathematics and social science based subjects. The curriculum, briefly stated,
should contain the following areas:

1. The conception of data, data processing and the function of computers.
2. Algorithms, introduction to programming, and problem solving.
3. Informatics in relation to economic processes and production.
4. Informatics related to the shaping of social relations/systems.
5. Informatics and its impact on political processes and structures.
6. Informatics and changes in qualification demands.
7. Informatics and possible effects on educational systems, on educational
   theory and practice, and on general didactics.

I have recommended the above 7 areas, in a more detailed and reasoned version, to the Danish Ministry of Education as a basic curriculum, both for student teachers and for in-service training.

CONCLUSION

I hope that this paper gives an impression of how I, as a social scientist both studying information technology and using it with pleasure, assess the possibilities and dangers connected with informatics. I look forward to the dialogues to come at the Birmingham conference. That is one good way of getting wiser.

Discussion - Rapporteurs: R E J Lewis and K G Ahlstrom

Taylor asked if the papers by Van Weert and Kristel related only to the training
of teachers of informatics, to which the reply was affirmative. In their
reference to standard software, Millin asked how one could cope with the large
volume of software coming from software companies and how one would make a
choice.   Van Weert replied that because of the design features of the course it
was largely irrelevant exactly which software was used but, as it takes a long
time to develop a course, it was essential that one used software with a long
life expectancy, such as that written for CP/M based systems.

Aigner asked about the pre-requisites for teachers attending the Netherlands
courses. It was expected that they would be computer literate but there would
be a variety of backgrounds; course members could come from any discipline.
Martin asked about any evidence on the value of didactic methods on the courses,
which were the same as those which teachers would use in school. Kristel
replied that as the courses had only just started, no evidence had yet emerged,
but that they were convinced that the methods of the training courses should be
the same as the methods of the classroom.

The problem over the variety of hardware systems in the Netherlands, at the
moment, was raised by De Kruif who went on to say that machine transfer of
software can be attempted in different ways, for instance by cross compilers and
development systems. The authors agreed that chaos would result, but that this
was one reason for using an industry standard. Software for the computer market
was most insecure, as companies frequently went of business.

Christiaen asked about courses for teachers of other disciplines, which would be
referred to in a later session by Gorny. As was suggested by Millin, teachers
who have attended courses are seen as experts by their colleagues and this was
likely to be a short term problem. This problem already existed in schools
(Tagg) in the context of assistance in mathematics being required from the
specialists. The solution seemed to be (de Kruif) that more than one or two
teachers from each school should be trained so that consultancy tasks could be
spread around.

Raymont asked about the statistics on the number of teachers needing training
compared with the capacity to provide courses. The authors replied that it was
still not clear in which direction the Government would go in respect of
informatics as a school discipline. Until that was known the size of the task
could not be assessed.

Lee asked why Wordstar was chosen and was it expected that this would
change as other software packages emerge. Petursson indicated that the choice
was made to take advantage of the wide commercial use of Wordstar in Iceland and
teachers were able to make use of professional printing facilities. Wibe asked
Johansen why computer literacy courses were not started before the fifth form
and was there a connection between this introduction and the use of informatics
concepts in other disciplines. It was an ambition in Denmark to introduce
informatics into the fifth form in the late 1980's. The only decision so far
taken was that an optional course be available in forms 8, 9 and 10. The
rationale for an early introduction to informatics was first and foremost to
resist later problems when some pupils, especially girls, would find computers
threatening. Kristjansdottir believed that the only difficulties that girls
might have with computers stemmed from their parents. She went on to ask how
overlap of informatics use could be avoided if it were used across the
disciplines. This issue was raised again later by Kristel who asked how a
school was to manage the contributions from a variety of teachers. Johansen
agreed that a school group or a coordinator was necessary but that the idea of
informatics as a tool in many disciplines could be achieved.

Johansen identified two classes of teachers; those who had been involved in experiments over the last ten years and those who had recently attended courses. A base line of training was needed. Some regions have refused to introduce the optional courses before all teachers have had adequate training. The author agreed with this policy indicating that a great deal more money as was needed for in-service training. Gorny asked if the author disapproved of the optional nature of the informatics courses. Johansen confirmed his disapproval of optional courses in comprehensive schools; they should be compulsory so that both boys and girls were involved. Initial teacher training in informatics should be undertaken at the beginning of the training programme in order that concepts could be used across the disciplines.

SESSION 2

Chairman: Peter Bollerslev

INFORMATICS AND TEACHER TRAINING
F.B. Lovis and E.D. Tagg (editors)
Elsevier Science Publishers B.V. (North-Holland)
© IFIP, 1984

INFORMATICS LITERACY FOR TEACHERS THROUGH LOGO

S.H. von Solms and Mrs M. Friedman

Rand Afrikaans University
Department of Computer Science
Johannesburg, S. Africa

There is a dire need in South Africa, as in other countries, for teacher literacy in Informatics. A group of people, convinced of the benefits of the computer language LOGO, started a project to expose teachers and school children to computers and computer literacy using LOGO. This group consists of computer specialists as well as school and university teachers.

Our teachers' course consists of about 40 teachers using LOGO. The course material has evolved over the last 2 years and at present consists of a manual which contains instructional material and problems to solve. No lecturing is done and the groups of two work through the manual at their own pace.

A full course lasts about 30 hours, usually over a period of 10 weeks. In the paper we will discuss the contents of this manual as well as the LOGO orientation program we run for schools.

INTRODUCTION

In South Africa, as in all other parts of the world, the advent of the computer and particularly the micro computer, has had a tremendous impact on all aspects of everyday life.

Education became one of the prime areas of interest as schools began to consider acquiring micro computers for administrative as well as instructional purposes.

Because of teachers' lack of knowledge and experience with computers, many outside people began offering computer courses to teachers and schools. Most of these courses emphasised the teaching of the syntax of the BASIC language. Suppliers, eager to sell their new computers to schools, convinced all and sundry that a course in BASIC was a prerequisite in the preparation of teachers for their new role as computer instructors in the education system.This approach mostly failed in its intent as it concentrated merely on the syntax of a computer language and did not address the spectrum of problem solving activities needed, namely algorithm development, top down design and the general integration of computers into the school syllabus.

Because most of the courses offered failed in the above objectives, teachers became extremely negative as far as computers were concerned. Thus a group of concerned people, consisting of academics, teachers and business men, realising that a more positive approach must be considered, began looking for a more suitable vehicle by which teachers could be made computer literate in an acceptable and pleasant way. A suitable vehicle was found - the computer language LOGO.

LOGO provided all the necessary facilities to make teachers self confident and enthusiastic about introducing a computer language into the school curriculum.

The reasons for this are manifold -

LOGO can be used by people who do not necessarily have to be mathematically inclined. This is an important aspect as many teachers equate computers and mathematics and those teachers with minimal mathematics exposure were extremely afraid of becoming involved in a computer world. The BASIC language approach, more often than not, exacerbated this fear.

LOGO is not simply a computer language, but is, as Seymour Papert takes pain to point out, a philosophy of learning based on sound developmental and pedagogical principles. It is firmly based on Piagetian cognitive psychology, making it an ideal vehicle for children to develop problem solving skills. The language necessitates interaction with the environment, making the process of learning an active one. This interaction begins at a very concrete level and gradually allows the learner to proceed to much more abstract methods of problem solving.

Incorporated into LOGO is a facility for imparting the ideas of problem solving, algorithm development and top down design. This is all important as teachers must realise that computer literacy or, in a wider sense, programming, consists of 70-80% problem solving and only 20 - 30% coding.

LOGO allows for the development of intrinsic motivation, as well as encouraging a positive attitude to error making. Another feature of the language is the allowance for individual creativity and LOGO permits the learner to retain his own particular cognitive style.

Another important aspect of the language LOGO is its ease of use. LOGO is so structured that it proceeds from the simple to the complex. Any child or adult can immediately tackle simple commands and because of the hierarchical nature of the language, can build those simple commands into complex programs. This is important as teachers can easily and painlessly begin writing their own programs, which is a tremendous spur to further computer activity and works wonders in building up self confidence.

The commands are written in a familiar type language and can be easily related to one's mother tongue. For instance, LOGO commands are very English-like in character, eg. FORWARD, BACK, REPEAT, CLEARSCREEN. These commands can also be easily translated into most languages and LOGO is available in Spanish, French, and even Afrikaans and Wolof.

Thus it can be seen that to implement LOGO in a classroom, one does not need a highly specialised knowledge of computers or mathematics, especially at the elementary school level.

INTRODUCTION OF LOGO TO ELEMENTARY SCHOOL TEACHERS

In all cases where computer courses were offered to teachers, similar problems were encountered. The main one being a very real fear of the computer and all it stands for. This was due to a general fear of an unfamiliar, almost alien technology, as well as an awareness that often the children were more familiar with a computer than they. As most elementary school teachers are non-specialists, their lack of self confidence was even more pronounced.

Those in the secondary school with some mathematical background were more ready to try their hand at a new "mathematical" tool. However, those trained in the Humanities felt that this aspect of education should be left to their more science minded colleagues, the "boffins" on the staff.

The introduction of LOGO did much to overcome these inhibitions because most educators, who have interests of children at heart, felt that LOGO with its unique, structured approach to problem solving was a very valuable adjunct to the school curriculum.

THE FIRST ATTEMPTS TO ORGANISE TEACHER COURSES

A robot turtle plus a number of micro computers were acquired and the first course was put into operation. The material was presented mainly through the medium of lectures. The teachers were given the opportunity of putting their turtles into action, but most of the theoretical aspects were given in lecture form. Although the teachers immediately took to LOGO, they soon began to flounder. Most of them had very different backgrounds, interests and their understanding of the material presented varied widely. It became clear that it was essential for teachers to work at their own pace and assimilate the material at their own rate.

From this experience, a set of course material evolved, designed in such a way that anyone could handle the material at his own pace and in his own way, yet still be taken through all the theoretical requisites, without becoming frustrated or being pushed too hard.

METHODS FOR CHOOSING TEACHERS TO ATTEND A LOGO COURSE

A useful method is to arrange a series of orientation lectures for the entire staff of a school, if possible. A short lecture, outlining the cognitive benefits of the language is usually given, plus a brief account of the different ways LOGO has been implemented in other schools.

A video or live presentation of children in a LOGO classroom creates a very positive impact as teachers can see for themselves the ease with which children use LOGO and most are amazed at the excitement generated in a LOGO classroom. They see for themselves the active learning that takes place.

Using a computer and a demonstration screen, it often helps to have the whole group try and solve a simple LOGO problem and thus they very soon lose their inhibitions about error making. Most importantly, each teacher should be allowed "hands on" experience at a computer and given another simple problem to solve. Most teachers become enthusiastic about the problem solving characteristics inherent in the language and even those who are still hesitant about their own capabilities in the field, are able to appreciate the benefit of LOGO to school children. This is important as a LOGO teacher must be allowed to teach in an atmosphere of support and appreciation from his or her colleagues.

After the orientation class, those teachers who have shown enthusiasm and interest in LOGO, may apply to their principal for permission to join a Teachers' LOGO course. These courses are usually held in a central area and take place in the evenings or late afternoons.

There have been cases of schools situated in far flung areas of Southern Africa evincing an interest in teaching LOGO in their schools. In these cases, a LOGO teacher, together with as many microcomputers as he or she can carry, travels to these schools and operates a very intensive LOGO workshop which may last several days.

THE TEACHER TRAINING COURSE

1. LEARNING THE LOGO LANGUAGE

This usually takes 20 to 30 hours of tuition. The course is structured similarly to that learned by the children. This enables the teacher to develop insights into problem areas that will arise when the children proceed through their lesson plans. The teachers usually work in pairs as do the children. A LOGO workbook designed for elementary school children is used and this workbook is so structured that the adult or child can work his way through the material virtually unaided. The concepts are presented in a hierarchical fashion, so that the student builds his knowledge on previously gained experience with the language. It is thus extremely suitable for a group, be it young children or adults, because they are able to work at their own individual rate.

Once they had attained some familiarity with the language, it was realised that they still needed help in their efforts to implement LOGO in the classroom and thus some aspects were still presented in a lecture format, although the emphasis is always on interaction between the "teacher-students" and lecturer.

2.   HOW TO IMPLEMENT LOGO IN THE CLASSROOM

This was divide into various sections depending on the standards being taught.

2a.   LOGO IN THE JUNIOR OR INFANTS SCHOOL (GRADE 1 AND GRADE 2)

Topics under discussion include directionality training, "playing turtle", the use of the robot turtle itself and hints on how to overcome problems such as a lack of reading ability in the younger children. In the lower part of the school, teaching LOGO is very teacher intensive, the children need a great deal of personal supervision and advice on how to divide the classes into working groups is discussed at length.

2b.   LOGO IN THE ELEMENTARY SCHOOL (Std 1 - Std 5)

In this area, much discussion is given to the pretesting of the children. Through experience, we have found that it is advantageous to have two children to a computer. This facilitates talking to one another in a mathematical language, an activity that appears to cause difficulty throughout most children's school careers as they cannot translate English, for example, into mathematical symbolic language. "Word sums" have often been a nightmare situation for both children and teacher. Talking "LOGO" becomes a valuable tool in overcoming this linguistic problem. Also the old adage that two heads think better than one is almost always true and this exchange of ideas serves to prevent computer frustration, but this implies that the children should be carefully matched, both academically and emotionally, to achieve a co-operative and positive interaction.

Thus ways and means of attaining "good matches" are thoroughly explored. Pretesting is also used to screen for specific learning disabilities, such as visual perceptual disorders, spatial disabilities and symbolic language problems. The teacher is then in a position to monitor the effects of these in the LOGO programme and often finds that many of the disabilities are ameliorated by the therapeutic effects of the child attending LOGO lessons.

3.   STRUCTURING OF LESSON PLANS

Time-table problems are aired - how often should the children attend LOGO classes and how long should each session be?

The emphasis should always be on "discovery learning" and yet the lessons should be planned in such a way that the process is inductive - i.e. the child should build up his knowledge in a natural progression, so that what is experienced or discovered in the initial work is used and applied in order to solve the next more abstract problems.

The teacher should be advised that LOGO should not be taught in a vacuum, but rather that it should be used to complement the existing school curriculum and to reinforce concepts learned in the other disciplines. It aids teachers if examples of the above are illustrated, because many fear that once the language is mastered by the child, LOGO will be dropped by the wayside. Thus a great deal of thought must be given to the integration of the micro computer into different school subjects.

4.   THE ROLE OF THE LOGO TEACHER

There is a subtle change in the role of the teacher within a LOGO classroom. He must get down from his podium and learn to become a FACILITATOR, one who structures materials in accordance with cognitive learning principles, a GUIDE who is sensitive to his students' needs and steers the pupil in his voyage of discovery and yet who prevents him from crashing on the rocks of frustration and lastly a COLLABORATOR and COLLEAGUE who shares together with the students a true learning interaction.

Monitoring of a student's progress is also given an important place in our teacher seminars. It is thought that it is inadvisable to test pupils formally as one can easily gauge their progress by merely looking at their work. However, a record of the students' work should be kept, whether in a journal, or on tape or diskette. This enables the teacher to evaluate whether cognitive growth is taking place.

5.   PROBLEM SOLVING TECHNIQUES

Perhaps for the embryo LOGO teacher, the most important lesson is one in which he is given hints on how to design an algorithm or recipe, in order to solve a problem. The ability of LOGO to design new commands, which are built up from simpler ones, provides a magnificent and easily understandable demonstration of this all important topic.

6.   OBSERVATIONS ABOUT CHILDREN WHO HAVE BEEN THROUGH A LOGO LEARNING PROGRAMME

Many teachers feel encouraged to hear of other teachers' experiences as well as the reactions of children who have spent some time in a LOGO classroom and most of our teachers request permission to sit in during a LOGO lesson.

7.   THE CREATION OF SPECIAL INTEREST GROUPS

As more teachers become conversant with the practice of teaching LOGO, it was suggested that special interest groups should be formed, each with their own particular interests and specialities. These groups could then pool their experiences and ideas thus giving a greater impetus to the teaching and learning of LOGO in our schools.

"Clearly the computer revolution is having a significant impact on education. But the revolution is only worthwhile if it liberates people, which it can by offering educators two remarkable opportunities! With computer technology teachers will be able to help children expand their love of learning; in turn, teachers will achieve a kind of professional status long denied them. Teachers, programmers and other micro-world designers will be the architects of inner space, proposing ideas and creating tools that will enrich our minds".

(R.W. LAWLER,BYTE MAGAZINE - AUGUST 1982, Pg. 160).

INFORMATICS AND TEACHER TRAINING
F.B. Lovis and E.D. Tagg (editors)
Elsevier Science Publishers B.V. (North-Holland)
© IFIP, 1984

TEACHER TRAINING IN LOGO

Rumen V Nicholov

Department of Computer Science
Centre of Mathematics
Sofia, Bulgaria

This paper discusses an experiment carried out by the
Research Group in Education at the Bulgarian Academy of
Sciences for using Logo as a training tool in programming,
mathematics, physics, foreign languages, drawing and
music at some schools. Special attention is paid to the
problem posed by the insufficient training of teachers for
the purposes of computerized education. There is a
brief summing-up of the experience in organizing the
education and preparation of teachers for their work with
Logo at schools.

INTRODUCTION

Due to the fast development of microelectronic technology, low prices and a wide
range of microcomputer application, society is faced with hard problems to solve.
Undoubtedly the most important of them is the lack of training of non-
professionals in operating the new equipment. The education system should create
a new approach to the training and education of the rising generation who will
live in the future computerized society. Programming, considered as a form of a
dialogue with man's new intellectual assistants, acquires the importance of a
second form of literacy (1) which should be learned during the early school years.
In our opinion the question "Who will be the new enlighteners?" has only one
answer: teachers. Along with the introduction of computers in schools, training
courses for teachers should be organized by specialists in informatics,
supervised from the point of view of methodology by specialists in pedagogics and
psychology.

The general purpose of Bulgarian education is to produce versatile and, in
prospect, harmoniously developed people. This purpose has become the starting
point in the activity of the Research Group in Education (RGE) at the Bulgarian
Academy of Sciences and the Ministry of Education. Under the guidance of the
Vice-President of the Academy, Professor Blagovest Sendov, a new, quite
ambitious project was launched, aimed at reforming Bulgarian education, covering
all the stages of the Unified Secondary Polytechnic School (USPS). This project
reflects the idea that training in informatics should be considered as an
integral part of the educational process as a whole. Special attention is paid
to teachers' training courses. This paper describes the author's experience in
organizing and teaching a course in programming, based on Logo, for teachers
within the RGE system.

RESEARCH GROUP IN EDUCATION (RGE)

The RGE started its work in 1979 when a group of well-known scientists, writers,
artists and other specialists created a primer for the first form (six-year-
old children). This primer was used experimentally in three pilot classes.

At the same time, a program plan was offered for a complete educational documentation from the first to the tenth year of the USPS. At present, the experiment of the RGE covers about 1 per cent of the whole educational system in the country.

In the course of its work the RGE has created a complete system of concepts and principles of teaching, which reflect the characteristic features of our times and take into consideration a number of shortcomings of the previous system of training and education.

The basic principle which guides the activities of the RGE is the principle of integration (4,5). When this principle is applied schoolchildren see the objects and phenomena of the world from many sides and can get a better knowledge and understanding of them. They solve many problems themselves looking for the answer in various fields of human knowledge. A computer, considered as an automatic executor of algorithms correctly written in a mathematical language, could be a valuable assistant to schoolchildren. Proceeding from these considerations, the research scientists from the RGE have come to the conclusion that mathematics should be studied as a language. Moreover, it should be studied in integration with other language subjects, i.e. natural human languages, dead languages and programming languages. In this way schoolchildren will understand what kind of information can be automatically processed. These ideas are embedded in the integrated textbooks from the first to the fourth form, in teacher's manuals and a number of other documents of the RGE.

This year, 1983/4, teaching within the system of the RGE has entered a new stage. Studies in a few integrated school subjects, i.e. Language and Mathematics, Society and Nature are being introduced. For the first time a foreign language (English) and a programming language (Logo) have been included as companion subjects to the new school subject Language and Mathematics. A new textbook, unique in its nature and contents, called "Language and Mathematics" (6) was created. It has two appendixes: an English primer and a textbook of programming (7). The textbook of programming aims at combining the RGE concepts and principles of teaching with Papert's approach to using computers in education.

THE ROLE OF THE TEACHER OF PROGRAMMING IN THE SYSTEM OF THE RGE

The concepts and principles of teaching in the system of the RGE are completely different from those of the traditional schools in our country. When they were applied the place and role of the teacher in the educational process were changed. As Professor Sendov likes to say: "The teacher in the RGE system is like a sports coach who teaches his trainees how to reach the top sport achievements, while he himself cannot reach them". The pupils learn the material by themselves from richly illustrated and aesthetically designed textbooks, use a lot of reference materials, solve problems, design, draw, play, sing, play games. Teachers coordinate school activities, strive to bring every pupil up to the necessary minimum of knowledge, encourage versatile interests of the pupils. Teachers do not give their pupils knowledge ready to assimilate, do not test them or award marks, but only show them the way to knowledge. Schoolchildren take on the role of researchers, who observe and measure, create and revise hypotheses, reach scientific generalizations and forecasts, which are the first step to formal knowledge. Teachers become tutors and good persons to talk to about many topics of interest.

In the first year of the secondary school (the fifth year) schoolchildren have access to the advanced microcomputer equipment for the first time. The effective use of this equipment depends to a great extent on the teacher of programming. By means of Logo he should guide his pupils smoothly into the interesting world of computers and guide them expertly in it. Using computers, the teacher of programming should create a kind of intellectual environment in which the pupils can develop their creative abilities to the full. The computer should become a new friend of the pupil, his partner in games and a good assistant in solving a lot of problems. The teacher of programming should ensure a closer integration of the pupils' knowledge and create new cognitive skills and abilities. Schoolchildren should have possibilities to reveal the secrets of simulation computer-based microworlds (2) through observations and measuring, creating hypotheses (programs) and their revision (debugging). In Mathland (3) they should talk with computers in a mathematical language. Mastering the foundations of programming, schoolchildren should learn by teaching computers to draw, to calculate, to play, to tell interesting stories, to show animated cartoon films, to understand new Bulgarian, Russian and English words.

In order to control and guide the study process the teacher of programming should:

- know and properly apply the concepts and principles of teaching developed by the RGE;

- know the role of computers in society and their influence on educational system;

- know the basic methods of using computers in education;

- know Papert's methodological principles and successfully combine them with the RGE concepts and principles of teaching;

- know Logo basic constructions;

- have the basic skills and abilities for operating the advanced microcomputer equipment;

- be able to solve problems from various areas of science and art by using computers;

- be able to define by himself the problems connected with the school material which can be solved with the help of computers;

- know to a definite extent the up-to-date principles and methods of programming which should play the guiding role in his work;

- be able to read programs and make corrections in them;

- be able to create by himself problem-oriented language extensions of Logo for specific teaching purposes.

The requirements for the teacher of programming have defined the objectives and material of the course. They became the basis for the choice of the specific strategy for teacher training in programming.

ORGANIZATION OF THE COURSE

A two-week teacher training course in Logo was included for the first time in the course system of the RGE. The lack of tradition in studying informatics foundations at school and the lack of teachers having the necessary qualification has posed the following question: Who could be a good teacher of informatics? Our choice was determined by the close connection between informatics and mathematics: it should be the teacher of mathematics. In order to ensure a fuller integration of informatics with other sciences and arts, the teacher of informatics should work in cooperation with other teachers. Due to a number of causes it was impossible to train all the teachers of the three pilot classes. We chose a more rational hierarchical organization of the course. Only

teachers of mathematics were trained. These teachers will train not only their
pupils but other teachers as well. In this way every teacher using the textbook
of programming and the available microcomputer equipment will be able to acquire
the necessary knowledge, with the assistance of the teacher of mathematics and
programming, at a convenient time. When taking classes using computers, the
teachers can count on the assistance of advanced pupils. Within the framework
of the RGE a team of specialists in informatics has been formed which in
cooperation with other specialists will create software and educational
documentation for the needs of teaching. They will give consultations on
programming and throughout the year will give assistance in teaching methods to
all the teachers using computers in the teaching process and in the administrative
activities of the schools. The course organization will be even more effective
in the coming years when the Logo courses will cover teachers of all the basic
schools of the RGE.

PROBLEMS IN TEACHER TRAINING IN LOGO

In the process of teacher training in Logo a number of problems faced the
organizers. The success of the course depended on their correct solution. Here
are some of them:

- it was the first time that the teachers had worked according to the
  principles and concepts of the RGE. Many years of practice at
  traditional schools created an inertia of thinking which was hard
  to overcome;

- the teachers were not acquainted with the teaching documentation
  from the first to the fourth year, which made them unable to
  determine the starting level of their pupils by themselves;

- the teachers' knowledge of informatics did not exceed that of
  their pupils;

- the teachers had no "keyboard" skills. They could not even type;

- the teachers did not know English, which created additional
  difficulties in their dialogue with the computer in Logo;

- different teachers had different paces of material assimilation,
  which required an individual approach to every one of them;

- there were a number of psychological barriers with reference both
  to the computer and the contacts with the course lecturer. They
  were embarrassed by the fact, that although teachers with many
  years of practice, they showed ignorance and had to be instructed
  by a person much younger than themselves;

- it was difficult for them to accept the methods of computer
  utilization in non-mathematical subjects;

- the short duration of the course did not allow for a better
  assimilation of programming. The level of difficulty of the
  problems solved by the teachers did not exceed that foreseen for
  the pupils.

TRAINING STRATEGY

The objective of the course was to help the teachers to assimilate the basic knowledge and skills only, which could be improved later through self-training. The chosen training strategy had the following characteristic features:

- the course was based on the textbook of programming for schoolchildren;

- a number of principles of child training were applied in the training process and later those principles were explained to the teachers;

- the peculiar features of training pupils in Logo were made clear to the teachers.

The advantages of this strategy are as follows:

- the material and problems in the textbook of programming can satisfy the interests of even the best pupils. The material assimilation and independent solution of many "difficult" problems give the teachers the necessary minimum of knowledge, skills and self-confidence;

- the textbook of programming offers knowledge in a form easy to understand which makes it easy for the teachers to assimilate;

- this approach makes it possible, while training teachers, to model an educational environment very near to that at school. Every lesson becomes a demonstration of the new concepts and principles of teaching. The discussions help the teachers to specify their own approach to training;

- basing it on their own experience as "pupils", the teachers see for themselves the effectiveness of the new teaching principles;

- the teachers understand better what kind of problems will arise when teaching their pupils, after they have analysed their own difficulties in working with computers and the textbook of programming;

- the teachers often fall into problem situations (especially when solving non-mathematical problems) which could later be faced by some of their pupils. This helps them to choose the instruction necessary to overcome the difficulties;

- the minimum knowledge which should be acquired by each pupil is discussed and specified with the teachers. Topics for discussion with the pupils and the range of problems to be solved are determined as well;

- the critical remarks of teachers concerning the textbook of programming contribute to its future improvement;

- improvised discussions provide the material for writing a teacher's manual of programming which will include a theoretical part, distribution of the material and explanations on the way the pupils' activities should be integrated.

HOW THE COURSE WORKED

During the course each teacher had at his disposal a personal APPLE II
microcomputer, a copy of the textbook of programming, a notebook and diskettes
with the necessary software. This software included a Logo interpreter (Terrapin
Logo version) and a set of utilities, i.e. games, simulation computer models,
problem-oriented extensions in Logo. The teachers assimilated the textbook
material by themselves, worked strictly on the examples, solved a lot of problems,
made up new problems themselves, asked questions, had arguments, took part in
general discussions. In their notebooks they put down some technical details,
made notes of their problems, wrote their remarks on the material of the course,
put down solutions of many problems.

As a lecturer I had a lot of things to do: I organized the "game" of pupils and
teacher, demonstrated, narrated, explained, persuaded, answered a lot of
questions, clarified new concepts and principles of teaching, organized
discussions, prompted, encouraged, helped to debug the programs, solved problems
myself and made mistakes (sometimes on purpose), studied the problems of every
teacher and took them into consideration, organized general discussions of the
solutions of some problems, provoked the use of new ideas, etc.

In order to illustrate the above, I shall describe some lessons with the teachers.

EXAMPLE 1

The first lesson included the demonstration of a number of computer games, after
which the teachers took part in some of them. Through computer games they got to
know in an easy way the rich possibilities of microcomputers, overcame to a great
extent their fear of this new equipment, got accustomed to the keyboard. The
demonstrations gave rise to a number of debatable questions connected with the
introductory chapters of the textbook of programming: what the computer is, how
the computer operates, what it can do and what it cannot do, the role of the
computer in society and education, programming languages, programs and
programming, etc. Through suitable examples I explained the role of the
educational computer games as a major way of providing motivation for the pupils.
We draw a line of clear distinction between games aiming at consolidating the
already acquired knowledge of the pupils and others aiming at assimilating new
knowledge. The teachers got acquainted with the educational computer games
described in the textbook "The turtle and the laws of movement" and "The turtle
in the orbit around the Earth". These games contain simulation models of some of
the laws of physics. Taking part in the games the teachers solved problems
themselves, and made some previously planned experiments. While analysing the
difficulties they understood the need of a close cooperation with the teacher in
physics. There were discussions concerning the effectiveness of the simulation
models and the methods of applying them at school. The main task of the teacher
was clarified, i.e. not to let the pupils view the game as at an entertainment
only, but as a facility which helps everybody to assimilate the knowledge
inherent in it.

EXAMPLE 2

The textbook of programming includes a number of problems which can be grouped
under the common title "Discover the Pythagorean theorem by yourself". Those
problems are as follows:

Problem 1. Draw a right-angled triangle with arms of 60 and 80 feet.
Problem 2. Write the word МИP (peace) with the help of the turtle.

The teachers were supposed to "forget" the Pythagorean theorem and, like their pupils, to discover it by themselves. They made a number of experiments, giving commands to the turtle and received the approximate values of the hypotenuse (or the arms) length of the acute angles. The results of the experiments were taken down in the notebooks and analysed. We discussed the recommendations which could be given to the pupils. The teachers themselves found the Pythagorean triples and formulated new problems. New ideas sprang up spontaneously concerning the experiments which could help the pupils to reach the formal knowledge. We have come to the conclusion that through such problems the pupils make their first steps in trigonometry without realizing it.

EXAMPLE 3

During the course I was trying to convince the teachers that they should always take into consideration the individual aptitudes of their pupils and adjust their approach dynamically to each of them. In my work with the teachers I also acted in accordance with this rule. Some ideas, principles and methods of programming can be assimilated with greater ease if they are connected with solving problems which sparkle a personal interest in pupil or teacher. One of the teachers had a bent for music and took a great pleasure in programming music. The basic notions, i.e. procedure, function, REPEAT-statement, IF-statement, recursion, etc. were perceived by him through some appropriate examples from music. The same refers to some methods of programming, i.e. solving the problems by dividing them into subproblems, top-down programming, structured programming. The teacher began to program his favourite melodies. While listening to them he debugged his programs easily. He assimilated a great part of his knowledge of programming through solving problems connected with mathematics and music. In cooperation with the music teacher the teacher of programming could achieve a closer integration between mathematics and music. That is one of the principles of the RGE: "Symmetry and rhythm in art give the child the sense of space and time, but he can investigate these categories only through mathematics and physics". (5)

When a pupil solves interesting problems by himself, or as a member of a group, he is proud of his results and demonstrates them with pleasure to his friends and relatives. In order to satisfy the natural aspirations of his pupils, the teacher of programming should help them in organizing a final "computer concert". In this way the pupils will get another urge to work with the computer.

CONCLUSION

The results of the course give rise to optimism. The teachers not only overcame the initial difficulties and assimilated the planned minimum of knowledge but also got a motive for further self-perfection. In spite of a delay in delivery of the computer equipment the course of training in programming in the three pilot classes started successfully.

Seymour Papert states that his objective is not to improve the existing school but to create a new type of school (3). It might be that the school he had in mind resembles the schools of the RGE system.

ACKNOWLEDGEMENTS

I should like to express my gratitude to Professor Blagovest Sendov for the confidence he placed in me and his competent help. I thank Professor M. Yanakiev, R. Novachkova, Bojidar Sendov and all the members of the RGE for their valuable advice and cooperation in the organization and implementation of the course.

REFERENCES

(1) Ershov, A P, Programming, the Second Literacy, in: Lewis B and Tagg D (eds)
     Computers in Education (North-Holland, Amsterdam, 1981).
(2) Lowler, R W, Designing Computer-Based Microworlds, BYTE, V. 7, No. 9 (1982).
(3) Papert, S, New Cultures from New Technologies, BYTE, V. 5, No. 9, (1980).
(4) Sendov, Bl. et al. Principles in the Work (Manuscript, RGE, 1982,
     in Bulgarian).
(5) Sendov, Bl. et al. Teachers book for the first form. Sofia, RGE, 1980.
     (in Bulgarian).
(6) Sendov, Bl. & R Novachkova, Language and Mathematics (A textbook for the
     5th form). Sofia, RGE, 1983. (in Bulgarian)
(7) Nicholov, R, LOGO- An experimental textbook. Sofia, RGE, 1983. (in Bulgarian).

INFORMATICS AND TEACHER TRAINING
F.B. Lovis and E.D. Tagg (editors)
Elsevier Science Publishers B.V. (North-Holland)
© IFIP, 1984

INFORMATICS IN THE EDUCATION OF YOUNG CHILDREN

June L. Wright

Microcomputer Discovery Project
Center for Young Children
University of Maryland
College Park, Maryland
U.S.A.

The microcomputer allows the young child to process information in new ways. True interaction demands that the child
manipulate a code understood by the machine. Naturalistic
research on children's concept development, as observed in
their exploration of the microcomputer, suggests that teacher/
child/microcomputer interaction can promote both convergent
and divergent thinking.

INTRODUCTION

The influx of microcomputers into pre-school classrooms has followed several years
behind their entry into secondary and elementary schools (Becker, 1983). In many
instances the decision to purchase them was spearheaded by parent committees or
directors of private pre-schools (Chen, 1984). Educators were fascinated by the
emergence of a phenomenon best described as "family sampling". Families were
visiting special facilities at parks and museums where they could play with computer programs designed for "kids". Next, short term parent-child classes, such
as "computots", appeared on the scene. With the emergence of the low cost personal computer, many middle and upper class families in America are purchasing
microcomputers. Because these microcomputers are located in the home, children
have ready access to this technology. Young children learn by interacting with
their environment (Piaget, 1970). Much of their learning takes place in the family
milieu (Coleman, 1966; Jenck, 1972).

The microcomputer is becoming part of the young child's environment in both home
and school. Approximately 25% of the licensed preschools in the United States
now have microcomputers and there are approximately 7 million in private homes
(Bowen, 1984). It becomes essential that teachers be adequately prepared to
facilitate the natural learning process of the young child in this technological
environment. Educators must maintain a proper perspective and resist premature
conclusions. Instructional decisions have definite consequences for children's
learning. It is necessary to investigate thoroughly a variety of implementations
and, for each of these implementations, to record the observed impact on children.

In order to study the impact of the microcomputer on the young child, the Center
for Young Children at the University of Maryland equipped a Computer Discovery
Room for its pre-school (September, 1981). The action did not reflect a
philosophical decision that microcomputers should become a part of the total pre-
school curriculum. Rather, it was a means of investigating whether young children
would be able to, and would wish to use the microcomputer. The microcomputers were
first introduced to three, four, and five year old children in the Computer
Discovery Room where careful observations could be made of the children's
responses to this new experience. Jersild (1946) defined the child development
approach to curriculum as "an effort to apply to the education of young children
the lessons learned from the study of children themselves" (P.1). Logs that

recorded the ongoing behavior of the children as they interacted with the microcomputers have been maintained throughout the first two and a half years of the
project (supplemented when possible with videotapes).

During the second year of the project the microcomputers were also placed in the
classroom environment. Two microcomputers were positioned next to each other so
that the children working with them could see both monitors and share their experiences. No initial disruption of classroom activities was produced (Fein, Campbell,
& Schwartz, 1984). Novel objects, such as the Tasman Turtle, and new input modes,
such as the Koala Pad, continue to be introduced to small groups of children in
the Discovery Room to prevent the potential disruption of the classroom caused by
each child wanting immediate access.

COMMAND CODES

A spiral curriculum approach would suggest that there is the potential for learning
any subject at any stage of development assuming that the components of the subject are well defined and the presentation is developmentally appropriate (Bruner,
1962). A computer can be defined as a "general-purpose, symbol-manipulating
machine" (O'Shea and Self, 1983, p. 24). If the intent is to allow the child to be
in command of the machine so that the child discovers its potential himself, then
it is necessary to establish a sequence of symbolic representations, or codes, that
the child can comprehend and utilize in the operation of the microcomputer. Observations suggest that motor based devices, such as a joystick or mouse, allow for
command of the microcomputer in the child's most easily understood mode, bodily
motion (enactive mode). Icons used as overlays on the keys and picture card
indexes which are numbered to correspond to the number keys serve as a second level
of command for the child (iconic mode). As beginning reading skills emerge, four
and five year old children enjoy exploring the full keyboard and inputting file
names and single letter Logo commands (linguistic symbol).

Early childhood educators who have a clear sense of the process of growth and
development of the young child must take responsibility for establishing a
relationship between the young child's development and the microcomputer experience. The goal is to design a curriculum (and software) that begins at the child's
developmental level and replaces each level that is mastered with the next level
of complexity. If the spiral is well built, it will allow the child to choose
modes of interaction that reflect his learning style. To the extent that the
child determines his activities, the child will see the microcomputer as a
tool or machine that he commands. Open-ended tool use in a pressureless environment can lead to creative behavior that might never be realized under functional pressure (Bruner, 1972).

CREATIVITY

Children's earliest microcomputer explorations at the CYC were graphic arts
experiences. An enlarged control panel promoted maximum awareness on the child's
part of the relationship between the movement of the joystick and the movement of
the cursor on the screen. Because the eye-hand coordination was purposefully
simplified, the child at age three or four could focus attention on the symbols
being created.

The discovery that the creations were their own came to the children in the first
fifteen minutes of interaction. Once aware of how the cursor could take on four
widths and four colors and would move in eight directions, the children shifted
into the involvement stage during which initial modes of expression were explored.
Typical modes included outlining a shape and filling it in, overlaying one color
with another, and filling and erasing the screen. The self confidence phase was
reached when the children were able, at will, to execute a plan, no longer hindered
by a trial and error approach to the necessary command sequence. True creativity
emerged shortly thereafter. Children, working side by side on matched computers,

began to share their ideas and invent new ways to use this simple but powerful program called "Scribbling". The initial pattern of discovery, involvement, self-confidence, and creativity was observed repeatedly in the logs of graphic arts, language arts, and Logo interactions (Wright and Samaras, in press). It has become the acronym for the now emerging DISC curriculum model.

The following list illustrates some of the many different strategies explored by the children with an open-ended drawing program:

1. Moving the joystick in a circular fashion to color in spaces.
2. Changing the cursor to the background color to erase.
3. Changing colors while drawing, resulting in a multicolored line (in some cases with all segments equal in length).
4. Pushing the button intermittently to leave squares on the screen; then connecting them.
5. Changing the color of the cursor to find it when it got "lost" in the same color area.
6. Floating the cursor without leaving a line and telling stories about what it was doing.
7. Creating a jumping line effect by drawing and clearing intermittently.
8. Creating games (eg. guessing games, hide and seek, spaceship, follow the maze). (Keenan, 1983)

These novel uses of the commands could not have occurred without an environment that fostered spontaneous exploration. One of the components of creative thinking is the promotion of "non-evaluative ideational productivity" (Dansky, 1970, p. 577). The microcomputer may well offer a new avenue for fostering divergent thinking. The children at the CYC surpassed expectations as they used graphic input to both define and execute their own pastimes.

PROBLEM SOLVING

The ease with which children move from one program to another depends upon the individual child's ability to discriminate between the varying sets of commands. Just as the children exhibit unique learning patterns when beginning to read, so too with computer literacy. There is a need for the teacher to be aware of each child's readiness to operate a more complex program requiring unique input by icons, indexes, and words. The level of the problem solving skills needed to implement the program must also be assessed.

When interacting with a simulation called "Electronic Easel", children are challenged to grasp a consistent cause/effect relationship. One child (age four) was able to understand that each one of the three primary colors represented in the paint cans must be mixed (input by number code) with each of the other primary colors sequentially to create the secondary colors and "fill" the six available paint cups on the easel. To reach this level of expertise, the child internalized not only the functions of the overlaid keys and the sequencing of the commands to execute the program, but also the principle of combinatorial thinking.

Seymour Papert (1980), in discussing the challenge of forming all possible combinations of beads, suggests that our culture has traditionally been lacking in models of systematic procedures. Well designed microcomputer programs can offer each child a chance to move up the spiral to a more complex input mode and to further concept attainment while accepting the child's current knowledge base. Too often this power for flexibility is ignored by the designers.

During a three month unit on "Instant Logo", some children exhibited novice programming skills. The Tasman Turtle has a two tone horn (high and low). The teacher wrote a procedure which alternated these sounds in a high-low sequence in response to the S key. One child (age 5) interpreted this sequence as the turtle's speech. He reasoned that there should be more patterns of turtle talk and requested procedures to yield specified patterns of sound (eg. four short

high sounds, two long, low sounds) when single keystrokes were entered. Manipu-
lating two attributes, he increased the robot's vocabulary in a very inventive man-
ner. Thus this child had conceptualized the potential of procedures. Young
children will work very hard at problems and questions which they invent. Teachers
who encourage this style of inquiry find that the difficult problems children set
for themselves are problems they would never think of suggesting.

INFORMATION ACCESS AND CONTROL

The conviction that the child should understand the microcomputer as a machine
which is programmed by people underlies all of the experiences at the CYC. The
children at the Center meet the programmers and artists who work with the teachers
on program development. They make suggestions about how they would like a program
changed. Several children wrote to the artist who created the farm shape table
for a make-a-picture book program and asked, "Gwendolyn, will you please give us a
program to make a picture book?;" the children knew that they were accessing information over which they had had some control. The programmers had also allowed the
children to decide the title of the index page.

Encouraged to make suggestions about commercial software as well as programs developed at the CYC, these children become a new breed of software evaluators. One
child, age 5, wrote to Spinnaker Software to explain that "Delta Draw" has two
problems: 1) to change (ie. edit) a saved picture (ie. its procedure) you have
to erase lots of commands and 2) to fill with white is listed as a choice but is
not possible. Another child, age 4, piloted "Hodge Podge", an alphabet game. Two
issues concerned her. The R Rabbit hopped up the screen as she hit the key but "he
has no legs" (the picture is of the head of a rabbit). Her second concern was that
some pictures had words under them and others did not. She tried to type in the
word "apple" - but the program went on to show her a pony for her P. The child
concluded that Betty and John, graduate student programmers, would have to fix
it (ie. put labels under all the pictures). In this atmosphere, information cor-
rection becomes a natural part of the child's growing concept of the power of this
new tool. It is interesting to speculate how these experiences will effect the
children's perspectives on information they encounter in the future. Will they
have a better conception of information as something that is processed by people,
not a static entity?

TEACHER AS LEARNER

In theory, all educators believe in continuing education. But the feelings of fear
and inadequacy which many adults experience when confronted with the microcomputer
often overshadow their sense of adventure. Introducing teachers to the power of
the microcomputer as a new thinking tool is significantly more difficult than
introducing young children, who have no fear, to the microcomputer as a plaything.

Perhaps the key to success lies in convincing the teachers to play! Play can be
any activity that is totally self motivated and enjoyed. It is crucial that
teachers experience enjoyment of the microcomputer in some way before they are
immersed in a structured inservice designed to teach microcomputer components,
curriculum design, hardware and software evaluation, and teaching techniques. The
process of moving from awareness of an innovation to personal involvement and then
to concern with the impact of the innovation on students (Hall, Loucks, Rutherford,
& Newlove, 1975) is a basic consideration for teacher training.

Rich peer interaction and peer teaching have been cited in many reports on microcomputers in the classroom (Hawkins, Sheingold, Gerhart, & Berger, 1982, Hawkins,
1983, Wright and Samaras, in press). Observations of the Teacher Training Workshops, Parent Workshops, and Inservice Days conducted at the University of
Maryland reveal the same phenomenon. Adults most often approach the microcomputer

first with a friend. "I'll try it if you'll help me", is a typical response.
Undergraduate and graduate students ask to assist in the preschool microcomputer
program, admitting later in the semester that they felt it was a safe way to "try
out the micro" where it would not be "too hard". At the CYC the children serve
as models for the adults, demonstrating a lack of fear and a sense of mastery.
The observation of children might provide a powerful introduction to teacher
training modules. Many early childhood educators have been convinced of the
creative potential of the microcomputer by watching from the observation booths
at the CYC or viewing the children on videotape (Wright and Midkiff, 1983).

A review of computer education inservice programs reveals that the focus is often
on the teacher as a learner of new content. It is necessary to balance objectives
and provide time for groups of teachers to design lesson plans (MECC, 1982). Joyce
and Showers (1982) highlight the importance of a practice component involving the
teaching of peers and small groups. Ferris (1983) suggests that the instructor
offer a support structure by visits to the schools during the teachers' first
implementation stage.

It is important for those who teach about the microcomputer to remember that it
has not been an integral part of many adults' environments and to provide time
for each adult learner to move through the Discovery, Involvement, and Self-
confidence stages observed in the children, before they can focus on the Creativity
of this new thinking tool and implement it into their own curriculum.

References

1   Becker, H. J., School Uses of Microcomputers: Reports from a National
    Survey (Center for Social Organization of Schools, The John Hopkins University,
    Baltimore, MD) I (1983) 5-10.

2   Bowen, B., Computers and Young Children: Future Trends and Opportunities.
    Paper presented at University of Delaware Conference on Microcomputers and
    Young Children (Newark, DE, 1984).

3   Bruner, J. S., The Process of Education (Harvard University Press, Cambridge,
    MA, 1962).

4   Chen, M., Computers in the Lives of Our Children: the Legacy of Television
    Research, in: Rice, R. E. (ed.), The New Media: Practical Communication
    Research (Sage Publications, CA. 1984).

5   Coleman, J., Equality of Educational Opportunity (U. S. Government Printing
    Office, Washington, D.C., 1966).

6   Dansky, J. L., Make-believe: A Mediator of the Relationship Between Play and
    Associative Fluency, Child Development. 51 (1980) 576-579.

7   Fein, G., Campbell, P., & Schwartz, S., Microcomputers in the Pre-school: Effects
    on the Cognitive and Social Behavior, in: Campbell, P. F. & Fein, G. G. (eds.)
    Young Children and Microcomputers: Conceptual Issues (Reston, VA, Reston
    Publishing, in press).

8   Ferris, G. W., Training and Implementation Strategies Appropriate to the Intro-
    duction of Logo Into Teachers' Curriculum and Instruction. PhD. Thesis, College
    of Education, University of Oregon (September, 1983).

9   Hall, G., Loucks, S., Rutherford, W. & Newlove, B., Levels of use of the innova-
    tion: A framework for analyzing innovation adoption. Journal of Teacher
    Education 26 (1975) 52-56.

10 Hawkins, J., Learning Logo Together: the Social Context. Technical Report #6
    (Bank Street College of Education, New York, Nov. 1983).

11   Hawkins, J., Sheingold, K., Gearhart, M., & Berger, C. Microcomputers in
     Schools: Impact on the Social Life of Elementary Classrooms. Journal of
     Applied Developmental Psychology. 3 (1982) 361-373.

12   Jencks, C., Inequality: a Reassessment of the Effect of Family and Schooling
     in America. (Basic Books, N.Y., 1972).

13   Jersild, A. T., Child Development and the Curriculum (Teacher's College,
     New York, 1946).

14   Joyce, B. & Showers, B. The Coaching of Teaching, Educational Leadership 40
     (1982) 4-10.

15   Keenan, K., Four Year Old Children and the Microcomputer in the Graphic Art
     Mode: A Pilot Study (Computer Discovery Project Report #3, University of
     Maryland, 1983).

16   Minnesota Educational Computing Consortium. Planning Inservice Training, a
     MECC Special Workshop (St. Paul, MN, 1982).

17   O'Shea, T. & Self, J. Learning and Teaching With Computers: Artificial
     Intelligence in Education (Prentice Hall Inc., N.J., 1983).

18   Papert, S., Mindstorms: Children, Computers, and Powerful Ideas (Basic
     Books, Inc., N.Y., 1980).

19   Piaget, J. Science of Education and the Psychology of the Child (Orion
     Press, N. Y., 1970).

20   Wright, J. & Midkiff, F., Early Learning With the Microcomputer (videotape)
     (Computer Discovery Project, University of Maryland, College Park, MD, 1983).

21   Wright, J. & Samaras, A., Playworlds and Microworlds, in: P. F. Campbell
     & G. G. Fein (eds.), Young Children and Microcomputers: Conceptual Issues
     (Reston Publishing, Reston, VA, in press).

INFORMATICS AND TEACHER TRAINING
F.B. Lovis and E.D. Tagg (editors)
Elsevier Science Publishers B.V. (North-Holland)
© IFIP, 1984

TEACHING LOGO TO TEACHERS:
A LOOK AT THE ISSUES

C. Dianne Martin
The George Washington University

Rachelle S. Heller
University of Maryland

Computer literacy has become the watchword in American
education over the past five years. There have been many
approaches to this new curriculum item, but no other approach to computer literacy has generated more controversy
than has LOGO. Right in the middle of this controversy,
as usual, are the classroom teachers who need training and
guidance if they are to implement LOGO in their classrooms.

This paper will describe the philosophical background of
LOGO. It will examine the ensuing controversy over how
LOGO should be used with children. Finally, it will describe a graduate level LOGO course for educators designed
to help them deal with all of these issues at the implementation level.

BACKGROUND

The philosophy underlying LOGO is that presented by Seymour Papert of M.I.T. in
his role as consultant to the National Science Foundation LOGO Project funded
over a decade ago. At that time Dr. Papert was horrified by the uses for computers with children that he saw being developed - computer assisted instruction (CAI), as exemplified by the PLATO project at Illinois, computer-managed
instruction (CMI), being developed by Suppes in California, and so on.

Papert saw computers being used to control children's activities, rather than the
other way around. He viewed the computer as a valuable tool for teaching children
how to formulate and solve problems, how to be inventive and resourceful, and most
importantly, how to describe their own solution processes articulately. Papert en-
visioned an educational system in which

"technology is used not in the form of machines processing
children, but as something the child himself will learn to
manipulate, to extend, to apply to projects, thereby gaining a greater...mastery of the world...and a self-confident-
ly realistic image of himself as an intellectual agent."
(Papert (1969))

Papert's work is a technological extension of the ideas of Dewey, Montessori, and
Piaget that children learn most effectively by doing and discovering. It is a
radical departure from the CAI and CMI approaches to computer use in education
where the computer is generally a mechanical administrator/drill master, rather
than a tool for the pupil to use and control.

The essential ingredient to Papert's view of computer usage is a computer language
easily accessible to children. Such a language should be very English-like and,
therefore, a very high level language. Thus LOGO, an easy-to-learn, interactive

programming language with graphics, string manipulation, and numerical capabilities, was developed. It has been found that children with average reading abilities can gain rapid mastery and self-reliance in communicating with the language. It has "provided the student with an active, operational universe for constructing and controlling a...process." (Feurzig, et. al., (1970)). The appeal of LOGO for children is the ease of accessibility it allows between user and computer.

RECENT CONTROVERSY

Many of the early proponents of LOGO were so enthusiastic that they appeared to evangelize it like a religion. It was often hard to pin them down with concrete evidence about the effectiveness of LOGO. Their stories were glowing anecdotes that tended to be subjective and difficult to measure in an objective sense (Young (1983)). The very nature of the LOGO experience, they say, defies quantification. LOGO was described as an "environment" rather than a programming language. As a result of this enthusiasm bordering on fanaticism many other educators became dubious about the true effectiveness of LOGO.

Another part of the LOGO controversy stemmed from the variety of ways in which it was introduced to children. On the one hand were those who believe that LOGO should be a completely open-ended, exploratory experience which was learner-directed. They would never teach LOGO in an organized fashion, but would let each child discover LOGO. The child would only be given the information and new commands that they asked for. Some children would never get beyond the "doodle" capability of LOGO - others would go on to accomplish wonderful programming feats. An implied assumption with this approach is that there was ample computer time available to allow for this exploration. The underlying philosophy of this approach was that LOGO should be a general problem-solving environment, a dynamic laboratory, to teach children how to think.

The opposite approach to teaching LOGO was typified by the materials produced by the Minnesota Educational Computing Consortium (MECC (1982)). Their LOGO packet consisted of a set of 10 modules containing directed activities. Each child would be told to do certain activities in order to learn to program in LOGO. There was some room for exploration by the child, but the materials were organized in such a way that every child finished with essentially the same learning experience. Inherent in such an approach was the assumption that computer resources were limited. Each child could accomplish the activities in a limited time slot on the computer. The underlying philosophy of this approach was that LOGO was a programming language which was easily accessible to children and which could be used to teach them how to control a computer.

There was yet a third approach to LOGO used by some school systems. This approach was to use LOGO for a specific purpose - to teach geometry concepts, as a tool for creative writing, to teach algebra, etc. In this approach LOGO was seen as a tool to help teach some other concept, rather than as an end in itself.

THE IMPACT ON TEACHER TRAINING

Whenever a new technology enters the educational arena, there is a flurry of in-service training activity. In the recent Office of Technological Assessment Summary Report (OTA (1982)), the importance of teacher training in bringing the new technology into the classroom was cited:

> "Widespread use of technology in the classroom will require
> that teachers be trained both in its use and in the produc-
> tion of good curriculum materials. Too few teachers are so
> qualified today."

LOGO presents the double dilemma of introducing a new skill to teachers as well as

the possibility of a radically different style for running their classrooms.
Many teachers feel that this is too much to expect of them and are very hostile
to the idea of LOGO in their classrooms. For any inservice training to be effective, it has been shown (McLaughlin & Marsh (1978)) that participants should have
input into the planning and implementation of that training. They should also
feel that the training will meet their perceived needs.

Teachers' attitudes are also affected by their classroom environment. The teacher who knows that the newly acquired skills are relevant and useful in the classroom will have a vested interest in the training. The teacher who sees the training as offering empty skills with no chance of incorporating this knowledge into
the classroom typically reacts negatively to such training (Hall and Loucks (1978)).
Availability of computers during training and afterwards in the classroom will
definitely affect teacher attitudes about inservice computer training.

With little "hard" research on the effectiveness of LOGO in the classroom, it has
been difficult to establish an inservice training model for LOGO. Teachers have
certain expectations about inservice training. For one thing, they expected to
be "taught". There were many negative stories from teachers who attended workshops conducted by some of the gurus of LOGO only to be disappointed to find out
that they were expected to "discover" LOGO on their own! They didn't want to
spend an hour struggling with a syntax error in LOGO - they wanted someone to give
them LOGO in a nutshell.

These teachers came away with negative attitudes about LOGO because their training
expectations had not been met. They still didn't know enough about LOGO to teach
it. What many of these teachers didn't realize was that they were being taught
LOGO in the way that it was hoped they would teach it themselves. The expectations of those doing the training and those being trained were definitely at cross
purposes. Even those teachers who understood why they were not being taught LOGO
in the traditional sense came away unhappy because they didn't have enough grasp
of LOGO to feel comfortable in the role of LOGO facilitator afterwards.

DEVELOPING A LOGO TRAINING MODEL

In June of 1983 the authors were approached by the Arlington County Virginia Public School System to develop and implement a LOGO training model for teachers.
The course was to be structured as a three-credit graduate course in Education to
be offered under the auspices of George Mason University. As we began to develop
such a course for Arlington County, the ramifications of this request became very
apparent. Our goal was to avoid the pitfalls of previous LOGO training models
while picking our way carefully through the politics of a local school system and
the bureaucracy of a local university.

There were at that time a few Apple Microcomputers in the school system, but the
hope was that the system would receive an Apple Foundation Grant which would supply each elementary school with one Apple Microcomputer. This meant that the
county might have computers in each school by the following spring or it might
not, depending upon outside funding. As has been previously pointed out, training 30 teachers in LOGO who might never have a computer in their classroom afterwards could prove to be a very negative factor on the outcome of such a course.

We were to have access to the Arlington Career Center which had 20 Apple Microcomputers linked together by a Corvus hard disk system. The traditional versions
of LOGO had never been implemented on a hard disk system prior to this course,
except experimentally. This meant that we would be using a newly released version
of the Terrapin LOGO on the hard disk for the first time. This new version of
LOGO didn't arrive until the third class session so that no testing time for the
instructors was available.

The course met once a week for 3 hours 15 minutes for 14 weeks. Our plan was to co-teach the course on alternating weeks. Both instructors were to be present for the first two weeks to get to know the participants and the last two weeks for the class presentations. The 20 computers were located in two classrooms so that the use of two aides for the course was essential. Both aides were parent volunteers who knew LOGO.

The concerns of the local university in setting up such a course involved the standards for graduate courses. What would the evaluation criteria be for the participants? There must be 45 contact hours in class. In a sense the criteria for establishing a three-credit course were at odds with the whole LOGO philosophy of learning by discovery. Our attempt to resolve this dilemma can be seen in the course syllabus.   We required annotated bibliographies, group projects, class readings, and a competency exam in LOGO as a way of measuring student participation and progress. We had to make it clear to the 30 participants from the beginning that this was to be a graduate level, three-credit course rather than a non-credit inservice course. However, in our teaching approach during the class sessions we presented LOGO using a guided discovery process.

CONDUCTING THE COURSE

The stage for the course was set the first night. During that session each participant was given a green folder and a red folder. They were told that the green folder was to be used for class handouts and would go home with them each week. The red folder was to be used for their tests, evaluations and homework assignments. It would always stop at the door and stay with the instructors. The first week they found the course syllabus and notes for the first lecture in the green folder. There was a Participant Profile Questionnaire and Weekly Evaluation in the red folder. Since the hard disk version of LOGO was not available until the third week, the first two weeks were spent on "getting to know the computer" and computer uses in education lectures.

Using the guided discovery process, a typical lesson lasted from 30-45 minutes. During the lesson certain LOGO commands were taught and demonstrated. The teachers were then given a worksheet which had two types of activities - directed and open. They could choose to do the directed activities which told them to do very specific examples of the commands presented that night. Or they could choose to do the open, exploratory activities which could take them in many directions. We always made it a point to stress the purpose of the two kinds of activities. It should be noted that there was never enough time for them to do both activities - they had to choose.

With 30 participants and 20 computers the teachers could choose whether to work in pairs or alone. Most of them found that it was beneficial to work on the activities in pairs. In addition to trying out the new commands each week, the teachers also were responsible for allocating some of their time to work on their group projects.

At the end of each session the participants were each asked to fill out a Weekly Evaluation as a way for the participants to provide input and direction to the course. Based on the teachers' comments each week, the instructors knew whether their lesson had been on target or not. The participants were also able to express their frustrations with the computers or their anxieties with the course. In this way the participants felt that their needs were being addressed by the instructors. The instructors went over all of the evaluations each week and put written responses on every one. Since the evaluations always stayed in the red folders, the participants would have them returned each week to read the instructor responses.

By the tenth week all of the LOGO content had been taught. On week eleven a LOGO language exam was given for the first 50 minutes of class. The rest of that week

and first half of week twelve were spent working on group projects. At the end of
week twelve a special lecture and demonstration of LOGO turtles was given by
June Wright from the University of Maryland. During weeks thirteen and fourteen
the participants presented their group projects to the class. The final week also
included a round table discussion of implementation concerns using LOGO in the
classroom.

EVALUATION

At the end of the thirteenth week the instructors compiled the results of the
weekly evaluations and prepared to share them with the students on the last
evening.

The weekly formative evaluations were coded, based on a content analysis of free,
self report responses to open-ended forms. An attempt was made to differentiate
a response which indicated satisfaction or pride of accomplishment from a response
expressing no difficulties and no special excitement. A further attempt was made
to differentiate between students who expressed a measure of disappointment in
their not finishing or mastering the material from those who felt strong
disappointment or frustration at not mastering the material.

A simple average of scores for each lesson was calculated. A plot of these
averages for each lesson shown in Graph 1 was prepared.

Content analysis was done on the difficulties students expressed after each
lesson. Graph 2 shows that while many reported no difficulties, the difficulty
level shows peaks when any new material was presented.

The students were polled each week to determine how much time they spent on the
course during the prior week. The results appear in Graph 3.

During the last session, the students were asked how the 12 weeks met their
conceptions of the objectives for the course. Graph 4 represents these findings.

CONCLUSIONS

Working in Pairs:

One of the first phenomena we observed was that those teachers who worked in pairs
were able to accomplish more, and discover more about LOGO than those who chose to
work alone. This fact became apparent to the teachers themselves who commented on
it in their Weekly Evaluations. There were several teachers that we encouraged to
pair up with others after they struggled alone for a week or two. There were
others who sometimes felt the need to work alone - there might be some concept
that they just had to work out by themselves, and fortunately sufficient computers
were available for them to do so.

Hitting the LOGO Wall:

Although LOGO was designed to be a language accessible to children, it is also

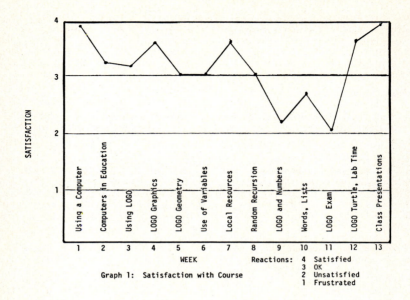

Graph 1:   Satisfaction with Course

Reactions: 4   Satisfied
            3   OK
            2   Unsatisfied
            1   Frustrated

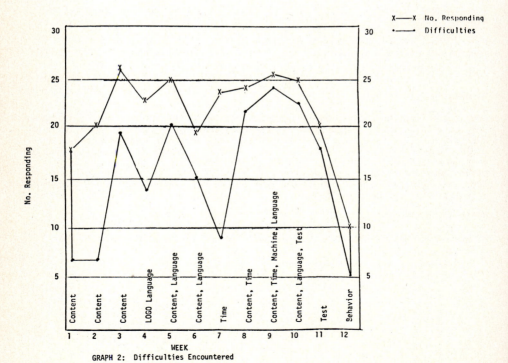

GRAPH 2: Difficulties Encountered

TIME SPENT DURING WEEK

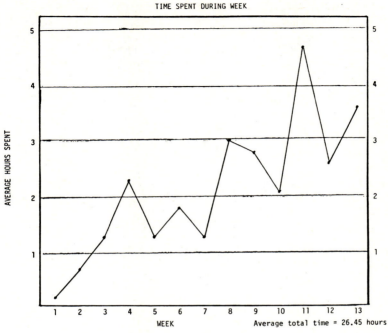

Graph 3: Time Spent During Week

Average total time = 26.45 hours

LEGEND

X———X Definitely achieved objective
•———○ Met objective to some extent
□———□ Did not meet objective

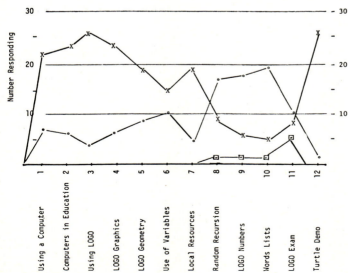

GRAPH 4: Participants'
perception of mastery
of course objectives

a very sophisticated and profound language from a computer science point of view. In any LOGO course that attempts to go beyond turtle graphics, there is a point when the participants hit an intellectual wall. This wall illustrated in Figure 4 was encountered in our course in week eight during the discussion about recursion and continued for the next two weeks in which the numerical and string manipulation capabilities of LOGO were presented. All of a sudden LOGO became more abstract and difficult for the participants, and they encountered a lot of frustration with syntax and logical errors. We had come to the limit of understanding for noncomputer-trained people.

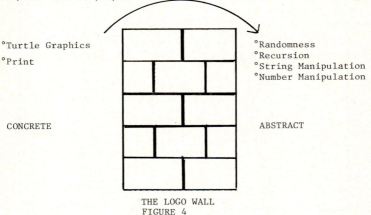

°Turtle Graphics   °Randomness
°Print   °Recursion
                                    °String Manipulation
                                    °Number Manipulation

CONCRETE   ABSTRACT

THE LOGO WALL
FIGURE 4

Computer Time Available:

Even though the participants had between 1 1/2 - 2 hours of hands-on computer time each week, one of the most common complaints was that the participants didn't have enough time to finish all of the activities. They felt that there was always some other idea that they wanted to try and never got to. They began to request sample answer programs from the instructors. This request was not granted until the end of the semester to give them the opportunity to solve the activities themselves. Toward the end of the semester they were becoming increasingly anxious about working on their group projects.

Part of the problem was that most of them did not, or could not, due to their own teaching schedule, take advantage of the one hour open lab time available before each class began. The other problem was that most of them did not have LOGO available to use at their own schools during the week. The course was originally designed with the hope that they would be able to start projects in class each week, put them on a floppy disk, and work on them in their own schools during the week. It should be noted that those teachers who were able to accomplish the most in the course did have access to computers during the week.

Open vs. Directed Activities:

In spite of all of our attempts to explain and foster the LOGO discovery philosophy, most teachers wanted to be taught LOGO rather than to discover it on their own. Most of them chose to do the directed activities rather than the exploratory ones. In the Weekly Evaluations they expressed the opinion that they didn't have enough time to waste "fooling around" with LOGO - they wanted to be sure they understood how it worked in a practical way. A significant follow-up of this issue would be to determine what techniques these teachers used to implement LOGO in their classrooms.

Inservice Training vs. Graduate Course:

One of the greatest difficulties the teachers had was in making the mental adjustment necessary to take a graduate course as opposed to a non-credit inservice course. As the semester progressed they became more and more anxious about how we were going to grade them. By the ninth and tenth week they were anxious about the LOGO exam scheduled for the eleventh week.

Our original intention was to de-emphasize the grading aspects of the course because we didn't want that to interfere with their discovery learning of LOGO. We came to realize that it was a great concern of the participants so we addressed this concern by explaining how we intended to evaluate the course. We also gave a practice test on the tenth week to help them prepare for the coming test. Many of them started to make comments that the course should have been organized as an inservice course, rather than a graduate course.

IMPLICATIONS FOR THE FUTURE

Based on our observations and on the teachers' weekly evaluations, we took the following actions. We felt that the syllabus was basically sound - we rearranged it slightly to move string manipulation capabilities with words and lists (lesson 10) before randomness and recursion (lesson 9). We eliminated the lesson on working with numerical problems in LOGO and added another week of project development time.

We established working pairs at the beginning of the course and then allowed individual computer work as participants gained more experience. All of the people who worked alone at first expressed the need to work with a partner. As the course progressed some people then wanted to work alone.

We were more specific about the requirements of the course from the very beginning. In the format of a graduate course, we required teachers to work on unfinished programs during the week so that when they returned each week their work on the computers would be more productive. The school system has purchased Apple II Computers with LOGO for each school. This has enabled teachers to work on their assignments during the week as well as in class.

In the final analysis, the importance of the course to the participants would be measured by the changes caused by the implementation of LOGO in their classrooms. The thrust of the teacher projects was practical - they were to develop a unit of study using LOGO at the level of their students. The projects they developed were very exciting - a fourth grade unit on American Indians, a Montessori unit on shapes, the formation of a LOGO computer club in one school, a unit on relationships (in, out, up, down, etc.) for special education students, a LOGO computer-assisted instruction program on averaging, and a unit on the international symbols used at the Olympics with LOGO

All of these projects involved the use and understanding of the procedural nature of LOGO. We shared a tremendous sense of satisfaction with the participants about how much they had accomplished. After all of the hard work and occasional frustrations, they had succeeded in developing some imaginative and worthwhile units.

REFERENCES

(1) <u>Apple LOGO in the Classroom</u>, (Minnesota Educational Computing Consortium (MECC), St. Paul, MN, 1982).

(2) Feurzig, W., and Grant, R., <u>Preliminary Course Guide for a Course in Mathematical Thinking</u>, (Bolt, Beranak & Newman, Cambridge, May 1970.

(3) Feurzig, W., Papert, S., Bloom, M., Grant, R., and Solomon, C., "Programming Languages as a Framework for Teaching Mathematics," (Bolt, Barenak & Newman Report No. 1889 to the National Science Foundation, November 1969).

(4) Hall, G.E. and Loucks, S., "Teacher Concerns as a Basis for Facilitating and Personalizing Staff Development," (<u>Teachers College Record</u>, vol. 80, no. 1, September 1978).

(5) "Informational Technology and Its Impact on American Education (Summary Report)," (Office of Technology Assessment, Congressional Board of the 97th Congress, Washington, D. C., November 1982).

(6) McLaughlin, M. W. and Marsh, D. D., "Staff Development and School Change," (<u>Teachers College Record</u>, vol. 80, no. 1, September 1978).

(7) Papert, Seymour, <u>Mindstorms</u>, (Basic Books, New York, 1980).

(8) Papert, Seymour. "Teaching Children Thinking," (National Science Foundation Grant CJ-1049. Bolt, Beranak & Newman, Cambridge, 1969).

(9) Watt Daniel, <u>Learning With LOGO</u>, (McGraw-Hill, New York, 1983).

(10) Young, G. P., "Children, Computers, and LOGO," (<u>AEDS</u> Monitor, August 1983).

ADDITIONAL BIBLIOGRAPHY

(1) Carter, Rickey, "The Complete Guide to LOGO," (<u>Classroom Computer News</u>, April 1983).

(2) Dryli, O. T., "LOGO, A Language that Empowers Children," (<u>Learning</u>, October 1983).

(3) Hall, G. E., "Issues Related to the Implementation of Computers in Classrooms: Where to Now?", (Research and Development Center for Teacher Education, University of Texas at Austin, February 1981).

(4) Harvey, Brian, "Why LOGO?", (<u>BYTE Magazine</u>, vol. 7, no. 8, August 1982).

(5) Martin, C. D. and Heller, R. S., "Status Report: Inservice Computer Literacy Training," <u>Informatics in Elementary Education</u>, (North Holland, Amsterdam, 1983).

(6) Martin, C. D., "LOGO and the Language Arts," (<u>University of Maryland Technical Report</u>, August 1971.

(7) Moore, Mary, "The Art of Teaching LOGO," (<u>Classroom Computer News</u>, April 1983).

(8) Solomon, Cynthia, "Introducing LOGO to Children," (<u>Byte</u>, vol. 7, no. 8, August 1982).

DISCUSSION - RAPPORTEURS TIM REEVE AND KIM FOSS HANSEN

Von Solms said that LOGO could be used with older pupils and at University level; it provides basis building blocks for programming (concepts of editing, loops etc). It is also a good starting point for specific courses and for studying computers in society (answer to Ahlstrom).

Kristel commented that he had been teaching LOGO to naive teachers and these courses had to be structured. He wondered about LOGO philosophy and its difference from normal didactic methods. Its base is in informatics but it aims to teach problem solving.

Martin said, in reply, that teaching LOGO effects children's thinking. Teachers must develop new styles - learner/coach relationship. Teachers need time to reflect on the dynamics of the classroom; self-observation and observations of pupils are necessary. This is part of the LOGO philosophy.

Von Solms said that the project had concentrated on the problem solving, which is part of informatics, but also used word processing and other processes. He commented that users do not design software but use it. He felt that LOGO was better than BASIC. People should generally use packages but consider what programming is and if necessary create their own software.

Gorny said that LOGO was more costly if used as a normal programming language (it needs storage for procedures) but it can be used like LISP for normal applications. In general, it needs more machine space (reply to Lee)

Lewis expressed concern that we should look beyond LOGO and consider 'tools for tasks'. A problem oriented language could be created using LOGO. However, Geologists, for example, need special features and we need a LOGO-like philosophy to develop the Mendelian world.

Martin (in response to Penter) said that follow-up evaluation was planned for next year. She commented that a disappointed parent found a teacher 'teaching' LOGO. There are also plans for an independent study.

Millin felt confused about the target audience for LOGO and wondered whether we should be teaching it to the young, 15-16 year-olds, or teachers.

Lee repeated the question 'What after LOGO?' and commented that teaching Computer Studies through LOGO could be transportable. He felt that this was an issue for research into the relevance of LOGO to various populations. At present, there were more questions than answers.

Van Weert said that these were strong points, in particular modularity. So far we have only look at turtle graphics but other aspects are available. Primitives can be developed for picture drawing and others can be defined.

Watson said we were making assumptions about algorithmic solutions. Group decision-making in humanities requires features which LOGO will not tackle.

Gorny felt that LOGO had limitations - no higher data structures - so far only turtle graphics has been exploited. The combination of LOGO and Small Talk had exciting possibilities. He felt that the disadvantages with most languages was that they were string based, but that we needed to use Icons more. We should not be too firmly attached to present programming languages and should keep our eyes open to the future. Algorithmic languages are awkward.

Pollak said that we had heard all this before; Fortran versus Basic; now we
have LOGO versus what?   He questioned the hypothesis that 'LOGO teaches
children to think' any more than the scientific method does.   The teaching
process involves many processes, inductive and deductive, and should use
whatever is appropriate for the moment.   What has to be done is to decide how
to approach the teaching process.

Lewis said that ten years ago we were restricted but now there is plenty of
software. All that has to be ensured is that we use the right software tool for
the present tasks.

SESSION 3

Chairman: Tom van Weert

INFORMATICS AND TEACHER TRAINING
F.B. Lovis and E.D. Tagg (editors)
Elsevier Science Publishers B.V. (North-Holland)
© IFIP, 1984

The Work of ATEE in the Field of Informatics Education

Peter Gorny
University of Oldenburg,
Applied Informatics, P. O. Box 2503,
D-2900 Oldenburg,
F. R. Germany

The report presents the efforts of the Association for
Teacher Education in Europe (ATEE) during the last five
years to identify the effects and implications of the
new information technology on the European educational
systems and to develop common strategies to cope with
the connected problems. The ATEE working group
INFORMATION TECHNOLOGY has presented a number of reports
on informatics teaching, on applications of IT in
general and on special education, at the ATEE annual
conferences. In 1982 the subject was the key theme of
the conference.

The subjects of discussion ranged from societal
implications of IT, over informatics curricula in
school and in teacher education, to programming languages,
software development and software exchange.

A series of national reports published by ATEE describe
the state of development of informatics in teacher
education in European countries.

The latest effort of the working group is a model syllabus
for literacy in information technology for all teachers.

Introductory Remark

This report is presented by a member of the ATEE Working Group on New Information
Technologies and, therefore, gives only a personal view of the goals
and efforts of ATEE. The document does not represent an official statement of
ATEE.

1. The Association for Teacher Education in Europe

In the ATEE, institutions engaged in teacher education, as well as interested
individuals from 16 countries, are working together in order to exchange new
ideas and to compare the development of the European education system. From
these studies new ideas and methodologies for the teaching process have been
derived and the results have been transferred to the curricula of teacher
education. It is the goal of ATEE to further these developments also at the
international European level.

The Association has established - along with other working groups - a permanent
Working Group on New Information Technologies, which has been vividly discussing
the impact of information technology on education during recent years. In spite
of the great distances and the difficulties in supplying travel funds, the
Working Group has met in Switzerland, Denmark (2), Britain (2), Germany (2) and

Belgium (2). The results of these meetings were presented at the annual ATEE conference and partly also in print. A brief outline only of these activities will be drawn here.

2. The Implications of Information Technology for Teacher Education

The impact of Information Technology (IT) on society is bound to concern the educational system in several ways. In the ATEE reports listed in the appendix four main areas have been identified:

- Pupils have to be prepared to live in a rapidly changing society; they will have to master new skills and professions, and they will have to be able to control, democratically, the further development of IT applications in their social environment. So schools have to teach about IT and about its influence on society.

- Secondly, this new technology implies a new way of handling information, or more precisely, of handling data carrying some information. The new way of information processing is connected with new thinking methods and new problem solving approaches. Thus IT involves schools in granting (or refusing) the children a new ability: literacy in information technology. Consequently this literacy will change the contents and methodologies, not only of mathematics and physics, but will effect practically all subject matters.

- Thirdly, IT can serve as an aid in the teaching process, either as a tool, just as a calculator, a dictionary, etc., or as a medium, comparable with slides, tapes, films, etc.

- Finally, IT may be used as an aid for school management and the management of teaching (computer-managed instruction).

These topics have been more precisely defined in two ATEE reports /R1, R3/ and have been further substantiated by studies of the existing influence of IT in different European countries /R2, R4, R6/.

The Working Group was also involved in an extensive comparative research project that was implemented by the Institute of Education of the European Cultural Foundation, Paris, for the Director General of Science and Education of the Netherlands. The results of this project have been published in a special issue of the European Journal of Education (Vol. 17, No. 4 (1982)).

The work on the implications of IT has led to a number of invitations to members of the Working Group to participate as advisers in conferences held by international or supranational organizations or by national governments.

3. Exchange of Teaching Materials

A continuous concern of ATEE is the exchange of curriculum material beyond the borders of the different countries and cultural barriers. In regard to IT this means especially the transfer of programs for Computer Aided Learning (CAL). It is one of the goals of the Working Group to encourage the international and supranational institutions in Europe to establish one or several "clearing houses" for software.

A number of obstacles hinder the easy flow of software, e.g. incompatibilities in hardware and system software, legal restrictions (e.g. copyright), and especially the differences between the school systems and their cultural background, including the languages. For several years the Working Group was engaged in finding a programming language suitable for schools, in order to reduce at least one technical obstacle.

The Working Group discussed, within the family of procedural languages, BASIC and Pascal as "old" languages, and also the more recent developments COMAL, LSE and ELAN on one hand, as well as LOGO as a list oriented functional language, on the other hand. The group refrained from making a recommendation, since technological progress now leads to microcomputer systems equipped with several of the languages. Another reason is that any of the languages, even the most primitive dialect of BASIC, may have - under given financial restrictions - an application area at school. On the other hand, none of the languages and their respective programming environments will be satisfactory for all school purposes - from primary to upper secondary level, in different subject matters, for general, vocational or special education, for teaching informatics or IT literacy, or for the (professional) production of teaching software.

4. Information Technology curricula in Teacher Education

As pointed out in section 2, ATEE has come to the conclusion that the New Information Technologies will have at least a similar impact on mankind to the mass production of print media and the corresponding obligatory instruction in reading and writing had in the past. Therefore, the school should create insights which enable the pupils to develop a reasoned and balanced attitude toward IT, which at the same time will enable them to react appropriately to situations in which contact with automated systems take place.

Teacher education has to take this into consideration and has to include fundamental informatics or literacy in IT in the normal training of teachers. The Working Group is engaged in developing appropriate syllabuses and has recently published the first of a series of reports on "A Model Syllabus for Literacy in Information Technology for all Teachers". This report provides recommendations on how to educate teachers about IT /7/. Reports on teaching with the aid of, and by means of, Information Technology and on the teaching methodology (didactics) of IT are being prepared.

A description of the model syllabus will not be given here, because the ATEE report is available at this conference. Instead we may, at this place, refer to the papers of our Dutch colleagues, with special mention of Tom van Weert, who have contributed a great deal to the report and are presenting a corresponding in-service curriculum at this conference.

The Working Group is hoping that the model syllabus will give an extra impulse to the general introduction of literacy in IT into European teacher education, be it - depending on the teacher education system of each country - as pre-service (initial) education or/and as in-service education.

5. Cooperation

As a consequence of the discussions in the ATEE a number of instances of cooperation between teacher education institutions of different countries have developed, three major examples only will be mentioned here: the development of programming languages, the program exchange and the curriculum development. The countries involved were Denmark, France, Germany and Ireland, Great Britain and the Netherlands, and finally Denmark, Germany and the Netherlands, respectively.

The ATEE Working Groups on Special Education and on New Information Technologies are closely linked in investigating the application of IT in special education and are discussing in joint sessions the possibilities and limitations of this technology to promote the learning process of the handicapped.

New cooperative efforts are about to investigate the influence of IT on sex discrimination and the combination of audiovisual media and computers in the teaching process.

6.   Perspectives of the ATEE work

ATEE is a loose association of institutions and individuals working in the field of teacher education. The common interest is to exchange experiences, to develop new ideas and to gather together the diverse efforts, hoping that – solely by the power of their arguments – they may influence their colleagues, as well as the politicians and administrators in their home countries and in Europe as a whole.

In the near future the ATEE Working Group on New Information Technologies will concentrate on the further development of the model syllabus mentioned in section 5 and on the establishment of an effective system for the exchange of teaching material on IT and of material using IT as an aid or as a medium for teaching and learning.

There is also research under progress to investigate if, and how, the new telecommunication techniques provided by the telephone services, called interactive Videotex (Prestel, Teledata, Bildschirmtext etc.), can be used, for instance, in school or in teacher education, as a self-study medium or as a means of communication in distance teaching.

It is the ambition of ATEE to participate – within its modest resources – in the support of the administrators and political bodies responsible for the educational systems of our countries to attain a reasonable attitude towards the New Information Technology, so that it will not be thoughtlessly used in education but applied with due respect for the individual. Our goal is to point out where the pedagogical efforts of parents and teachers might be changed by IT applications and where they might be amplified, in order to enable all pupils to gain insight and ability to develop their lives 'in pursuit of happiness' and to be conscious of their responsibilities within our future society.

Appendix: ATEE Reports on Information Technology

1.   Rhys Gwyn:

 The New Information Technologies and Education – Implications for Teacher Education, Brussels, 1981.

2.   Elizabeth Oldham:

 The New Information Technologies – Implications for Teacher Education – Country Study: Ireland. Brussels, 1981.

3.   Rhys Gwyn:

 Information Technology and Teacher Education: Perspectives on Development, Brussels, 1982.

4.   Peter Gorny:

 The New Information Technologies and Education – Implications for Teacher Education. Country Report 2: Federal Republic of Germany. Brussels, 1983.

5.   Torsten Alf Jensen:

 New Information Technologies and Education in Denmark. Brussels, 1982.

6. Alan Smith (Ed.):

Teacher Training and New Information Technologies Proc. 7th Annual
Conf. of ATEE, Working Group IT, Birmingham, September 1982, Brussels, 1983.

7. Tom van Weert (Ed.):

A Model Syllabus on Literacy in Information Technology for All Teachers.
Brussels, 1984.
German edition in LOGIN, Vol 3, No. 4 (1984), French edition in preparation.

Reports can be obtained from ATEE - Association for Teacher Education in Europe,
51, rue de la Concorde, B-1050 Brussel.

INFORMATICS AND TEACHER TRAINING
F.B. Lovis and E.D. Tagg (editors)
Elsevier Science Publishers B.V. (North-Holland)
© IFIP, 1984

Methods and Dichotomies in Teaching Computing Science

Robert P. Taylor
Teachers College, Columbia University

Introduction

This paper is concerned with teaching computing, especially at the secondary school level. It outlines the methods course for secondary school teachers of computing science that is part of a teacher training curriculum outline that the ACM (Association for Computing Machinery) is currently considering for issue as an official curriculum recommendation. Several important dichotomies that arise in teaching computing and that therefore lie beneath the design of the methods course are then discussed. The prospective teachers must learn how to maintain a healthy tension between the poles of each dichotomy if their own students are to emerge as well-balanced candidates for the computing profession.

A Methods Course for Training Computing Science Teachers

The methods course suggested in the draft curriculum paper is one of six courses recommended as required prerequisites to secondary school teacher certification in computing. The minimum framework of six courses includes:

(1) R1. Computer Programming I

(2) R2. Computer Programming II

(3) R3. Introduction to Computer Systems

(4) R4. Organization of Computer Languages

(5) R5. Data Structures and Algorithm Analysis

(6) R6. Methods for Teaching Computer Science

Courses (1) through (5) are very much based on the ACM's Curriculum 78 and recent or pending updates, and would give the prospective teacher successfully completing them a minimum background roughly equivalent to an undergraduate degree minor in computer science. The draft's authors included the sixth course (Methods) because they felt some concepts essential to learning sound computing needed special emphasis, in addition to any attention such concepts might normally receive in courses (1) through (5). The methods course outline as drafted appears below, marked by additional indentation. (The original version of the methods course was by the author of this paper. In reviewing it, Arthur Luehrmann, Kathleen Norris, Jim Poirot, and Harriet Taylor all contributed to the draft shown here, the one finally presented for ACM review).

R6. Methods of Teaching Computer Science

The objectives of this course are:

a) to provide prospective teachers with insights that will enable them to improve computing skills of their students;

b) to introduce techniques of teaching topics of computing, particularly programming;

c) to adapt computer science concepts for presentations in programming languages commonly available in an educational setting;

d) to examine the role of the computing teacher in a secondary school setting.

The prerequisite for this course is R5 Data Structure and Algorithm Design. Because the prospective teacher will primarily teach programming, this course should reflect that focus. Though it will touch many of the topics from the other required courses, the emphasis here will be complementary rather than redundant, dealing with these topics and processes from the prospective of how they may best be learned, not what they are.

Throughout the course, strong emphasis should be placed on the learner's point of view and developmental level, and on its impact on how the abstract concepts of computing are best presented. It also presupposes strong emphasis on the role of the teacher in teaching computing, and familiarity with appropriate research and learning, particularly learning computing and problem solving.

The following are the topics of study basic to the methods course:

A. Methods of teaching students to see software and hardware as intermediaries in communication between human beings rather than as ends or sources of communication. This should help students to learn to create software, including documentation, sensitive to the user's point of view, not just the programmer's. It requires experience using and maintaining software created by others.

B. Methods of teaching students to understand how to work effectively within the individual and social human environment. This should help students to appreciate the intellectual limitations of humans as individual programmers, as well as help them to work effectively within software development teams. Requires familiarity with research on psychology of thought and social interactions.

C. Methods of teaching students to see how hardware and software limitations constrain the development of every computer-based problem solution. This should help students to see how limitations such as those associated with memory, disk capacity and access speed, response entry device flexibility, and operating speed, affect the degree of user support includable in current software. It requires students to experience different types of computer, representing different size and performance classes.

D. Methods of teaching students to see that good structure and modularity are essential in software systems, not only to arrive at an implementable design, but also to make possible any reasonable degree of maintenance or extensibility of that software. This requires students to work with systems too large to be implemented in a single module, to work on teams, and to maintain and modify software designed by others. It requires familiarity with research on how students learn to program and how structure affects design and maintenance.

E. Methods of teaching students to see the general aspects of programming across different languages, including how essentially similar logic must be implemented differently in alternative programming languages. Requires having students look at the formal structure (particularly control structures) of at least one, and preferably several, languages, in addition to the vehicle used in R1. (Programming I). This should include learning how to implement the best structure possible, even in languages which, though popular, may not have effective and well-designed general control structures. It requires familiarity with research on programming style, learning problems, and other matters associated with programming structure.

How institutions offering such a methods course will actually implement the details will vary. What topics in communication and psychology they choose to explore, what programming languages they decide to use, how they manage to structure team and group work, what sorts of computer hardware they make available, and so on, will all strongly shape the direction that teacher trainees will get from the course. The draft recommendations do not deal with these details, nor shall we here. Instead, we shall consider several of the underlying dichotomies that must be dealt with by anyone trying seriously to teach computing, particularly to prospective teachers of computing.

Underlying dichotomies that must be kept in balance

Dichotomies are often useful in providing insight because they force one to consider a situation or an issue from both sides. The following are no exception. Consideration of them can be particularly useful in helping prospective teachers of computing to appreciate the range of learning they want to encourage in their own computing students when they return to teaching. The balance required to resolve the real polarities each dichotomy represents is reflected in the design of the methods course.

(1) Eclecticism versus structure

(2) Being a coach versus being the Wizard of Oz

(3) Creating in one burst versus creating by refinement

(4) Creating versus using

(5) Textual versus graphic representation

Let us look briefly at each dichotomy.

Eclecticism versus Structure. Kids seem to favor an eclecic, hacking approach to program development. Using Logo or Basic, the 8 year old typically hacks away until he or she gets the picture or action wanted (or some satisfactory substitute for it). Adults, on the other hand, often want a strong sense of structure, to hold their thinking together, almost from the beginning. And professional adult programmers have certainly learned that structure and planning are essential to producing maintainable systems. Since the secondary school teacher is working with students who probably learned eclectically and who may not always be happy with developing a more structured style, he must work out a balance between eclecticism and structure in his teaching of programming. Considering that the professional programmer usually oscillates between eclectic and structural operation, developing a balanced view of the place of each mode is crucial for the teacher and should be encouraged. They should appreciate that the professional programmer exercises eclecticism to find out exactly how a particular feature in a language or a piece of hardware works, then reverts to rigid planning and structured progress to proceed with overall project or program development.

Being a coach versus being the Wizard of Oz. Since the role of the teacher is quite likely to change, as computers become more prominent through education, the prospective teacher should be encouraged to examine his role. He should explore recent research into teaching and recent speculation about how teachers might behave under the sorts of conditions more computing may foster.

For example, the traditional role of the teacher as a Wizard of Oz or expert on the subject of the day, might be less appropriate in a computer-oriented classroom than a role in which the teacher functioned as a coach. The predominant tendency for a teacher to exercise class control through emphasis on his supposed prowess as a font of all knowledge should be firmly balanced by efforts to help the teacher learn to function also as a coach. In that role the teacher encourages, cajoles, criticizes, warns, counsels and urges the students, all toward better computing; the teacher does not need to know more about programming than anyone in the class, and need not be able to outperform the students to prove who is teacher.

Creating in one burst versus creating by refinement. There often seems to be a misconception in the novice's mind about how software is developed, holding that the entire program (or even system) is conceived in a blinding flash and then coded from top to bottom, all correct and ready to produce the final results wanted, as soon as it is executed. In fact, software creation is a refinement process and may often be better characterized as a grinding process rather than the execution of a one-shot, blinding inspiration. The teacher must learn to help students appreciate the reality of both poles of this dichotomy, and to understand that refinement and revision should even be part of the planning of software. Creation in and out of computing may depend on the creative flash. There is no creation of significance, though, without the subsequent grinding process of refinement.

Creating versus using. As communication, all programs should reflect sensitivity to the user's perspective. Teachers should thus learn to encourage their students to appreciate this by using and criticizing appropriate existing software and by creating new software which reflect the user's point of view. In particular, they should be required to spend considerable time using software created by others, including software that does not take seriously the user's point of view.

The importance of thinking of the user while designing and implementing software has an important corollary in teacher behavior itself that should be underscored for the trainees. That is, they should be confronted frequently with the difference between (a) flaunting virtuosity with computers as a testimony of one's own competence and (b) employing computing fluency to simplify things for the novice.

Textual versus graphic representation. For too long we have underplayed the importance of graphic representation in teaching and learning programming. Textual representation of logic may be all right, but the need for diagrams, indentation, and other forms of visual aids indicates how much most humans are supported by graphic representation. Teachers should look for better ways to represent programming languages to novices, particularly now that computers can more ably handle graphics of all kinds. Extrinsic graphics such as windows on multiple events, or pictures of memory locations and their contents are fine, but a graphic representation of the language of programming itself certainly helps the learner to grasp the relation between his thinking and the process of programming.

For example, the FPL language and compiler we have developed at Teachers College incorporates a graphic representation of each major construct in classical programming. Thus the computer represents a rough idea, a segment of code yet to be refined, as a cloudy shape including a textual label as in Figure 1 and a simple conditional (IF..THEN..ELSE..) in the visually familiar form of a left/right choice as in Figure 2.

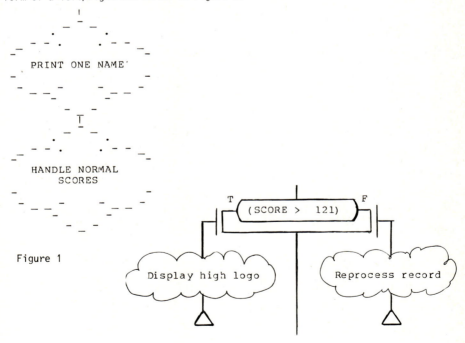

PRINT ONE NAME

HANDLE NORMAL
SCORES

Figure 1

Figure 2

Though some learners do not seem to support their logical thinking with a graphic representation, many do. The teacher currently has little to offer such learners; currently popular languages simply do not incorporate any graphical representation.

To better support the learner who does relate well to graphical representation and for whom such representation is a substantial learning aid, the teacher needs languages that do intrinsically incorporate graphics. Whether these languages are designed, like FPL, to teach classical programming as used with FORTRAN, COBOL, BASIC and PASCAL, or to teach some newer type of programming does not matter. The graphic support should be included.

Summary

This paper presents the outline of a new methods course for secondary school teachers of computer science. The course is under consideration by the ACM as part of a statement on recommended curricula for use in establishing state certification standards for such teachers. Five dichotomies that arise in teaching computing are discussed. Consideration of such dichotomies played a significant role in the design of the methods course and represent polarities of creative tension the prospective teacher must learn to keep in balance.

References

1. Austing, Richard, et al (editors), "Curriculum '78 recommendations for the undergraduate program in computer science, "CACM, vol 22, no 3 (March 1979), pp 147-166.

2. Brooks, Frederick The Mythical Man-month. Addison-Wesley, 1975.

3. Forsdale, Louis Perspectives on Communication, Addison-Wesley, 1981.

4. Kniefel, David, Arthur Luehrmann, Cathleen Norris, Jim Poirot, Harriet Taylor and Robert P. Taylor, "Proposed curriculum for programs leading to teachers certification in computer science," (under current review by the Association for Computing Machinery as a curriculum statement).

5. Luehrmann, Arthur and H. Peckham, Computer Literacy, 1983.

6. Macluhan, Marshall, Understanding Media, 1965.

7. Papert, Seymour, Mindstorms, Basic Books, 1980.

8. Polya, G., How to Solve it, Princeton, 1945.

9. Solloway, Elliot, J. Bonar, K. Erlich, J. Greenspan "What do novices know about programming?" Dept of computer science Research Report 218 (mimeo) Yale University 1982.

10. Taylor, Robert P. Programming Primer, Addison-Wesley, 1982.

11. Weinberg, Gerald Psychology of Computer Programming, Van Nostrand-Reinhold, 1971.

INFORMATICS AND TEACHER TRAINING
F.B. Lovis and E.D. Tagg (editors)
Elsevier Science Publishers B.V. (North-Holland)
© IFIP, 1984

TEACHER TRAINING IN THE U.K. — SOME CASE-STUDIES

introduced and edited by
Barry H. Blakeley

Centre for Science and Mathematics Education
Chelsea College
University of London

During the past decade the picture of teacher training, in particular in-service training, has changed markedly. A set of case-studies is presented to illustrate a number of the facets of the topic, with an introduction which aims to put the various types of activity in context.

Introduction

Many changes have taken place in the education system of the United Kingdom during the last twenty years, most notably the change to comprehensive schools and the attendant disappearance of grammar schools. The vast majority of children between the ages of 11 and 16 are now educated in non-selective schools. However, the technological revolution of the computer and, more recently the micro-computer, has produced changes which were not foreseen even a few years ago. In particular the enormous growth in the number of micro-computers in schools (both primary and secondary) has created a need and a demand for teacher training at pre-service and in-service stages. There is now a great variety of such training and the case-studies which form the bulk of this paper are intended to provide insights into a cross-section of that training.

Setting the Scene

It will help to set the various case-studies in context if there is first presented a brief summary of the structure of education in the U.K. Figure 1 shows the main elements in the provision of maintained schools and higher education in England and Wales.

There is compulsory schooling for children between the ages of 5 and 16. There are some 22000 Primary Schools, employing about 170000 teachers and catering for roughly 4.25 million pupils. At the secondary stage (ages 11-16) about 4200 schools, employing 240000 teachers, cater for roughly 4 million pupils. Special education is provided (in 1500 schools) for handicapped children, with educationally subnormal children being the largest category among the 120000 pupils who attend such schools.

The public education service is a partnership of national and local government. Although national government, through the Secretary of State for Education and Science, is responsible for all aspects of education in England (and some in Wales), it does not run any schools or colleges or engage any teachers. Much power is devolved to Local Education Authorities (LEAs) to provide education (other

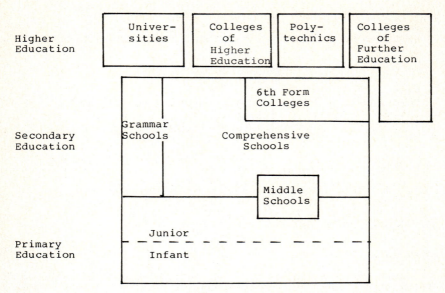

Figure 1

than in universities); they build schools, employ teachers, local inspectors of schools and education organisers; they also provide equipment and materials. (Local inspectors and Her Majesty's Inspectorate - the government's inspectors - have traditionally provided some of the in-service training for teachers.) At age 16 pupils have a number of options, including full-time education to 18 (in school or college), part-time education (in college) and seeking employment. Higher education (including universities and polytechnics as well as further education colleges) covers students from age 18 onwards. Universities are independent bodies in charge of their own awards, but the Council for National Academic Awards (CNAA) was established in 1964 to validate university-level courses outside the university system.

Public examinations (at present under careful re-consideration) broadly comprise the General Certificate of Education (GCE) (at ordinary and Advanced levels) and the Certificate of Secondary Education (CSE).

Teachers and Training

Teachers in maintained schools are required to be qualified, which means that they must have completed an initial course of training. In the past many teachers have qualified by means of courses at Colleges of Education, but many such colleges have been closed during the past few years. The main routes to qualification (in England and wales) are shown in Figure 2.

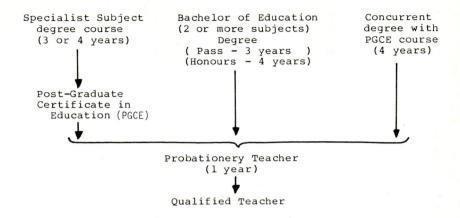

Figure 2

Government Initiatives

During the past ten years, government funded programmes have had an important effect on Informatics in schools and colleges. The National Development Programme in Computer Assisted Learning (1973–78) was the first major programme. The Microelectronics Education Programme (MEP), set up in 1981, formed 14 Regional Information Centres (RICs) to provide, in conjunction with LEAs, a means of disseminating information, curriculum materials, and software, and to provide in-service training for local authority advisers and teachers. The third major impact has been made by the Department of Industry who, first in secondary schools, then in primary schools, have provided half of the purchase price of microcomputer equipment. According to a recent report. secondary schools now have, on average, five micro-computers each; it is the government's intention that every primary school shall have at least one microcomputer by the end of 1984.

Under such circumstances it can be readily understood that the need for in-service training is enormous. In addition to the LEA provision mentioned above for many years courses have been provided by colleges, polytechnics and universities. Increasingly over the last few years, the Open University has been providing courses which have met the in-service needs of serving teachers, in addition to the part-time degree courses which many teachers have followed.

The case-studies which follow do not cover all aspects of teacher education, but it is hoped that they provide an impression of the quality and variety of the work now in progress in the U.K. I should like to express my sincere thanks to the authors of the case-studies for agreeing to write them, at a time when their work schedules were already over-crowded.

References

Department of Education and Science, The Educational System of England and Wales. (Her Majesty's Stationery Office, 1983)

CASE STUDY 1

POSTGRADUATE CERTIFICATE IN EDUCATION COURSE

P. Piddock

Faculty of Education, University of Birmingham

General Structure and Assessment

The Postgraduate Certificate of Education at Birmingham University is a one-year full-time course. It is assessed in two parts and candidates must satisfy the examiners in each of these. There are no examination papers. The Theory of Education requires two essays based on lectures given by members of the departments of Curriculum Studies, Educational Psychology, Social and Administrative Studies in Education, History and Philosophy of Education, and Special Education, together with two pieces of assessed work in the student's Main Method subject and a Special Study. The Practice of Teaching is assessed by observation of the student's teaching performance in two periods of teaching practice. The first of these ("School Experience") takes place in weeks 2-4 of the course, and the second occupies the whole of the second term. Supervision of teaching practice is undertaken by main method tutors. There are eight computer science students in the current year and this is a typical tutorial group size.

Main Method Work

The Main Method course in computer science occupies two half-days per week throughout the first term. There is also a further afternoon per week devoted to tutorial group work, which is used for main method by most tutors. In the third term, two weeks are dedicated to further main method work.

Seminar/discussion sessions are used to cover

(a) the role of the computer science teacher in the school;
(b) syllabuses and course planning;
(c) resources;
(d) marking and assessment;
(e) preparation, delivery and evaluation of lessons;
(f) teaching methods.

Students are introduced to the hardware and software available to schools by means of practical sessions in the computer laboratory. Throughout the first term they carry out a circus of experiments designed to give them this varied experience. In addition they pursue two optional fields of study (including various computer languages, and hardware devices such as bit-pads, light-pens and speech synthesis units, but with a complete and open-ended freedom of choice).

Visits are undertaken to Birmingham Educational Computing Centre (Local Education Authority information support and resources) and to the West Midlands Regional Information Centre of the Microelectronics Education Programme. During visits to local schools, each student teaches all or part of a lesson which is observed by the rest of the group and discussed in a later group session.

The assessed written work consists of an essay on the place of computer science in the school curriculum and a folder of notes taken during all of the activities described above. The essential philosophy of this main method work is that described in the IFIP booklet "Aims and Objectives in Teacher Training" (1972).

Subsidiary Method Work

Students are required to study one subsidiary method subject. Eight afternoons during the first term are devoted to this; it is not formally assessed. It is assumed that the students who choose the computer science subsidiary have a reasonable technical knowledge of computing so that the course can concentrate on teaching methods. Topics covered during the eight sessions are typically:

Week 1   Syllabuses and courses in computer science
Week 2   Resources - hardware, software, books, information
Weeks 3,4 "Structured Programming" approach to practical work
Week 5   Low level languages
Week 6   Using LOGO
Week 7   Using Prolog
Week 8   Information Retrieval

Special Study

In the third term, students pursue a special study project of their own choosing, supervised by the lecturer with whom the topic was agreed at the end of the first term. A two week period is devoted to this work, and a report (4000 words) is required for assessment after a further three weeks. About ten students undertake special study work in the area of computer-assisted learning, and this usually includes most of the main method computer science students. This year the topics are mainly concerned with extending and amending by software the facilities available on BBC microcomputers, to offer help to visually handicapped users and to their teachers. Previous work has included stereoscopic colour graphics, speech synthesis and the production of small pieces of software to support the teaching of various subjects.

Other Computer Science content

Optional work with the computers in the laboratory is offered on eight afternoons during the first term, and is open to all P.G.C.E. students. A lecture and discussion session of about two hours, on "Computer Education", is offered to all students in the third term. Main Method work in many of the subjects offered on the P.G.C.E. course now incorporates examination and discussion of the role of computers in the teaching and learning of those subjects. This trend is being strongly encouraged.

CASE STUDY 2

DIPLOMA COURSE IN HIGHER EDUCATION

S. Rumsby

Leicester Polytechnic, Leicester

The advent of microcomputers introduced the age of cheap computing power - the micro revolution. This led to a government initiative to place a microcomputer in every secondary school. Very many schools were then left to introduce some form of computer studies with teachers who had no formal (or informal) qualifications in the subject. The normal training was a few ad hoc short courses. It was because of these events that, in 1981, the British Computer Society (BCS) Computer Education Group designed a course [1] which would enable teachers to acquire sufficient expertise to teach up to C.S.E. or O-level. Leicester Polytechnic responded to the requests from LEA'S by adapting the BCS course and offering it as a One-Year full-time course leading to the Diploma in Professional Studies in Secondary Education (DPSE).[2]

The course was split into seven modules. Six of these were essentially the same as the course proposed by the Computer Education Group. The first module, "Systems Analysis and Computer Applications", was meant to introduce the skills of systems analysis and how they were applied in commerce. The second, "Programming and Problem Analysis", was intended to concentrate on how to produce well designed, reliable programs using a suitable language. The third, "Computer Architecture and Systems Software", was designed to give an understanding of the basic hardware, how it worked and what systems software was required to make it usable. The fourth and fifth modules, "Computers in Education" and "Curriculum and Pedagogy" dealt with the implications of computers in the educational environment. The sixth module, "Computers in Society", covered the areas of privacy, communication, freedom and protection of information, automation and so on. The last module, "Computer Graphics and Visual Communications", was an option in the BCS scheme and was a compulsory option in the Leicester Polytechnic scheme, as the team involved in producing the course considered graphics an essential element.

It can be seen that our belief is that teachers should have a sound base of knowledge integrated with skills. The course is aimed at giving the teacher confidence and the ability to work in the field at a viable commercial level. With this in mind the scheme enables successful diplomates to qualify for exemption from BCS Part I examinations. It also provides an adequate base for future staff education in computing. This is vital in a discipline which is undergoing such rapid metamorphoses. The diplomates should be able to hold their own with specialist and information technologists and be in a position to provide much needed "technical" expertise.

In the Spring of 1981, the Department of Education and Science (DES) wrote to the Polytechnic suggesting it should run a one-term "pilot" version of the course for the summer term 1982, and provided financial backing in the form of grants for the secondment of teachers. This course was a truncated version of the BCS Diploma Course consisting of the Systems Analysis, Social Implications, Computer Architecture and Programming modules. The initial response to the course was overwhelming and over 100 teachers were interviewed, mainly from Leicestershire and the surrounding counties. The DES allocated 30 grants for the course and as this number could not be exceeded, the course eventually ran with 27 students. At the same time as this course started, in April 1982, the One-Year DPSE course was validated by the Council for National Academic Awards (CNAA), and although efforts were made to recruit teachers for a September 1982 start, this proved impossible due to problems with secondment.

The one-term course was run again in the Summer term of 1983 and considerable effort was spent in promoting the DPSE course. The former course received little support from the LEAs, even though funding was available. We were therefore unable to make a case to the DES for continued funding and the course is no longer offered. The first intake of the DPSE course started in September 1983 with 18 teachers. Three of them were from Further Education, one from a junior school and the rest from secondary schools. Both the one-term course and the DPSE course appear to be satisfying an urgent need. Although the course involves intensive learning and a great deal of practical work, the lecturing staff have been impressed by the industry and enthusiasm of the students.

Great problems have been experienced in bringing the course to the notice of teachers. Different forms of advertising have been tried ranging from advertisements in the national press to circulars to Computing Advisers. The use of the Microelectronics Education Programme (MEP) as a vehicle for informing teachers about the course failed completely. The LEAs, generally, do not seem to regard the plight of Computer Studies teachers to be that severe, judging by their reluctance to second them, even though 75% of the costs of secondment can be recovered by the LEA from the DES. It may be that the teachers who would benefit most can be least spared for a year — a Catch 22 situation.

Other institutions are now producing their own versions of the DPSE course in both full and part-time versions. The Leicester Polytechnic DPSE places greater emphasis on the computing aspects than on the educational, because that is where the need is most urgent. We intend to produce a report evaluating the course in the summer of 1984.

References

[1] Diploma in Computer Education (Proposed) BCS Computer Education Group (available from British Computer Society).

[2] Leicester Polytechnic DPSE (Computing) course specification

CASE STUDY 3

LEA'S TEACHER TRAINING FOR PRIMARY TEACHERS

Leon Shuker

Inner London Educational Computing Centre

The present government's offer of half funding for a micro, monitor, cassette storage system and a package of primary age-range programs has enabled many primary schools to purchase one of the three British made machines offered by the Department of Trade and Industry. The DTI offer stipulated that LEA's must provide two days inservice training for two teachers from each recipient school, and this was supplemented by a 30 hour Open University-style distance learning package.

The response to this scheme by the LEA'S has been varied, and the most successful authorities have been those who were previously supporting micros in their primary schools. The Inner London Education Authority in particular had a pilot scheme of 22 primary schools who were supplied with a Research Machines Ltd. model 380Z and some of the software then available. Other authorities had individual schools experimenting with micros, and a few, for example Hertfordshire, had established a centre to support these schools.

To support LEAs, and particularly those with limited expertise and resources, the Microelectronics Education Programme, funded by the government, provided courses for trainers of teachers, and 2-day support material for them. Fourteen centres throughout the country had been previously established through the MEP, though very few of them had primary school expertise among their staff. This was to be expected as there was little expertise among primary teachers in any schools in the early days of the DTI scheme.

The '2-day' courses consist of whole days, half days or evening sessions, in which teachers learn the rudiments of operating the equipment, use of the current software and school management of the technology. Among the software used was one of the various data retrieval programs (e.g. SCAN, MICROQUERY, QUEST, FACTFILE), a LOGO program for showing problem solving possibilities, and a variety of uni-purpose programs of varying quality, including some which were in the Micro Primer Pack supplied free to schools as part of the MEP package. The MEP distance learning pack is considered by many teachers to be more suitable for those who have already had some form of training. Exceptionally, the Inner London Education Authority has a four-day training programme, concentrating on the educational aspects of the micro, with more time for teachers to study and use the best of the software and discuss its uses within the present primary curriculum philosophy, and the ways such programs may improve and change that curriculum.

In a few areas, again notably where pre-DTI scheme work had started, there are further courses for primary teachers to extend their expertise. Some MEP centres have longer courses and supplement the DTI scheme with a variety of day and evening topic based courses; Birmingham has a one-term residential course based in one of their colleges and London has several 150 hour certificated courses, organised by their computer education inspectorate and based in some of the further education colleges.

Several authorities have initiated self-help user groups, being aware of the need for continuing training but heavily committed to the DTI training scheme. These activities are supplemented by school based inservice training in some schools.

The activities in parts of the country known to the writer suggest that many British primary schools are being given a richer curriculum through the use of the micro, though the training programme put upon LEAs is straining their resources in staffing and funds.

CASE STUDY 4

IN-SERVICE TRAINING VIA CAL DEVELOPMENT

Deryn M. Watson

Computers in the Curriculum

Chelsea College, University of London

Introduction

The Computers in the Curriculum Project (CIC), based at Chelsea College, London University, has been funded by government agencies for ten years to research and develop computer assisted learning materials for secondary (11-18 years) schools in the United Kingdom. It has evolved a philosophy [1] that CAL materials should enhance and extend the existing curriculum, thus relating both to current classroom practice and also the moving curriculum. Accordingly it works increasingly with innovative educational projects [2] and has developed a model for CAL development to accommodate its main aims [3]. A key component of this model is the involvement of teachers from the classroom who form part of a discipline-based CAL development team.

The model at work

The team, operating in various locations across the country, has certain components:-

- local teachers, still working in the classroom, with regular support and secondment from their LEA advisers, who are often also involved in

- an innovative curriculum project, e.g. the History 13-16 Project based in Leeds. This group is supported by

- professional programmers (members of the Chelsea team) one of whom is often based locally, and

- CAL designers based at Chelsea. These individuals, who have been involved with CAL development for some time, act both as a catalyst for the group and as a bridge between potentially conflicting demands of the programmers and teachers.

The detailed mechanism for such groups varies with location. Some teachers have a period of weekly secondment (anything between half

and two days a week);   some a two or three day block release once or
twice a term, when the whole working group gets together for a
concentrated session;   others work at weekends in their own time.

After a lengthy development process, both resultant software and
related teachers' and pupils' material are tested independently in
schools and modified before publication.   The Leeds/Bradford Group
associated with the Schools Council History 13-16 Project, has been
in operation for three years;   at the end of this period 12 units
will be available for publication.   During this time both Leeds and
Bradford LEA's have been prepared to arrange regular secondment,
financed from their in-service training budgets.

In-service Implications

CIC considers that the publication of good educational software is
in itself linked to in-service work.   Software that is seen to be
sound educationally, that is related to the moving curriculum, that
gives various alternative strategies for interactive use through its
teachers' and pupils' material - all this makes such software units
exemplars for sound practice.   For the members of the development
groups, there are also overt in-service implications:

1.   Because the teachers are not removed from the classroom for a
     long period, their CAL development work takes place while they
     are still engaged in normal classroom activities.   Reality is
     never far away.

2.   As members of a working group, the teachers are actively
     involved in tasks for which they are responsible.   Indeed, it
     is stressed throughout that they are the key to successful
     development of educationally sound software.   This involvement
     is very different from being a passive recipient of information
     while attending a short course.

3.   Group members are forced to re-examine the content and concepts
     of their own discipline, in order to identify areas for CAL
     development.   Already used to curriculum discussions they now
     have to extend this for CAL work.   For instance, models, that
     have previously been adequately described, now have to be given
     an exactness appropriate for programming.

4.   CAL design forces a re-examination of teaching methodologies.
     Interactive CAL can reinforce existing practice or drastically
     alter it by opening up methods of learning not hitherto
     fostered in some classrooms.   Discussions and writing notes on
     the way a unit could be used involves each individual in wide-
     ranging methodological analysis.

5.   The organisational issues, with one or many micros to the
     classroom, and the design of attendant software, will be a key
     part of the discussions in the group.   How practical is it to
     design a CAL unit which will depend upon groups of two or three
     pupils all having access to a micro at the same time?   Should
     this be encouraged?

6.   Many curriculum development projects depend, like CIC, on team
     work.   The detailed discussion amongst a group of 12 teachers
     is most powerful because the peer review comes into operation.
     There is no hierarchy in the team.   They are forced to justify

their ideas to others; the sound educational ideas are the ones therefore that survive.

7. Team work is powerful in in-service terms. The individual teachers are forced to look beyond their own boundaries of experience and individual idiosyncracies. Active involvement with the writing group and receiving feedback from trials schools places their own ideas and concerns within a much wider context.

Conclusion

The CIC model of CAL development produces a small group of teachers who are thoroughly aware of the issues of what CAL is and how it relates to the curriculum and classroom. The long-term and detailed nature of their in-service learning suggests that these individuals could be key influencers, and possibly change-agents in schools as they assess the potential and implication of computers for the learning environment.

References

[1] Lewis, R. and Want D.   Educational Computing at Chelsea (1969-79), in Lewis, R. and Tagg, E.D. (eds.) Computer Assisted Learning - Scope, Progress and Limits. Heinemann. London.   1980.

[2] Watson, D. Some Implications of Micros on Curriculum Development, in Lewis, R. and Tagg, E.D. (eds.) Involving Micros in Education. North Holland, Amsterdam. 1982.

[3] Watson, D. A Model for CAL Development.   Computers and Education. 1983. Vol.7, no.3.

CASE STUDY 5

THE CHANGING FOCUS OF IN-SERVICE EDUCATION FOR TEACHERS

Lorraine Stone

Chiltern Region M.E.P.

The Advisory Unit for Computer Based Education, Hatfield, has been organising in-service activities for Hertfordshire teachers for a number of years and became the Chiltern Region Advisory Unit, serving eleven Local Education Authorities, when the national Microelectronics Education Programme began. In the early days, relatively few teachers were involved in computer education and most of our courses were designed with a strong technical bias to meet the needs of individuals. Now, the situation has changed dramatically: we have to consider the needs of whole school staffs, both primary and secondary, and the curricular implications of microtechnology in our schools has to become the focus of many of our in-service activities. One course designed to respond to these changing needs is described below.

Background

Although many of our secondary schools have been involved in computing for some time now, the falling cost of hardware and various government initiatives, as well as growing public awareness about new technology, have all exerted pressures on schools to extend the use of computers beyond the computer studies department. Schools obviously respond to these pressures in different ways but there is evidence that many schools now expect their heads of computing or computer studies to take responsibility for introducing and supporting the use of microtechnology in other areas of the curriculum. Heads of departments, however, may not always feel they have the necessary time, information or skills to help their colleagues make the best use of microtechnology. Headteachers and deputies of secondary schools, who have to decide on priorities in financial as well as curriculum terms, sometimes feel overwhelmed by the jargon-ridden world of computing and find it hard to identify the issues as a preliminary stage in the decision-making process.

With these in-service needs in mind, we planned a course designed to initiate a dialogue between these two groups of people so that together we could identify some of the major issues which secondary schools are currently facing.

Selection of Course Participants

Local Education Authority advisers were asked to nominate schools who had already made some progress in cross-curricular uses of microtechnology, so that the course members' own experiences could be used during the course. Two people from each of the schools nominated were invited to attend the course – the person with overall responsibility within the school for computer use across the curriculum and the member of staff with responsibility for curriculum and staff development. In most cases we anticipated that this would be the school's deputy head.

Aims

The course had three major aims:-

To identify and explore issues arising from the management of computer resources within course members' schools;

To broaden course members' experience of applications in different curricular areas;

To help course members identify ways of supporting members of their own staff who become involved in computing.

Course Structure

The course took place on six consecutive Tuesdays followed by a residential weekend. Each of the days was organised around a particular theme. The first day was designed to allow people to find out about each other and the particular stage their schools had reached. The next two days were spent on cross-curricular applications of microtechnology, followed by two days concentrating on the organisation and management of resources. The final day dealt with school-based in-service education. It was hoped that one of the outcomes of the course might be a document which would help other schools to explore some of the issues raised during the course, but the final decision about this was to be left to course members. In fact, the residential weekend was spent writing this document, which course members considered to be very important.

Course Venue

Course members were drawn from five different local education authorities , so a venue had to be found which was reasonably accessible to all. A teachers' centre was chosen, partly because of its geographical location but also because it provided a comfortable, flexible environment which emphasised education rather than machinery.

Methodology

Many of the issues which needed exploring required an honest appraisal of the schools' progress so far, from two separate points of view — that of the management team, represented by the person with curriculum responsibility and that of the computer 'expert', who was being asked to share his expertise with other colleagues. We were aware that this might involve a conflict of interests, which was unlikely to be examined unless a climate of trust and openness was established early on in the course and maintained throughout. Course leaders were chosen, therefore, on the basis of their ability to facilitate group discussion, as well as their technical expertise.

The course included some formal input sessions on text-handling, information handling and the management of resources, and computers were available for course members to try out the software which was demonstrated. The majority of the time, however, was spent in group discussions and group problem-solving tasks, since the most useful resource for learning was the combined experience of members of the group. We were concerned too that the course had some immediate effect within course members' own schools and that the group had access to the perceptions of other secondary teachers who were neither computer specialists nor part of the school management team. In the final session of each day we raised a small number of questions which related to the following week's theme, which course members discussed, altered where this was felt necessary and took back to school. They identified a small group of colleagues in their own school and discussed the questions with them, bringing back their responses to be discussed at the beginning of the following session. This strategy proved very useful since it broadened the scope of the debate at school as well as on the course and set a pattern of consultation within the schools that course members could subsequently build on.

Residential Weekend

A residential element was planned as part of the course so that there could be an intensive period in which the various strands of the course could be drawn together and course members could decide on reasonable actions they could take back in their schools.
Many questions had been raised during the six day sessions which we felt could usefully be asked by other schools, and the group decided to spend the weekend writing a document designed to help other schools who wanted to evaluate their practice in relation to the use of microtechnology.

The process involved in the production of the document was
considered to be more important than the document itself by the
course leaders because it allowed the group members to focus their
thinking and decide on future actions within their schools. Course
members, however, were concerned that the document should be a
'product' which helped schools to question their practice in a
constructive way. This proved to be a useful tension during the
weekend since the 'process' emphasis helped allay anxieties about
the task and the 'product' emphasis ensured that the task was
completed.

Follow-up

The course leaders undertook to structure and edit the writing
generated during the weekend and to produce a first draft of the
whole document. A follow-up day was arranged for a month later,
when course members would review this draft, make alterations and
additions and hence create a final draft. At this stage, the final
format of the document and the mechanism for dissemination within
the Chiltern Region was decided.

Strong links have been made between the Chiltern Region staff
leading the course and the group members, which we hope will prove
useful to everyone in the future. In a sense, this was a pilot
course, drawing on schools from a number of Local Education
Authorities, and we intend to maintain contact with the group partly
so that they can continue the process of examining developments
within their own schools and partly because the group is an
invaluable resource for course planning in relation to in-service
education for secondary teachers.

CASE STUDY 6

A SHORT COURSE — MICROELECTRONICS AND SPECIAL EDUCATION

John Garrett

Council for Educational Technology

Introduction

The Council for Educational Technology, as agent for the
Microelectronics Education Programme (MEP), cooperates with Local
Education Authorities, the MEP's Regional Information Centres (RICs)
and the Special Education Resource Centres (SEMERCs) to arrange a
limited number of five day courses, funded by MEP. The third of
such courses was held at the Whirlow Grange Conference Centre,
Sheffield, early in March, 1984.

Each local education authority in the area nominated a number of
experienced and enlightened teachers whom they had identified as
being likely to play a leading role in the authority's in-service
work on the use of micro-electronics in special education.

Aims of Course

The aims of the course were:

(i)   to indicate ways in which microcomputers can be educationally effective across a wide, well-balanced curriculum to be offered to children with special educational needs in ordinary and special schools;

(ii) to capitalise on microcomputer developments in order to further curriculum development in schools;

(iii) to refine teachers' curriculum skills by analysing learning tasks for children with moderate or severe learning difficulties;

(iv) to participate in producing program specifications ready for presentation to a program writer;

(v)   to evaluate some existing programs.

Pre-course Work

It was intended that working groups would consist of people from the same local education authority who had met before coming on the course and had agreed on a topic appropriate for children with similar special educational needs. If the LEA did not have a special education user group, it was hoped that their working group might form the nucleus of such a user group on the completion of the course. Course members were also asked to notify the course director of their proposed topics so that any existing program on similar topics could be brought to the course and used for guided evaluation sessions as well as providing ideas.

The following were some of the topics suggested before the course began:-

(i)   Language:- reading skills, remedial language work, stimulating "Cloze" procedures.

(ii) Number:- Subtraction by decomposition, telling the time, budgeting.

(iii) Social/Life Skills:- Signposts, street plans, signals, sequencing of household tasks, safety, survival skills, simulations of every day situations involving children in decision making, as individuals and also in collaboration with others.

(iv) General:- Software for use with concept keyboard, work with Turtle. Use of sound for children with severe special needs.

Programme

Day 1.   (i)   An overview of "Microelectronics and Special Education".

(ii) Curriculum Development 1.
a.   A Curriculum Framework for the School - its value and implications.
b.   Problem Analysis.

(iii) Working Groups.

(iv) Guided examination of some existing programs.

Day 2.   (i)   Curriculum Development 2.
                c. Hierarchies of learning.
                d. Assessment - Specification theme - examples of
                    'modified' and 'developmental' curricula.
          (ii) Videos showing microelectronics in use for children
                with special educational needs.

Day 3.   (i)   Program Specifications.
          (ii) Reporting back with plenary session discussions and
                exchange of views.

Day 4.   (i)   Demonstration of MEP funded project to produce a suite
                of programs for children with severe and moderate
                learning difficulties by local teacher and his program
                writer.
          (ii) Working groups (with support of analysts).
         (iii) Demonstration of programs produced by local teacher
                for children and adults with severe and complex
                special needs.

Day 5.   (i)   Demonstrations to other groups and explanations of
                completed program specifications.
          (ii) "What next?" Director of the South Yorks and
                Humberside Regional Information Centre.
         (iii) Concluding session when arrangements were made for
                follow up work.

Group Tasks

Each group was asked to complete the following tasks:-

   (i)   To state reasons for a curriculum framework in all schools.
  (ii)   To produce curriculum aims related to their group topic.
 (iii)   To select one aim to be broken down into a hierarchy of
         learning for a 'modified' or a 'developmental' curriculum.

One example of the curriculum aims, produced by the working groups
on Day 2, was:-

     To help children develop the ability to make decisions in
     social situations, based on an awareness of the possible
     consequences and the implications of an individual's
     actions.   To simulate real life situations in non-
     threatening situations (without peer group pressure or
     sanctions from authority).

Program Specifications

The groups produced the curriculum aims during the first two days,
finding some difficulty in stating objectives, in the abstract,
which indicated the route towards the achievement of their stated
aims.   Most were impatient, wanting to get on with the making of
their programs. As a result of the input during Day 3 the need for
clearly stated objectives and an awareness of task analysis
techniques became more obvious. Groups worked hard from then on,
late into the night, preparing flow charts, producing objectives
almost without being aware of it.   The comprehensive and complicated
flow charts which were completed by the morning of Day 5 were
retained by one member of each group, who is the correspondent with
whom contact will be made about further work to be done to produce a
finished program.

A brief outline of the program specification for the aims quoted above was:

Program Title:- DECIDE.

Aim. To develop the ability to make decisions in everyday social situations based on an understanding of the consequences and implications of one's actions.

Objectives Having been presented with a number of simulated incidents the pupils will make a choice between alternative courses of action presented on the computer and therefore in a non-threatening situation.

Outcomes. The computer package will include the program, adventure map, illustrations/photographs, teacher's guide. The teacher's guide will contain suggestions for use in an overall social skills scheme with starting points for discussions, creative writing, drama and project work.

This module will be part of a suite of programs which will be potentially content free so that individual teachers will be able to devise incidents appropriate for the needs of their pupils.

Conclusions

Course members were already convinced of the value of microelectronics for children with special needs when they came on the course and were anxious to get down to working with the computer. They worked enthusiastically to develop program specifications but many found the curriculum theory at the beginning of the course somewhat trying, even to the extent that some felt it to be a waste of precious time. However, when work was begun on program specification flow charts most saw the relevance. Stating behavioural objectives, however, still continued to present dificulties in spite of the fact that most, as experienced special education teachers, were well able to break down learning tasks into small steps with little trouble.

Consideration is now being given to the possibility of starting the next course with the program specification lecture and then, having established the need to define aims and objectives, to discuss curriculum development alongside the work being done on the programs. Hopefully this may bring out the importance of having a curriculum framework in every school which is known and understood by every teacher.

The need for the groups to continue to work together on their program was stressed and a date for a one day seminar was arranged for all course members to return and report on progress, as well as completing curriculum development proposals for consideration by one or more funding agencies.

CASE STUDY 7

TEACHERS LEARNING THROUGH GROUP EXAMINATION SCHEMES

Shirley Evans

Liverpool Polytechnic

In recent years the introduction of Computer Studies courses into British Schools has been made easier as a result of the Government support. This has helped to overcome one of the obstacles to the development of such courses - the restricted availability of equipment. However, another major obstacle and, in fact, one that is of even greater concern, is the lack of availability of suitably trained and experienced teachers.

The teacher training departments in the Colleges and Universities are beginning to offer courses in the new technology. This will provide a flow of trained teachers into the education system, but that will be a mere trickle in comparison to the needs of our schools. In order to satisfy the current demands it is necessary to supplement this input from the colleges by providing in-service training courses for teachers. Such courses, of necessity, must cater for a larger group of personnel.

The traditional form of in-service training is to provide courses which teachers attend to further their knowledge of the subject matter or to develop new teaching techniques. However, participation in workshop sessions, teacher exchange, curriculum development activities and group development work make a major contribution to teacher training.

The operation of a Group examination scheme provides one such means by which teachers can provide for themselves a form of in-service training. The present school examination structure in Britain permits the operation of courses that are different from those normally offered by the Examination Boards. These courses must be specially approved by the Boards. In 1972 Computer Studies was not available with the examination Boards. Thus, it was necessary to design a syllabus which satisfied the educational criteria laid down by the Examination Boards. Such an arrangement is possible within any subject area of the curriculum, but it is of particular benefit in Computer Studies and any other aspect of the new technology.

Rarely has a new 'subject' been introduced into the school curriculum for which the prospective teachers have received no formal training. It is in such circumstances that Computer Studies was conceived. It must be remembered that all teachers involved with the creation of this new 'subject' had already received formal training in some other subject area, and had a broad knowledge of educational principles and experience in the training of young people in the classroom. Thus the best qualities of all aspects of their experiences were combined to provide self-support. It was with this broad background that teachers in Merseyside initiated Computer Studies and Information Processing courses in their schools.

The schemes devised by the Merseyside Group of teachers were accepted by the Examinations Boards. This led to the formation of consortia of teachers who subsequently prepared their pupils for the examinations which they had devised.

The rapid change in technology has led to the need for the syllabuses to be
updated frequently. The teachers' consortia bear the responsibility of ensuring
that the syllabuses and forms of examination are always relevant to the present
state of the art. During the last ten years the syllabus has been revised five
times. The current views of Merseyside teachers are contained in the document
'Computer Studies at 16+', published by the Microelectronics Education Programme.

The introduction of Computer Studies into Merseyside schools began in 1972. At
that time it was not easy, particularly because the equipment used to support
the courses was expensive. Apart from the poor availability of computing
facilities and the lack of published material, there was little support from
education authorities. The early pioneering teachers were motivated by their
enthusiasm to succeed.

It is the pioneering teachers who are able to offer first hand advice to newcomers in this exciting field of educational development. The early pioneers
have experienced many of the problems in computer education which confront the
newcomer. They are able to advise and support their colleagues in a way which
has probably not been experienced in any other subject discipline. The exchange
of experience and discussion about problems is of high priority when Computer
Studies teachers meet. Discussions about syllabus content often lead to detailed
exchange of teaching methods. The more experienced teachers are able to respond
to the needs of their colleagues and provide appropriate support. In the
discussion about syllabus content the need to abandon out-of-date ideas and
teaching techniques is readily identified. When a group of people work together
to initiate educational development, a competitive element ensures that they are
continuously forward-looking and innovative. An effect of working as a
consortium has been to maintain high standards at all stages.

The Merseyside Group Examination Schemes operate under the above-mentioned special
syllabus arrangement ('Mode 3'). In this type of examination it is the teachers'
responsibility to carry out many of the functions involved with the production
of the examination papers and to provide the assessments of their pupils' work.
The teacher, in fact, works in the role of the examiner during the preparation
and assessment of the examinations, in addition to being responsible for
teaching the pupils in his charge.

Experienced teachers have a great deal to offer newcomers to the subject. They
understand the difficulties that are likely to occur, because they too will have
experienced those difficulties, only a few years previously. The exchange of
experience has helped this new subject to move forward rapidly, but at a pace
that is acceptable to the majority of teachers involved.

As a result of the experience obtained in the operation of the Group Examination
Schemes teachers become more competent:

a) in the technology;

    This is achieved by

    - continuous revision of the syllabus, so that it is relevant when it
      is presented to pupils

    - the production of a range of examination questions, which adequately
      examine the syallabus

    - the preparation of solutions to the questions set.

b) in presenting the new technology;

    This is achieved by

    - the sharing of expertise in the continuous debate with colleagues in other schools

    - involvement in the assessment of their pupils' achievements.

The wide range of activities experienced by teachers participating in a Group Scheme of this type is of immense value to the personal development of teachers and to the placing of Informatics courses in their schools, on a sound basis. This work has only been possible as a result of the support given willingly by Headteachers and colleagues in the participating schools.

For many years the training received from complete involvement in the Group examination Schemes has provided the major source of in-service training for teachers in the Merseyside Local Authorities. Teachers have developed their expertise by working together to benefit the implementation of informatics courses in their schools.

Discussion - Rapporteurs: S H von Solms and Mrs M Leuveren

Martin remarked that the FPL language seems to be very close to flowcharting. Taylor replied that the language is well-structured, with a 1 - 1 correspondence between classical program-structures and structures in FPL. He argued that to a certain extent flowcharts are still used to represent the logic of a program in a graphic way. Christiaen stated that flowcharts are a means of representation and do not help as far as methodology is concerned. For methodology, a Pseudo Code is better.

Raymont was worried that too much emphasis is placed on programming and languages, at the expense of more important concepts.

These more important concepts include:

How does one decide what to do with a computer?

How does one define the problem?

How does one implement these problems on a computer?

He felt that there is too little attention given to this higher-level type of problem.

Gorny replied that software engineering and requirements engineering are the areas that should address the concepts raised by Raymont.

Taylor stated that the Methods Course in the ACM proposal addresses these higher level areas.

Hammond wanted to know if European countries will conform to the ATEE syllabus, when it will be implemented, and if it had been tried out.

Gorny replied that some experiments are in progress, and that it is hoped that the syllabus will be implemented.

Hammond felt that it is not healthy for all countries to conform to the same syllabus. Taylor felt that some guidelines are necessary. Gorny supported this, and stated that in the absence of any guidelines, everyone is doing what he wants.

Johnson restated his earlier remarks that teachers should be made aware that unresolved issues do exist, and that there is no unanimous agreement amongst experts about syllabi, contents, etc.

INFORMATICS AND TEACHER TRAINING
F.B. Lovis and E.D. Tagg (editors)
Elsevier Science Publishers B.V. (North-Holland)
© IFIP, 1984

THE OPEN UNIVERSITY MICROS IN SCHOOLS PROJECT

Tim O'Shea

Micros in Schools Project,

Open University

This paper provides a general account of the history and
current activities of the Open University's Micros in
Schools project. Since early 1981 staff at the Open
University have been designing, preparing, testing and
distributing a variety of self-study packs designed for use
by serving school teachers. The topics covered by the packs
are "awareness", "educational software", "computers in
action in the classroom", "microelectronics" and "inside
microcomputers". The packs provide the teacher who studies
them with a course of practical work which relates directly
to classroom applications of microcomputer technology. The
paper concludes by discussing the problems involved in
maintaining the usability and relevance of these materials
for the remainder of the decade.

INTRODUCTION

The Open University supports a large Computer Assisted Learning (CAL) Research
Group whose primary activities include experimentation with different forms of
delivery systems and the evaluation of existing computer based teaching systems.
[1]. In 1980 some of the members of this group decided to bid for resources from
the newly established National Microelectronics Education Programme (MEP) to
finance the production of a series of self-study packs for teachers. The MEP
itself was in part a response to the scheme whereby the Department of Trade and
Industry was subsidising the purchase of two microcomputers per British School.
As the Open University has a large percentage (currently 23%) of teachers amongst
its 100,000 strong student body its staff already had considerable experience of
preparing materials for teachers. Distance learning techniques are particularly
appropriate because new teaching methods are best learnt 'on the job' and because
many older professionals prefer the anonymity of self-study to the perceived risk
of making a fool of themselves with new technology in front of younger colleagues
on a conventional course. The main motive of the CAL Research Group for seeking
MEP funding was to continue large scale studies in the design and teaching of high
and low level languages to novices [2].

HISTORY

In 1981 a grant of £30,000 was awarded to support the design and testing of an
awareness pack supporting forty hours of study with the RML 380Z microcomputer.
This pilot project was successful and in 1982 a grant of £486,000 was given to
support the production of four more packs on the topics of "educational software",
"computers in action in the classroom", "microelectronics" and "inside
microcomputers". The first two packs named above and the awareness pack were to
be produced in editions for the Apple II, Sinclair Spectrum, BBC model B, Research
Machines RML380Z and RML LINK480Z. The microelectronics and microcomputers packs
were to be supported by a special purpose microcomputer named by the terrible but

memorable acronym DESMOND (Digital Electronics System Made Of Nifty
Devices). By mid 1984 all five editions of the awareness pack, three editions of
the software pack and the microelectronics pack were available. The complete
range of packs is planned to be available in early 1985 and to remain on sale till
at least 1987. There is a possibility that further packs will be produced dealing
with the topics of special education, the LOGO programming language and the social
implications of microcomputers. Some of the existing pack material is being
supplemented to provide the basis for an undergraduate course in educational
computing to be available in 1987. Another long term plan is the provision of a
diploma in educational computing which would incorporate this material, conventional Open University computing courses and   a large element of guided project
work.

THE AWARENESS PACK

The awareness pack is designed as a very first introduction to the use of
microcomputers in education. It includes photographs of the sockets and leads
used to connect the microcomputer to the electricity supply and the monitor or
television. This makes it possible for a teacher who has never previously
touched a keyboard to set up the microcomputer and run the programs included in
the pack without asking more experienced colleagues for help or advice. The
pack includes software on disk or cassette which shows how computers can be used
in a variety of educational roles including these of electronic blackboard, database, teaching package, and drawing. No single educational computing line is
promoted and, for example, the drawing activity is based on a subset of LOGO
turtle graphics,but simple programs are explained by means of a BASIC program
that steps through and illustrates its own operation. After the teacher has been
guided through the use of the programs included with the pack via a study book,
they then read a set of 13 case studies.   These are written by teachers and
describe different ways of using computers across the curriculum, how classes are
organised and the teacher's own views on the educational value of their work.
Finally the teacher carries out projects in their own classroom using the software provided in the pack. They are helped in the planning and running of these
activities by a project book.

Early versions of the awareness pack were tested with teachers without any prior
computing experience. The tests were carried out in both group teaching and self-
study contexts. The first drafts did not adequately support the initial practical
work, contained an excess of cross references between the three print items (study
book, case-studies book and project book) and lacked educational context and
motivation in the case-studies. These problems were solved as follows. Firstly,
a 'three column' design was adopted for the practical work. The first column
being the key(s) to press,with each key being set individually boxed on the page
(eg the character 'R' and the command 'RETURN' have a single box). The second
column provides a screen photograph of the outcome and the third column gives a
commentary. This is an expensive form of printing that guarantees a close and
accurate relationship between print and keyboard activity. Secondly, the print
items were designed to 'stand alone'. This made life easier for the students and
also made it possible to change only a proportion of the print for each new
microcomputer edition. Finally,all case-study material had to be based on actual
classroom experience and standard questions relating to age of pupils, curriculum
and logistics had to be addressed in each account. At the time of writing about
2,500 copies of the awareness pack have been sold and some individual packs have
been used by more than 10 teachers. The reviews of the pack have been very
positive and it seems to meet its objectives of making teachers aware of the
potential of microcomputers and helping them overcome their fears and inexperience
of this new technology.

PACK DESIGN PHILOSOPHY

The awareness pack has served as a model for our other four packs. Each pack is

designed to support private, personal and classroom practical computing work.
First of all the teacher student acquires specific skills and builds up experiences. This is supported by elaborately designed print material using the three
column key/screen/commentary format based on 'so type this', 'you will see
this' and 'the computer responds in this way because .....'. Then the teacher-
student widens his experience via print or video cassette based case-study
material. Finally the teacher-student applies his new skills in his own
classroom setting.

Each print item is designed to be stand-alone and a study guide is provided as a
'route map' for each pack and a separate document provides an overview of the
relation between the packs. The awareness pack,or an equivalent experience, is
assumed as a prerequisite for the study of the other four packs which can be
studied in any order. The educational software and computers in action packs
concentrate on the software side whilst the other two packs concentrate on
microelectronics and microcomputing. An absolute novice would probably be best
served by studying the packs in the sequence awareness - action in the classroom -
educational software - inside microcomputers - microelectronics. However, the
ideal sequence depends on the teacher-student's long-term goals and the facilities
in his or her classroom. When the awareness pack was first tested a number of
experts expressed concern that teachers might dislike the extreme hand-holding
approach used. In practice teachers with prior computing experience just study
the early material more quickly. The primary concerns that teachers raise are the
accuracy of the reference material and the reality of the classroom work
described. Teachers are especially sensitive to University Lecturers masquerading
as teachers in video cassette material. The video material in the packs is
designed to support a group viewing by teachers during which five minute segments
are played, replayed and discussed. This is supported by printed video notes with
still frames and discussion frames and is modelled directly on the successful.
Open University course 'Developing Mathmatical Thinking' [3]. The notion of a
prototype pack (in this case the awareness pack) is also taken from the production
history of this course. The practical computing work and the DESMOND is a
development of a style pioneered in a course for managers entitled
'Microprocessors and Product Development'. This course [4] included DESMOND's
'grandfather', a microcomputer for learning about assembling programming and real
time control based on the INTEL8049 . So the design of the packs largely depends
on marrying techniques developed in the School of Education for teaching teachers
and in the Faculty of Technology for teaching practical computing skills to
industrialists.

PACK PRODUCTION PHILOSOPHY

The key notion is that the material must be developmentally tested by real
students in real conditions. This test is run by a member of the Institute of
Educational Technology who is a 'students' advocate' independent of the team
producing the pack. The testers are isolated from the producers and it is the
job of the educational technologists to tell if the testers become really stuck
with the material and what intervention, if any, is appropriate. Novices
encounter a whole variety of conceptual [5], practical and affective problems [6],
with computing work and there is no way of determining a priori what given way
    of explaining assignment or sub-routines will work with some class of novices.
The strategy adopted in our project has been to keep testing versions of the
material until it works. Apart from educational technologists a variety of staff
with distinct roles must work together as a team to produce the packs. Over 30
staff have made substantial contributions to the project including programmers,
authors (from the School of Education and Faculty of Technology), a course manager
(responsible for scheduling), secretarial staff, BBC production staff, an information officer, market researcher, an editor, designers, staff tutors and sales
staff.

Our production process is typical of Open University course development work.

Firstly a pack team is assembled and it circulates an outline design for
external and internal critical comment. Then a first draft of the print material
is circulated with the school based material being developed in collaboration with
serving teachers. Then a complete version is developmentally tested with a
carefully selected range of teachers. The material (print, video, audio and
software) is then revised and the editor and the graphic designer develop the
print materials to fit to project and University standards and conventions
Just prior to printing,the page proofs are checked against the computing practical
work because a single wrong key press could cause many problems for the individual
learners.

In parallel with the pack production,market research is carried out on the type
of teacher and institutions likely to purchase the packs and the range of acceptable fee levels. In the case of this project the MEP grant covers the design and
development of the packs but not the printing and distribution costs. These latter
costs have to be recouped via fee income. Once a pack is available it is
advertised via brochures, leaflets and conference presentations. In each Open
University Regional Office an individual staff tutor spends some time on making
the packs availability known to local institutions. The Open University is still
at an early stage of learning how to market distance learning material and its
skills in this area cannot be compared to its highly professional approach to
developing distance learning materials.

THE SOFTWARE PACKS

Both the educational software and the computers in action in the classroom packs
require access to LOGO. The project team made this commitment because we felt
strongly that LOGO (unlike BASIC) represented a coherent and pleasing educational
philosophy [7] and could be used to illustrate the structure and operation of a
variety of types of educational programs. This design choice has caused us some
practical difficulties as LOGO is not currently available for the Sinclair Spectrum
and BBC model B microcomputers. Our Academic Computing Service has produced an
elegant chip based implementation of LOGO for the model B and this is currently
being developmentally tested.

The educational software pack is designed to help teachers become critical
consumers of the types of programs touted for school use [8]. It enables teachers
to 'look under the bonnet' and answer questions like 'will this program run properly on my schools microcomputer?' or 'does this program fit my current curriculum?'
The practical work includes modifying existing programs and appraising commercial
software.

In contrast the 'microcomputers in action' in the classroom pack focuses on the
integration of microcomputer use into classroom practice. The types of application covered include simulation, special purpose programming languages, word
processing, information retrieval and teaching packages. The print and video case
studies include details of organising learning activities and overcoming
organisational difficulties. The video material makes it possible for teacher-
students to watch closely and analyse the activities of other teachers and pupils
using microcomputers.

THE MICROELECTRONICS AND MICROCOMPUTERS PACKS

Both these packs depend on the use of DESMOND to provide practical experience and
give confidence. DESMOND is a portable battery powered microcomputer. It is
programmed via a simple calculator style keyboard and liquid crystal display. It
includes a variety of sensors for heat, light, touch, magnetism and and tilt
and output devices such as lamps, a buzzer and a motor. It can be used to
simulate a set of electronic components to 'build' (without soldering) devices
such as an electronic spirit level, a digital thermometer or a burglar alarm
Alternatively it can be programmed in an assembly language as a computer to

illustrate the uses of microcomputers as components of other devices operating in real time (eg cameras, washing machines, sewing machines) as well as for inform-ation processing tasks. DESMOND is designed so that in either mode it is easy to examine and step through the simulated electronic components or assembly language program.

The microelectronics pack also includes a highly illustrated book which introduces basic principles including circuits which can remember and make decisions, a detailed practical book for DESMOND using the three column format and classroom case studies which include real teachers' experiences of DESMOND. The video material is based on a documentary of a group of teachers learning to use DESMOND in the classroom and its highlight is the way an english teacher employs DESMOND in her language teaching.

The pack 'inside microcomputers' has similar components and it enables teachers to understand and explain to their pupils a wide variety of microcomputers applica-tions. Having mastered the practical work the student teacher is able to appreciate some of the ways in which high-level programming languages vary, and how the parts of a computer communicate with each other and the outside world. Examples of specific concepts encountered include subroutines and device driving.

OUTSTANDING PROBLEMS

We are currently faced with distribution and maintenance problems. The three software based packs already come in five microcomputer flavours. The packs continue to proliferate in different editions because we must try to help the student who has already acquired a DESMOND, a LOGO system or some of the software packages included in a pack. In addition we find ourselves assembling special 'bulk orders' for U.K. and foreign training institutions who may, for example, wish to teach batches of 20 students at a time providing all students with print material but only requiring 20 DESMONDS and one video tape.

The most acute problem we face is maintaining the software components of our packs. We have already had to deal with one microcomputer which suffers a reduction in available memory when it is upgraded for use with disk drives or networks and another whose operating system upgrade resulted in problems with a whole variety of programs. Screen resolutions and dialects of BASIC and LOGO vary from microcomputer to microcomputer and versions of existing packs for different microcomputers can require 50% of the original design development effort. At the same time as computers become more familiar at home and the place of work our students' expectations and characteristic initial behaviour and errors change. There is no simple solution to the maintenance problem. We need always to test new packs developmentally, continually monitor the microcompter manufacturers' initiatives with new software and peripherals and evaluate student use of the packs. This requires an annual staff effort of approximately 20% of the original development effort properly to maintain the packs.

SUMMARY

The Open University is providing teachers with a range of self-study materials for a variety of skill levels. Each pack is based on private and classroom 'hand-holding' practical work that is subject to extensive developmental testing. The teacher-student gets an opportunity to build up confidence privately and observe (usually via video) the work of other teachers before carrying out his own projects. The packs are not pro- or anti- microcomputer use in education but rather designed to help teachers develop into intelligent consumers and users of the new technology.

The costs of developing robust good quality materials in this area are severe and in this project have averaged £2,500 per student study hour. The only justification for these costs is the large audience eventually reached. There are acute maintenance problems in distributing packs with software components, while the microcomputer manufacturers complete with each other in the development of their incompatible product lines, these problems will continue.

This is an area in which rapid change and innovation are routine, yet at the same time the teaching profession is conservative, suspicious and afraid of any new technology apart from a small number of enthusiasts   who advocate new gadgets or packages as universal panaceas. To be successful in providing teaching materials in this area it is necessary to develop them in real educational settings in collaboration with real teachers, to test the practical work ruthlessly in development and to monitor continually for maintenance problems.

ACKNOWLEDGEMENTS

I thank my colleagues on the project and wish particularly to acknowledge my debt to Marc Eisenstadt, who led the team that produced the pilot awareness pack, and Helen Boyce, our project manager.

REFERENCES

[1]   Jones, A. Scanlon, E. and O'Shea, T.   'The Computer Revolution in Education: New Technologies for Distance Teaching', Harvester, in Press.

[2]   du Boulay, B. O'Shea, T. and Monk, J. 'The black box inside the glass box: presenting computing concepts to novices'. Int J of Man-Machines studies 1981.

[3]   Floyd, A. and O'Shea, T. 'Prototype led course production', Distance Education in Press.

[4]   Monk, J. and O'Shea, T. 'Planning and role differentiation in course production', Teaching at a distance vol 19 1981.

[5]   du Boulay, B. and O'Shea, T. 'Teaching Novices Programming' in(Coombs and Alty Ed) Computing Skills and Adaptive Systems, 1980.

[6]   Jones, A. and O'Shea, T. 'Barriers to the Use of Computer Assisted Learning'. British J of Ed Tech 1982.

[7]   O'Shea, T. and Self, J. 'Learning and Teaching with Computers'. Harvester, 1983.

[8]   Jones, A. and Preece, J. 'The educational software pack for the Open University micros in schools project'. Published in this volume.

INFORMATICS AND TEACHER TRAINING
F.B. Lovis and E.D. Tagg (editors)
Elsevier Science Publishers B.V. (North-Holland)
© IFIP, 1984

THE EDUCATIONAL SOFTWARE PACK FOR THE OPEN UNIVERSITY PROJECT
'MICROS IN SCHOOLS'

Ann Jones   Jenny Preece

Lecturer, Institute of Educational   Lecturer in Computer Based
Technology.   Education, Micros in Schools Project

Open University
Walton Hall, Milton Keynes, MK7 6AA, England.

One of the biggest problems which faces teachers using microcomputers is the lack of good educational software. Yet few
courses succesfully tackle the problem of training inexperienced
teachers to develop the skills necessary to choose educational
software wisely. Most courses lack an appropriate framework
which would provide teachers with the skills and experience
necessary to judge software critically. The Educational software
pack (Open University, 1984), produced by the Open University does
provide such a framework. In this paper we discuss both the
philosophy and design of this pack and describe how the pack was
produced and evaluated.

INTRODUCTION

Educational Software (Open University course code P541) is one of the packs
produced by the Open University Micros in Schools Project which is funded by the
Microelectronics Programme. Like all the Open University courses, the packs are
designed for learning at a distance and use a variety of media including
correspondence texts, T.V, Audio visual, home kits and CAL. The courses are
produced by Open University course teams. This system of team production results
in several drafts which are commented on by a number of people at different stages:
these commentators include both project and course team members and external
readers. In the Micros in Schools Project, we have sought two different kinds of
comments. The first is from other experts in the field who act as critical
readers and the second kind of comment comes from practising teachers (developmental testing): the intended audience of the pack.

Like many other Open University Courses, the packs include a large number of in-
text exercises and self-assessement questions. In particular, because the packs
are aimed at an audience who are working on their own, they include features to
make it as easy as possible for teachers to work through the computer activities.
For example, the practical activities are laid out, step by step, in 3 columns:
the first column contains instructions for each step, the second shows a screen
photograph indicating how the screen looks after carrying out each step, and the
third column provides an explanation. How well these activities work is evaluated
by the teachers who work through the pack when it is in its second draft.

THE COURSE

The main aim of the course is to help teachers to become critical consumers, so
that they can choose wisely from the increasing amount of software on sale.
Selecting good educational software is not a trivial task. Teachers need to be
encouraged to expect more from software than just bug-free programs with 'whizz-
bang' graphics which keep children busy and quiet . The philosophy underlying
this pack is that teachers need to know about program design and to consider the
'trade-offs' between what is educationally desirable and what is technically

feasible when designing software for small machines. Exercises which involve browsing through software, which form part of many short INSET courses, do not provide sufficient background knowledge and experience for making sound judgements about software.

The course, therefore , starts by introducing some key programming concepts. The teachers modify and write short Logo procedures. The idea behind this approach is not to teach programming per se but to make teachers aware of program structure. Logo is used because its procedural nature fosters good program designs. Logo has a modular structure where separate routines, that is procedures, can be written to perform different functions and are called up when needed. Programs are put together in a building block fashion and long variable names also help to make the programs easy to follow. By the end of this part of the course, the student should be able to:

* make a critical appraisal of existing educational software
* contribute to the design of educational software
* have an appreciation of fundamental programming concepts so that he can construct small programs, modify existing programs and estimate the size of a programming task
* appreciate which kinds of educational software are suited to which learning tasks

and he should have a good understanding of

* some of the principles underlying educational software design
* the various design techniques and tools used to implement educational software
* the roles played by different people in producing educational software.

The next part of the course includes a series of small Logo programs in which the teacher runs, and examines the design of, a variety of programs, including simple drill and practice, modelling, information retrieval and an adventure game. The teachers are also asked to consider the educational role of each program.

Figure 1 gives an example of one of these exercises.

Exercise 35

(a) NUMBER has built into it the idea that some numbers are easier to translate than others. Say as precisely as you can what the idea is. (This is its task difficulty model).

(b) NUMBER keeps some information about a pupil's competence. Say as precisely as you can, what this information is. (This is its pupil model).

Figure 1

One of the exercises from the section on a drill and practice program, NUMBER.

The pack contains a reader which includes articles written by well known authors, which provide information about tutorial computer assisted learning systems such as PLATO and TICCIT, simulations, using Logo in the classroom, and intelligent teaching systems such as MYCIN and SOPHIE.

Articles about various programming languages (e.g. PROLOG, SMALLTALK, BASIC and authoring languages) are also included for those teachers who wish to extend their knowledge of programming.

In the next section of the course the teacher puts the concepts and skills that he has learnt into practice in evaluating three commercially produced software packages. The course emphasises the distinction between software evaluation , which involves examining software in use in the classroom and software selection , in which the design of the program and accompanying materials is examined. Although we feel that both activities are very important, this course deals only with selecting software. The packages which teachers examine include a drill and practice program, a simulation game and a problem solving program. They are all typical examples of commercially available packages. The packages were chosen because they illustrate a variety of different types of program structure, error handling and help routines, graphics and educational material.

Six categories of criteria for judging software are introduced and discussed in the text: educational documentation, achievement of stated aims, appropriateness of the micro and the program, screen presentation, friendliness and flexibility of the program and technical documentation. The activity which is set in this section requires the teacher to read and answer questions about how the program has been used in the classroom. She is then asked to explore the package and to complete a set of 'Software Selection Criteria sheets'. These sheets require the teacher to give a rating to each item in the six categories. (see figure 2).

Software Selection Criteria

Complete this sheet by awarding a score for each aspect which describes how well you consider it has been achieved by the package, place a √ in the appropriate column. 5 is highest, 1 is lowest, N/A is not applicable. Use the blank space to record your additional comments.

You may wish to photocopy this sheet.

Name of package _____

Name of program _____

Additional comments

		5	4	3	2	1	N/A
1	**Educational documentation**						
1a	Statement of aims and objectives	□	□	□	□	□	□
1b	Information about the content and background	□	□	□	□	□	□
1c	Statement of intended type of use and audience	□	□	□	□	□	□
1d	Suggestions of ways to use the program	□	□	□	□	□	□
1e	Pupil activities or worksheets	□	□	□	□	□	□
1f	Instructions for running the program	□	□	□	□	□	□
1g	Presentation of a typical run	□	□	□	□	□	□
1h	*General impressions*	□	□	□	□	□	□
2	**Achievement of stated aims** *(as far as you can tell without actually using the program with a class)*						
2a	Aims/objectives	□	□	□	□	□	□
2b	*General impressions*	□	□	□	□	□	□
3	**Appropriateness of the micro and program**						
3a	For teaching this topic	□	□	□	□	□	□
3b	For the suggested audience and type of use (e.g. group whole class, etc.)	□	□	□	□	□	□
3c	*General impressions*	□	□	□	□	□	□
4	**Screen presentation**						
4a	Use of graphics	□	□	□	□	□	□
4b	Use of colour and animation	□	□	□	□	□	□
4c	*General impressions*	□	□	□	□	□	□

Software Selection Criteria

		5	4	3	2	1	N/A	*Additional comments*
5	**Friendliness and flexibility of the program**							
5a	Helpful messages to correct user errors	☐	☐	☐	☐	☐	☐	
5b	Help to pupils in understanding the program	☐	☐	☐	☐	☐	☐	
5c	Versatility so that the user can control what the program does	☐	☐	☐	☐	☐	☐	
5d	Feedback to pupil	☐	☐	☐	☐	☐	☐	
5e	Program adapts to pupils' performance	☐	☐	☐	☐	☐	☐	
5f	Record of pupils' performance kept by program	☐	☐	☐	☐	☐	☐	
5g	Program model accessible to pupil	☐	☐	☐	☐	☐	☐	
5h	Suggestions or help for teacher to modify the program	☐	☐	☐	☐	☐	☐	
5i	*General impressions*	☐	☐	☐	☐	☐	☐	
6	**Technical documentation**							
6a	Information about machine requirements	☐	☐	☐	☐	☐	☐	
6b	Information about the model used	☐	☐	☐	☐	☐	☐	
6c	Information about the program structure	☐	☐	☐	☐	☐	☐	
6d	Listing and readability of the program code	☐	☐	☐	☐	☐	☐	
6e	Portability, i.e. ability to transfer program to a different computer	☐	☐	☐	☐	☐	☐	
6f	*General impressions*	☐	☐	☐	☐	☐	☐	

Summary of overall impressions
Give an overall score for each of the categories 1–6

		5	4	3	2	1	N/A	
1.	Educational documentation	☐	☐	☐	☐	☐	☐	
2	Achievement of stated aims	☐	☐	☐	☐	☐	☐	
3	Appropriateness of the media and the program	☐	☐	☐	☐	☐	☐	
4	Screen presentation	☐	☐	☐	☐	☐	☐	
5	Friendliness and flexibility of the program	☐	☐	☐	☐	☐	☐	
6	Technical documentation	☐	☐	☐	☐	☐	☐	

Figure 2: Software Selection Criteria Sheets

The course is drawn together at the end by a discussion of the principles of software design used by material software development projects.

FORMATIVE EVALUATION

As with the other Micros in Schools packs we carried out a formative evaluation via critical commenting from internal and external readers. The pack was also developmentally tested by practising teachers who worked through the pack and commented on it. Educational Software was tested by two groups of teachers. It formed the basis of an inservice teacher training course run over two weekends and it was also used by six teachers working independently. It might seem that using distance learning materials as the basis for a face to face course is a strange thing to do! However, at this stage of development, having direct and immediate contact with teachers and being on hand to sort out any real difficulties can be very helpful. In this case we discovered that we had pitched some of the course at too high a level. Having one of the course team members present enabled us both to get detailed feedback on what the problems were, and to help the teachers over the difficulties so that they could continue to the next part of the course. In general the teachers' reactions were very positive, but they indicated some areas for change. We mentioned above that some of the course was too hard: the teachers needed more structure and guidance with some of the programming activities. It also became clear that we were unsure about whether the video should be aimed at groups or individuals.

We were able to address both these issues by breaking the programming activities into smaller segments and providing more guidance and structure, and by deciding that our video, like the rest of the pack, should be aimed at teachers working on their own. Groups of teachers studying together are catered for through tutor notes.

SUMMARY

In this paper we have argued that selecting suitable software to use in the classroom is a difficult task. We have described the philosophy and production of a course designed to provide teachers with the appropriate skills for selecting good educational programs.

The Micros in Schools project benefits from the Open University's extensive experience of producing high quality distance learning material. Unfortunately, producing packs in this way is time consuming, which is a disadvantage at a time when both hardware and software are changing fast. However, we believe that this is offset by the advantages of this method of production. In particular, one of the advantages is that the pack is subjected to the rigorous commenting and testing procedure. The resulting material is of a high academic quality whilst also meeting the needs of practising teachers.

Reference:
Open University Press, 1984, Micros in Schools: Educational Software (P541Z)

Acknowledgements:
The Educational Software pack was produced by the Micros in Schools Project P541 Course Team chaired by Dr. John Self and Jenny Preece. The Micros in Schools Project is directed by Dr. Tim O'Shea.

Discussion

The discussion started with a question from Taylor who wondered why the presenters thought the teachers evaluating the software were not critical enough. Jones said she had meant they were not critical enough about commercial software; Preece added that evaluation of software for teachers most certainly is a difficult task. O'Shea compared software with textbooks and said there was not the same professionalism in evaluating software as books.

Pollak mentioned the cost of producing the OU packages and said the cost would be ten times as much in the USA. He wondered if re-using the software had been taken into account. O'Shea said that their price was calculated from the sale of packages and the normal time it would take to go through a package. He mentioned that some parts, LOGO and others, could be re-used and in a wider context.

Taylor wondered how many people were involved in the "software factory"; O'Shea answered that there were about 30 specialists. Lovis added that not all the programs were made there - some were taken over from other projects within or without the Open 'niversity.

Which philosophy do you have in choosing the software to look at ?, was the question from Wright. What do you choose, good or bad? Preece said that they had chosen 3 pieces of software, simulation, fairly sophisticated drill and practice and an electronic blackboard. They had been chosen to be understandable to teachers of all subjects, illustrating different features (graphics, providing help, and so on) but the choosing of the software had been quite difficult. O'Shea mentioned that merely choosing software of a good standard was dangerous, as teachers were neither programmers nor maths specialists. He said it was certainly not difficult to find bad programs, but more difficult to get them documented.

Gorny asked what kind of software packages they used for evaluating intelligent CAL (ICAL); Preece answered that they did not go any further than trying to make teachers aware of the existence of ICAL.

Finally Kristel asked for the reason why teachers were taught programming and if any sources were given. Preece said that they wanted the teachers to be able to understand programming design and modify existing software, so they taught the teachers to use the editor.

Rapporteurs: Anna Kristjansdottir and David Walker

SESSION 5

Chairman: Peter Barker

INFORMATICS AND TEACHER TRAINING
F.B. Lovis and E.D. Tagg (editors)
Elsevier Science Publishers B.V. (North-Holland)
© IFIP, 1984

TEACHER TRAINING FOR EDUCATIONAL COMPUTING
IN PRIMARY SCHOOLS IN SCOTLAND

A. Russel Wills

Computer Education Department
Dundee College of Education
Dundee, Scotland

Despite earlier attempts, significant progress in getting
computers into the primary schools has only been made since
the arrival of microcomputers in 1978. Research at Dundee
College of Education showed the need for: teacher training
to give confidence, a commitment of time and effort to
overcome potential difficulties and a supply of good quality
curriculum based software. Computing in the classroom made
slow progress until the Department of Industry's Micros in
Primary Schools Scheme overcame the problem of lack of
equipment by offering primary schools selected hardware at
half price, plus a starter pack of software. Schools and
teacher training are now in a state of transition with the
arrival of computers in the classroom and the advent of a
new four year B.Ed. course in primary education, with a
strong computer content. The future looks promising, with
computer related innovations potentially leading to the
development of a curriculum with more active pupil
participation. There will be problems but with appropriate
software and in-service training teachers can use modern
technology to prepare pupils for the challenge of the real
world outside school.

INTRODUCTION

This is an exciting time for those interested in computing in the primary school.
After a number of years, during which a few enthusiasts struggled to overcome the
inertia and apathy of the majority, the situation has drastically changed. Most
primary schools now have, or are getting, at least one microcomputer. The problem
now is to train the teachers so that maximum benefit from the microcomputers can
be had by the pupils.

The present transitional stage in educational computing in primary schools in
Scotland suggests consideration of teacher training in the area. This is
conveniently viewed in the context of background events and future plans.

BACKGROUND EVENTS

It is necessary to appreciate that Scotland has its own education system, totally
separate from the rest of the United Kingdom, under the control of the Scottish
Education Department. Within this education system pre-service teacher training
is provided by centrally funded colleges of education.

In the summer of 1967 the Secretary of State for Scotland set up the Computers and
Schools Committee "to consider the implications of computers for schools and to
make recommendations." This committee, under the chairmanship of Mr B. T. Bellis,
reported finally in 1972 recommending:

1. An introductory course in computer studies should be provided for the great
    majority of pupils, with teachers of various subjects encouraged to
    co-operate in presenting the course.

2. Further work related to computers should be incorporated into the teaching
    of various school subjects. Computer Studies should not be developed as a
    subject discipline in its own right.

3. All inspectors, advisers and teachers should be made aware of the
    applications of computers in their own subjects.

4. The provision of computing facilities on a regional basis should be expanded
    to meet the growing needs of schools.

5. A national committee should be set up to guide the development of computer
    education.

This report had both positive and negative outcomes. The recommendation that
computer studies should not be a specialist subject but be incorporated into the
various subjects meant that computing was every teacher's business. Unfortunately
"that which is everybody's business is nobody's business." Computing did not take
off in secondary schools, but was left to a few dedicated enthusiasts.

Regional computing facilities were established at the four largest colleges of
education, giving every school a regional centre to call upon for advice and
computing services. These mainframe computer facilities were most consistently
used for administrative packages for timetabling, marks processing and report
generation. A minority of schools used them to teach programming.

With considerable computing facilities in the colleges of education pre-service
students and in-service teachers were offered courses in both computing and
in specific applications. Non-graduate students entering the colleges, to train
as primary teachers, embarked upon a three year course leading to a diploma in
child education.

The more able of these students had the option after two years of transferring to
a B.Ed. degree course taking a further two years. Both diploma and degree
students could take computer studies options.

In the primary schools themselves, computer work was limited to computer
appreciation as long as access to computers depended upon visits to college
mainframe computers or using temperamental terminals to the mainframe via the
telephone system. The beginning of the breakthrough came with the arrival of the
first microcomputers from the USA in 1978. The author developed a number of
educational programs for the PET microcomputer at this time, which was the start
of a growing interest in the possibilities of using computers in the primary
school.

This research led to a major research project at Dundee College of Education,
Microcomputers in Primary Education - Using a Microcomputer in a Primary
Classroom. This research began in April 1980 and was completed in September 1982.
The project investigated the possible ways in which a microcomputer might be
integrated into the primary school classroom, using PET microcomputers supplied by
the Scottish Council for Educational Technology. A number of essential factors
for successful use of the microcomputer emerged from this research. These were:

1. Teachers require training and preparation in order to be sufficiently
    confident to handle the microcomputer and to cope with program errors or
    unexpected difficulties.

2.   Teachers need genuine commitment to use computers and must be prepared to spend considerable time and effort if they are to integrate the microcomputer fully into the classroom.

3.   The availability of educationally good software is crucial to the successful integration of the computer into the curriculum.

Besides the problematic areas of training, time, commitment and the software gap, positive signs of teacher interest, of curriculum development and of pupil initiative in a learning context also appeared within schools involved in the research.   In addition, scores of teachers attended evening courses, summer schools and national conferences on the computer in the primary school.   Awareness and interest grew, but the cost of a microcomputer still placed it beyond the budget of most primary schools.

In October 1982 the Department of Industry announced the Micros in Primary Schools Scheme whereby all primary schools in the U.K. were offered selected hardware configurations at half price. As well as the hardware they were offered the Micro Primer multi-media distance learning pack designed to familiarise the teachers with information technology and help them cope with the difficulties of introducing microcomputers into their classrooms.   The third element in the scheme was the software, a collection of about thirty programs covering a wide variety of program types and user ability ranges.

This Department of Industry initiative effectively broke the self defeating circular argument that ... there is not enough appropriate software to justify buying a microcomputer for a primary school and there are not enough microcomputers, of any one type, in primary schools to warrant writing special software for them.   The demand from primary schools for these half price micros was immediate and overwhelming, particularly for the BBC microcomputer, which the majority of schools chose in preference to the cheaper Sinclair Spectrum or the more expensive, RML 480 Link.

With the Micros in Primary Schools Scheme, a microcomputer suddenly became a realistic possibility to the "ordinary" primary school teacher, not just the idealistic preoccupation of the enthusiastic and computer initiated teacher. Microcomputers were about to invade the primary schools.

THE CURRENT SCENE

The present situation in Scotland is very much one of transition for both primary teacher training and for computer use in primary schools.   From October 1984 all non-graduate students preparing to teach in primary schools in Scotland will take a four year full-time course leading to the award of an ordinary degree of Bachelor of Education, carrying the Teaching Qualification (Primary Education). This is a major step towards an all-graduate teaching profession.   Computer content of the new degree is discussed below.

Before 1982 only a very small percentage of primary schools had a microcomputer but by the end of 1984 most, if not all, primary schools will have one and many will have several.   Providing appropriate in-service training to enable teachers to manage the newly acquired computer effectively is proving difficult.   The stringent financial restraints on both local education authorities and colleges of education impede the release of teachers to attend in-service courses and the provision of staff to run such courses.   One of the conditions set out by the Department of Industry in its Micros in Primary Schools Scheme was that the local education authority should arrange an initial two days in-service training course for two teachers from each school when the computer was first collected.   This training has been done by various agencies: colleges of education, local authority colleges and employees specially recruited for the task.   Two days, for teachers who have never before used a microcomputer, is pitifully inadequate to give the necessary instruction for teachers to use the computer confidently and competently in the classroom.

The follow up to the initial courses has been varied. Some authorities have been active and organised further meetings not only to resolve problems that have arisen, but to move forward. Such authorities have recruited programmers, provided additional hardware, run awareness courses viewing the latest software as it becomes available, taken out licences for and run special courses on particular items of software such as turtle graphics and information processing. Other authorities have been less active.

The degrees of enthusiasm with which individual primary schools have welcomed computers are extremely varied. It is easier in the smaller school where there is greater access to the computer.

Similarly some teachers have attended programming courses in their own time and at their own expense, and bought their own computers, while others desperately hope the microcomputer will vanish from the primary scene as rapidly as it arrived.

Pupils, almost without exception, have eagerly welcomed the microcomputer. They are always fascinated by new devices and with the computer are anxious to experiment with all the available software.

THE FUTURE

Predicting future trends in such a rapidly changing area as computing in primary schools is difficult. What is certain is that the present sporadic enthusiasm will be replaced by a more widespread realistic acceptance as computers settle into regular use. Computers are not going to go away.

The increasing numbers of computers in secondary schools will mean that more of the students embarking upon teacher training courses will be familiar with the potential and limitations of computers. The new four year B.Ed. degree course will include significant computing elements to ensure that all students are aware of the theoretical and practical aspects of microcomputing and information technology.

The course will aim to make students:

1.   Aware of the functional components of computer systems.

2.   Able to assemble and use them with safety and confidence.

3.   Aware of the importance of software, its different types, uses and evaluation.

4.   Able to integrate the use of the microcomputer into the school curriculum using appropriate hardware, software and classroom management.

While a new generation of student teachers is becoming better prepared to utilise the computer in the classroom the present teachers will be experimenting with current software. Various colleges are involved in cooperative projects with local teachers, designing, programming and testing new educational packages. The Scottish Microelectronics Development Project (SMDP) has teams of teachers from all over Scotland supplying ideas which are then programmed, tested and documented. The packages so produced will be available to all primary schools in Scotland.

Software is the vital key that unlocks the potential of the microcomputer. The quantity and quality of software is rapidly improving. It is necessary to get the newly arriving quality software into the schools to evaluate how it can be used to the best advantage. The earlier emphasis on the then available drill and practice programs can now change to a focus on more sophisticated work such as simulations where pupils work within interesting learning situations created by the computer. Similarly strategy programs, where pupils develop their decision-making and problem-solving skills cooperatively are now available. More content free programs like LOGO will become available; in these the children program the computer to solve their own problems. Information retrieval programs where pupils have to discover, enter and process their own data also afford new learning situations. Language programs where the teachers or pupils enter especially relevant material relating to their own favourite book, local environment or school are also possible. New software and peripheral devices facilitating simple computer control applications in the primary school are appearing.

All these innovations lead to the possibility of developing a new curriculum in the primary school incorporating the flexibility and potential of the computer for active participation by the pupils which will enliven, enrich and extend experience beyond the limitations of the traditional curriculum.

CONCLUSION

Teachers as a profession, and primary teachers in particular, are notoriously resistant to change. There will always be difficulties when trying to make innovations in such a conservative situation. How can we make room in an already overcrowded curriculum for any innovation? How can we overcome ignorance, inertia and prejudice about the computer? With computers in the primary school in Scotland we have begun to succeed. The number of machines has now passed that critical mass at which an explosion is inevitable. With this proliferation of computers will come trying and frustrating times and an ever increasing demand for more software and in-service training. These demands will never be completely satisfied. Nevertheless from the urban school in Inverness with a network of micros with one in each classroom, to the one teacher, one pupil school on the Western Isles with its BBC microcomputer and disc drive, modern technology has arrived, and is helping our pupils prepare to meet the challenge of the real world outside.

REFERENCES

Elder, R., Johnstone, M., Gourlay, J. and Wills, R. Microcomputers in Primary Education (Dundee College of Education, Dundee, 1982)

Wills, R., The Use of a Microcomputer in the Primary School, M.Sc. Thesis, (Department of Computational Science, St Andrews University 1983)

INFORMATICS AND TEACHER TRAINING
F.B. Lovis and E.D. Tagg (editors)
Elsevier Science Publishers B.V. (North-Holland)
© IFIP, 1984

INFORMATICS AND TEACHER TRAINING IN NORWAY

Jon Walstad

Trondheim College of Education
Breidablikkveien 39
N-7000 Trondheim
Norway

Jan Wibe

Trondheim Katedralskole
N-7000 Trondheim
Norway

The primary aim of this paper is to present the plans for
the introduction of informatics in Norwegian schools. This
is a development project supported by central authorities.
Extra resources will be given by the government for buying
computers, for education of teachers, software development
and projects at certain schools.

Further, we shall describe the teaching of informatics at
various stages of the school system and finally go into
the education of teachers, as the second main subject of
the paper.

1. INTRODUCTION

The pupils start school in the year when they are seven. The first nine years
are compulsory and are called "grunnskole" (elementary school). They are
divided into:

- The first six years called "barnetrinnet" (the child stage -
  corresponding to primary school).

- The last three years called "ungdomstrinnet" (the youth
  stage - corresponding to lower secondary school).

The pupils can then choose if they want to continue for another three years in
"videregående skole" (corresponding to upper secondary school). This school
offers a wide variety of subjects ranging from the theoretical (general subjects
which aim at preparing the pupils for entrance to a university), to practical
subjects giving different kinds of vocational education.

In this article we shall not go into the teaching of informatics in all parts of
the school system, and shall keep within the following limits:

- Age: 14-19

- Type of education: General education

We shall not include any kind of practical, vocational education.

The history of informatics in school is quite short. It started around 1970
when informatics was introduced as an optional subject. For many years the
teaching was concentrated only on mathematical problems with emphasis on
programming in BASIC. At the end of the seventies there was an extensive
assessment and we shall be looking at the resulting variety of available subjects.

2.   THE TEACHING OF INFORMATICS

2.1   Compulsory curriculum

All pupils who have chosen to concentrate on general, theoretical subjects in the
upper secondary school are supposed to get a compulsory minimum education in
informatics.   A plan has been developed for a course which will last for ten
lessons and include these topics:

- Computers, how they are constructed and how they work.

- How to use computers.

- How can we control the development of society?
  Through regulations and restrictions.
  Through political awareness.

It must be emphasized that this course does not include programming.

In future it is likely that parts of this course will be dealt with in lower
grades. We have just started the discussion as to which topics should be taken
at the various stages. As the schools get their own computers, we must develop
appropriate material for demonstrations and practising. Searching in library
data-bases could provide suitable tasks.

2.2   Full-year courses in informatics

Pupils who have chosen general, academic subjects in "videregående skole" are also
offered an optional informatics course of two lessons a week for one year. The
three leading topics are:

- Use of computers and its social aspects.

- Computer science.

- Programming.

Basic has been used most often, but Comal and Pascal are becoming more popular.

This course can be extended by another three lessons a week during the last year
at school. The contents of this course are a continuation of the topics already
mentioned. Two important areas are added:

- File processing

- System development

So far we have very limited experience with this course. But although it has been
tried for only one year, it has already proved to be a very popular choice for the
pupils.

In elementary school, too, informatics can be chosen for two lessons a week. As
very few schools have the computers needed, few pupils get the chance to choose
the subject at this stage. There is also current discussion whether we ought to
use informatics as an optional subject in compulsory school. There is a fear that
this will create new class divisions in the school. Very few girls choose the
subjects compared with the number of boys, and it has been pointed out that the
emphasis on programming will favour the clever pupils.

Finally, some comments on the choice of programming language. There is a clear line of development from Basic to more structured versions like Comal or BBC-Basic.

But there is a widespread opinion that programming is becoming a less interesting way of approaching informatics. Other ways can be just as useful, such as word processing, data base management systems and visicalc.

So far these ideas are very theoretical as we have a bare minimum of experience in the field.

2.3 The computer as an educational aid

Very little has been tried in this area so far. Through international conferences and magazines we have a clear impression that most countries are far ahead of us. We have some experience, though, in mathematics, social subjects and science subjects.

In the near future, the use of computers as a tool in different areas of education will be rapidly increasing. However there are many obstacles that will prevent the development from going too fast:

- The schools lack computers
- We lack suitable software
- The teachers do not have sufficient education
- We have not yet been through a pedagogical debate of how computers
  can be used as a natural aid in the various subjects.

3. TEACHER EDUCATION

Very few teachers in the schools have had a formal education in informatics. This is the most important single factor preventing the development of the subject in a school connection. So far there has been no plan for the education of teachers who are in school. We also expect few new teachers to have competence in informatics. The decreasing number of children starting school will lead to a decreasing need for new teachers.

To obtain teachers who are better qualified in informatics, it is necessary to invest in in-service training.

We also need teachers with more informal qualifications. Courses of variable extent must be arranged to meet special needs. A good illustration is the use of computers as an aid in different subjects. How can we use computers in the social subjects? How do we adapt the use of software to the aims of the subjects?

Here there are a lot of important tasks for the education of teachers. Our traditional education in this area does not properly tackle these tasks.

3.1 Formal teacher education in informatics

Formal requirements for teaching informatics have just been outlined by central authorities. The framework of this education is quite wide, but the following topics must be represented:

- Programming

  A high level language, Pascal or a similar language, must be used. Basic (as well as Comal-80) is regarded as insufficient.

- Informatics and society

    The problem of controlling the development of society through laws
    and regulations and through agreements with the trade unions must
    have considerable emphasis. There is a great need to develop
    suitable educational material in this subject. Working with
    projects must be an important aspect of any plan. The hope is that
    the students will achieve the necessary attitudes to the problems
    through individual work.

- Computer science

    This includes knowledge about how computers are constructed and how
    they work. It is a point of discussion how far one should penetrate
    into this topic. In an elementary course it is impossible to go
    into details - the aim of teacher training is not to educate
    specialists. But in this area as in others it is relevant to ask
    the question: What basic knowledge is necessary for teachers in
    elementary school?

- Didactics of teaching informatics

    Choosing the contents of this topic seems to be the most difficult
    part. Education in programming, informatics and society and
    computer science can be based on several years of experience. But
    for the method one has to search for new ideas. In our opinion
    the subject must aim at creating attitudes. The students must
    achieve a considered attitude to how we use informatics in school
    through demonstrations, practical tasks and discussions.

    So far we have very little experience with this actual plan.
    There has been some disagreement on the question of programming
    and the part this topic is going to play. A course in Pascal
    programming, for example, is said to be too exclusively directed
    towards science students.

3.2   Informal teacher training

Teachers who are going to teach informatics as an individual subject, are
supposed to have the formal education described in section 3.1. But we assume
that an increasing number of teachers will use computers as an aid in the years
to come. These teachers need an in-service-training which is quite different
from the formal education. We have just started the discussion on what the
contents of this training should be. The groups of teachers who are involved will
need knowledge in a wide variety of fields, so if it is going to correspond to
the actual needs, the offered education must also be varied.

Even so, we can distinguish between some main types of education.

- Informatics education for all teachers

    In Norway we have decided that all pupils should receive a
    compulsory education in informatics. The consequence of this
    is that all teachers must also be given an education in the
    subject.

    So far we have neither carried out nor planned such an education.
    But if this idea succeeds, we think that the in-service training
    must be given in each school. The starting point must be the
    individual needs of each school and the aim is to instruct the

teachers how to use the computers in their own schools. Furthermore, there must be an aim to inspire them to use the computer in their own teaching.

- The use of computers as an aid

The former section gave a brief sketch of an educational plan where the teachers were inspired to use the school's computers in their own subjects. If we want teachers to do this in a more serious and professional way, we cannot avoid giving them an appropriate education for it. We can imagine an education within the following frameworks:

1. Give varied examples of use.
2. Give instruction in the use of appropriate software. This must include the necessary instruction in using computers.

The attitude to using software in the teaching of other subjects is just as important. This new medium must be submitted to the general principles of teaching and the special aims of each subject.

- Developing software

The supply of a sufficient quantity of software is no problem in Norway, but the programs usually lack quality. They are mostly developed abroad and are not well adjusted to the Norwegian school. As a consequence, we must invest in developing our own software and in this connection the teachers will be a central factor. Interested teachers must be given access to an education which qualifies them for this. A programming course in Pascal does not automatically qualify one for developing programs.

What kind of education is needed to take part in software development? The needs are numerous and varied. Developing good software is no work for one man alone. This is a task for co-operation in a team where each member has a specialised function. The first course for an education based on these principles is planned for the summer of 1984.

The educational tasks we are facing are great and exciting. Other countries have done a good job in this area and we hope we can extract the best of others' experiences and use them in our own country.

- Evaluation of software

What is good and what is bad software? It is important to train teachers to have a critical attitude to the software they receive. We need criteria for evaluation of suitability, what technical and pedagogical effects are used, and first of all, software must be evaluated in relation to the aim of each subject.

4. DEVELOPMENT PLANS FOR INFORMATICS IN THE NORWEGIAN SCHOOL SYSTEM

The Norwegian government will - in the years to come - make great investments in introducing computer science into the schools. In January 1984 a governmental report called "Computer science in the school" was published. This report is to be debated by the Parliament (in Norwegian: "Stortinget") during the spring of 1984. At present (March 1984) we do not know the result of this. Therefore we are going to refer to the main points of the governmental proposition:

- A four-year long development project will be started.

- The country will be divided into 6 regions. Within each region co-operation is to take place between primary schools, secondary schools, teacher education institutions, research institutions, various occupational groups and trade unions.

- 40-50 schools will be given financial support in order to participate in the development project. These schools will get both computers and software, and all the teachers will be given appropriate education. It is important that every teacher is stimulated to make use of the computer as an educational aid. This is especially important in vocational education in which - in many people's opinion - Norway is lagging behind.

- The entire project will be managed by a secretariat in Oslo. By this means, one avoids the ordinary administration systems in school, and hopes to get higher efficiency.

- The success of a project like this depends on the available economic resources. One is therefore willing to give financial support to a wide spectrum of activities:

   * Computers

      The central authorities are now negotiating with the distributors of 2 different computers concerning delivery to the schools. The prices achieved will be valid for all schools. The central authorities themselves are buying 300 computers for distribution to the project schools.

   * Teacher education

      All the teachers involved in the projects must take part in an education program. This will include both formal and informal education as described in section 3. In addition to this education program, several meetings and seminars will be arranged in order to discuss the layout of the different parts of the project, as well as how they should be carried out.

      What about the teachers who are not working at a project-school? They will form the majority and also need all types of education and information. It is the aim that these teachers must also benefit from the experiences attained in the project, but it is too early to say how this should be done.

   * Development, use and evaluation of software

      In section 3.2 we have described the design of such projects. As whole schools will be involved in the project, it is very important to start developing Norwegian software. Unfortunately,

we have not much experience in doing this and must build up
competence. This will, of course, take some time. We must
therefore extract the best of what is done in other countries.
The governmental report underlines also the importance of
international contacts in this and in other areas.

* Evaluation of computer science in school

The computer is a new aid in school. In what way will it change
the content of different school subjects? What new principles
of teaching will be adopted? Will the pupils' ways of learning be
changed? In Norway we are now starting a new epoch in school.
It is therefore of great importance to observe and evaluate what
is happening as a result of these new aids. Will we be able to
maintain the superior aims we have for all education? We are
here facing great and challenging evaluation tasks.

- Regional planning

Both authors of this paper are involved in regional planning, and
we are therefore going to tell a little about the development
project from this point of view. Norway is divided into 20
countries (norw.: "fylker"). Referring to the data development
program, our region consists of three neighbouring countries. We
should therefore expect about 7 project schools to be picked out
within our region. In other words: 2-3 schools in each county.
This illustrates the fact that the central authorities want to
give good financial support to a small number of schools. One
obvious question is therefore: What about the rest of the
schools?

In our country we have established a basis for cooperation between
the groups that are involved. Further, we have started to make plans
for a local development project. A main idea has been to start
smaller projects in various schools. We assume that most of the
school subjects will be represented, but we intend to spread the
projects over many schools. This is in contrast to the model given
by the central authorities. Whether this idea will be accepted or
not remains to be seen. We hope to clarify this in Birmingham.

Finally, let us say something more about the contents of this paper.
It has mainly dealt with planning and organising. Maybe we have
told too little about our experiences from projects that have already
been carried out. Partly, this is because of the fact that we are now
going to start the largest development project in Norwegian school
history, and partly it is because we have a negligible number of
projects and experiences to refer to. Accentuating these results too
much would give a false picture of the situation in Norway.

Other countries have carried out similar projects on a larger scale.
We hope to get reactions both to this paper and to the presentation
which will be given in Birmingham. In particular, we should
appreciate receiving reports from similar projects in other countries.

INFORMATICS AND TEACHER TRAINING
F.B. Lovis and E.D. Tagg (editors)
Elsevier Science Publishers B.V. (North-Holland)
© IFIP, 1984

Teacher Training and Education for Mathematics and Informatics
in the German Democratic Republic

I. O. Kerner

Paedagogische Hochschule,
Dresden,
German Democratic Republic

1. Introduction: The Education System of GDR

The 10-year general polytechnical secondary school (allgemeinbildende
polytechnische Oberschule POS) is attended by all children in the German
Democratic Republic. The training of teachers for this type of school is a task
of the universities and colleges of education, in general, and of teacher
training institutes. In 1965 we passed the law on the Integrated Socialist
Education System, the effectiveness of which increasingly influences the quality
and rate of development in all spheres of social life. The first component of
this system comprises pre-school education. Children up to the age of three go
to crèches (controlled by the Ministry of Health), and children aged three to
six go to Kindergarten (nursery school) controlled by the Ministry of Education.
All children attend the 10-year general polytechnical secondary school. Since
1959 this has been the basic type of school in the GDR. After finishing at
this school - divided into a primary level of four years and a secondary-(I)-
level of six years - the pupils can continue their training either in the
institutions of vocational training or in the extended secondary schools
(secondary-II-level, erweiterte Oberschule EOS). Vocational training generally
takes two years. The skilled workers' certificate entitles a student to study
at a technical school (Fachschule). The period of training there is three years.
Passing the final examination at such a technical school entitles the students
to go in for higher education. The pupils who continue their education at the
extended secondary school (EOS) sit for the matriculation examination (Abitur)
after two years (see Fig. 1).

If and how the social functions of education are fulfilled depends largely upon
the standard and the effectiveness of the work done by teachers. That is why
the training and further education of teachers has been made a key task in the
overall development of society in our state. The teachers are highly respected,
i.e. the reputation and the social standard of teachers, teacher educators, and
teacher training institutions has become good and high.

I.O. Kerner

```
Age
23                          Universities or Colleges
22                                    ----------------------------
21
20                                    Technical Schools
                                      (Fachschulen)
19   Grade
----------------------------------------------------------------------
18   12 Extended Secondary Schools    Vocational Training Institutions
17   11        (EOS)              or
----------------------------------------------------------------------
16   10
15    9
14    8  Secondary level
13    7
12    6                          10-year general
11    5                          polytechnical
---------------------------      schools (BOS)
10    4
 9    3  Primary level
 8    2
 7    1
----------------------------------------------------------------------
 6
 5              Kindergarten (nursery schools)
 4
----------------------------------------------------------------------
 3
 2              Crèches
 1
----------------------------------------------------------------------
```

Figure 1. The integrated socialist education system of the GDR.

It is our aim to enable future teachers to utilize modern pedagogical science as a productive force, as it is necessary to prepare all pupils for their later work in the interests of society. The rising generation of teachers will be able to meet the growing professional and pedagogical demands made upon the training and education of the young and they will be able to provide creative instruction on the basis of new curricula and syllabuses.

The teachers for the primary level (lower classes) of the 10-year general polytechnical secondary school (grades 1 to 4) are trained at Institutes for Teacher Training (Fachschulen) in three-year courses. The requirement for admission to such a course is the successful completion of the 10-year general polytechnical secondary school. They have a somewhat different vocational training from that shown in figure 1.

The training of 'Diplomlehrer' ('Diplom' roughly corresponds with the degree of M.A.) or so-called subject teachers teaching in the upper classes of the 10-year general polytechnical secondary school (grades 5 to 10 or secondary level) and in the classes 11 and 12 of the Extended Secondary School (secondary-II-level) is provided by universities and colleges of education (Paedagogische Hochschulen). The training course lasts five years. The prerequisite for admission is the successful completion of the Extended Secondary School (EOS) with the Abitur or matriculation standard. The teachers are trained in two subjects and graduate with the first academic degree, the 'Diplom' (diploma).

Our educational system has evoked great interest in developing countries. The well-known Entebbe-system for African mathematics education has failed in many countries. I am working at a college of education or teacher training centre with a lot of international connections. Some of our colleagues have worked in Algeria, Somalia, Ethiopia, Angola, Congo, Guinea, and Mozambique. It is true that Entebbe-Mathematics enables the pupil to study in western Europe or America. But this is a small minority and an even smaller minority comes back to the country of origin – because of the brain drain. Through Entebbe-Mathematics, a cultural import takes place as can be seen by a single look into the teaching materials, i.e. the majority of books are often simple copies of English, French or American ones.

What young African nations need is sufficient Mathematics for vocational training even for jobs and trades which do not yet exist. Our help consists in developing such educational programmes in Mathematics, and by training teachers in these fields. But we know and see further problems. After training a lot of pupils for four or six years and giving them a foundation of knowledge as a basis for vocational training there must be enough vocational training facilities. Establishing such centres and, furthermore, places of work are the next steps; on this depends the success of our kind of help.

2. General Curriculum for Teachers: The Mathematics Part

As already mentioned, the training of subject teachers for the secondary I and II levels takes five years. The training programme for the first four years covers the following disciplines:

- training in the two subjects to be taught;
- training in educational sciences; (pedagogics, psychology, health education, methodology of the subjects to be taught);
- fundamentals of Marxism-Leninism;
- general education (foreign languages, sport, cultural and aesthetic education).

In the fifth year of the training course the students work as trainee-teachers (Praktikanten) in schools in order to gain experience in the teacher's main

activities. This period of training is especially designed to promote the
development of independence and to facilitate a continuous transition to full
employment.

As mentioned above, subject teachers (Diplomlehrer) for the secondary I and II
level are trained in two subjects. Possible combinations with mathematics are
'mathematics and physics', 'mathematics and geography', 'mathematics and
chemistry'.

field	year			
	1	2	3	4

Basic course for mathematics	///////////////////////////
	30 hours pre-course for
	      fundamentals
	225 hours analysis
	165 hours algebra
	150 hours geometry
				////////////////////
				45 hours meta-
				      mathematics
				30 hours free
				      specialized fields

Graphical geometry (drawing, figuring)		/////////// 60 hours		
Numerical analysis and informatics		////////// 120 hours		
Probability and statistics		///////// 75 hours		
History of mathematics			////////////////// 30 hours	
Methodology for mathematics teaching			///////////////////////////// 135 hours	

Figure 2: The training programme for teachers: The mathematics part.

The basic course in mathematics lasts two years and covers 645 hours with a
ratio between lectures and exercises of 390:255.

The study course takes 8 semesters, each of 15 weeks, each consisting of nearly
30 hours. That means 3250 hours in total. We have 1065 hours i.e. about one
third, available for teaching mathematics. A second third is for the second
subject, and almost the last third is for the other disciplines mentioned above.
There is a volume of 180 hours during the third and the fourth year for
preparing a paper for the diploma (Diplomarbeit, diploma-thesis, master-thesis).
The students can choose a theme from mathematics, from the second subject or
from another discipline such as pedagogics, psychology. Choosing mathematics
or the second subject includes its didactics, of course.

We consider the 60 hours available for informatics a fairly small amount and
think the training in the third year is too late (cf. figure 2). But the
lecturers of the basic courses are concerned to show the interface with
informatics and to familiarize the students with algorithmic and dynamic
thinking and methods (procedures instead of formulae). There are similar
opportunities in numerical analysis and in probability and statistics. Mostly
we are demonstrating the three fields

> numerical analysis
> informatics
> probability and statistics

as a block of 195 hours to the students, and we do this with a strong use of algorithms and computers. Furthermore, the time when no lectures are held (remember a semester has only 15 weeks with lectures) is not a time of holiday. A great part of this time is devoted to self-study and important practical courses. So we have three weeks of computer practice, equivalent to nearly 120 working hours, at the middle and end of the third year.

3. The Curriculum in Informatics

In this field the students acquire a basic knowledge of problems and methods in informatics. They learn how to apply mathematics and powerful mathematical instruments to other sciences, to the national economy and other areas of society. The students acquire further fundamental knowledge and become qualified to conduct some departmental courses or lead working groups of pupils in our schools. They acquire a basic insight into the possibilities of communication between human beings and machines; they also learn of the limits. The whole complex of problem-analysis, design of algorithms for solution, programming and a critical look at the computed results is shown to them. The teaching process consists of five topics:

1. The computer as an information processing system

    - the operating system of a computer
    - design and function of a computer
    - stages and tendencies of computer structure
      (history and future)

2. Control of computers by algorithms

    - examples of numerical and non-numerical algorithms
    - intuitive notion of algorithms, requirements and properties of
      algorithms
    - flow diagrams, structograms
    - examples of algorithms in school (elementary) mathematics.

3. Programming languages

    - introduction to an algorithmic language (PASCAL preferred)
    - syntax and semantics of programming languages
    - classification of the chosen language

4. Elements of data structures

    - fields or arrays
    - lists (stacks, queues, trees)
    - applications in mathematics and non-mathematical algorithms

5. Application of computers

    - operating systems (batch, multiple remote access, dialogue)
    - examples of application.

During the three weeks of computer practice the students work at problems given to them during the lectures in numerical analysis, informatics, and probability and statistics. They also have the opportunity of using the computer in some problems of their diploma thesis. Furthermore they can join themselves into

project groups - up to five members - dealing with a freely chosen problem.
At the end of the computer practice they have to submit a minimum program of
about 50 lines, debugged and with results.

4. The Situation of Informatics in School

At present we are in a process of reformation. Next year - 1985 - we shall
introduce the pocket calculator, starting with grade 7. The school books or
text books have been prepared. We plan to skip the period of programmable
pocket calculators and to introduce video computers in all schools. These
home or personal computers are of our own production and very similar to
international standard models at an average level. A curriculum for informatics
in schools is in preparation. The first step will be a new arrangement of two
courses in practical mathematics and in data processing. These courses are
provided for interested pupils. The number of realizations of these courses and
the number of participants will increase during the next years.

Since 1972 teachers have been trained according to the curriculum mentioned in
paragraph 3. This means there are nearly 12,000 teachers, or 2 in each school,
with a minimum of knowledge in this field. But they have not been able to
use this in their daily work, so far. So it will be necessary to start with a
great programme of in-service training for refreshing and modernizing this
basic knowledge. Therefore all institutions for teacher training are equipped
with a number of video computers and have access to a more powerful computer.

5. Computer Aided Teaching and Learning

The equipment of schools with video computers opens up the possibility of using
them as a pedagogical and didactic medium of teaching and learning, instead of
merely as an object. Teachware, i.e. software for pedagogical processes as
instruction/training/drill/exercises/examination, is to be prepared. For
facilitating this, we have in our research programme at Dresden a higher
language LEFO (Lehrprogramm-Formulierung, teaching program formulation) which
will enable most teachers in most teaching subjects to design, prepare and
test their own programs. This language is open for all pedagogical, didactic,
and methodical ideas and processes. The control of teaching and learning can
be chosen from a wide spectral range based on a lot of data which was assembled
while teaching the respective learning process. We have made a strong
distinction between program data, i.e. instructions, questions, answers, and
the statements of the program. So we can write from the same program data
several programs with different structures, and we can give to the same program,
with a good pedagogical basis,several sets of program data for teaching and
learning other subjects.

Furthermore program data is easily exchangeable with data in another (foreign)
language. In this way an export of teachware is very simple. In avoiding a
cultural export - not wished by the importer - it is possible to exchange the
German names of LEFO statements with names in other languages. Teachers from
foreign nations are then enabled to write their own programs. Only a simple
part of the compiler - the scanner for lexical analysis - has to be exchanged.
Examples of this method are being implemented with colleagues from Cuba and
Poland.

The basic or background language of LEFO is Pascal, which is available on a wide
spectrum of micro computers. So LEFO is fairly simply transportable to other
computers.

For the future we intend to incorporate more methods and ideas of artificial intelligence into the tools of LEFO. So we are on the way to intelligent computer aided teaching and learning. We shall give some of the control of the process into the hands of the learner, so that the computer will no longer control the learner, but vice versa, and the human being will have first priority.

INFORMATICS AND TEACHER TRAINING
F.B. Lovis and E.D. Tagg (editors)
Elsevier Science Publishers B.V. (North-Holland)
© IFIP, 1984

Toward a Theory of CAL: Some Benchmarks for Teachers

Seong-Soo Lee

University of British Columbia, Canada

Abstract

The problems of CAL applications are traced to lack of research based guidelines for courseware development and evaluation. In particular the attempts of teaching professionals to evaluate poorly developed CAL materials seem to reflect the current practices in a "cart before the horse" order. It is suggested that we should first clarify what can be done better with the computer than with the human teacher, by way of developing a CAL theory.

A.   Teaching Professional Readiness for CAL

In this micro-electronic information age, many large local educational systems appear to have responded to calls for computerizing their operations by placing appropriate computing resources in school classrooms. We do not yet have an overall picture of the impact of such innovative efforts on the actual teaching and learning processes in each learner. But we are not readily convinced that the computer instructional materials developed for microcomputers are of an acceptable quality, regardless of the area of instruction (Roblyer, 1983). A strong case against courseware evaluation was also made by Ragsdale (1983). The problem of the lack of quality courseware can be compounded for the teaching professional by the absence of instructionally useful guidelines for making judgements about courseware quality. This is because theory-based concepts, concerning the learning processes involved in the acquisition of the new material being presented, have yet to be formulated.

We might be able to guess what is going on in the schools by looking at some possible barriers against effective utilization of computers. To elaborate upon only one of them, we know that teachers are the very computer users whose professional competence constitutes the most important ingredient for successful computer application. In this regard, a relevant question I should like to pose is: How many of our teachers can make professional judgements about the quality of available courseware with reliability and validity? To begin with, our teachers are in a way induced to look at some commonsense surface characteristics of computer aided learning (CAL) materials, but not to make judgements about the substantive qualities of those materials. This can be seen in two contrasting sets of evaluative criteria (Figure 1). The latter set was advocated as the preferred one by Sall (1984).

*Necessary Attributes to Consider
in Designing Courseware for the Microcomputer[2]*

Generic to Instructional Design
1. Target audience specified
2. Learner entry competencies specified
3. Rationale, goals, and objectives specified
4. Objectives stated behaviorally
5. Objectives stated in terms of the learner
6. Objectives include higher-order skills
7. Learners informed of objectives
8. Range and scope of content adequate
9. Preinstructional strategies used:
    Pretests
    Advance organizers
    Title at beginning of unit
10. Instructional text formatted for easy reading
11. Concept learning employed in instructional approach
12. Vocabulary used appropriately for learner
13. Graphics embedded in content
14. Graphics used appropriately
15. Demonstration of the exercise provided
16. Teacher's Manual provided
17. Instructions clearly stated for student
18. Evaluation components provided

Necessary for Design Courseware
1. Curriculum role used:
    Adjunct
    Mainline
    Management only
    Other
2. Mode of interaction employed:
    Drill and Practice
    Tutorial
    Game
    Simulation
    Problem-Solving
3. Student sequenced through the content:
    Nonlinear
    Varied by teacher/student
4. Instructional text formatted for screen display
5. Graphics embedded in the content
6. Graphics used appropriately
7. Cues and/or prompts used
8. Action occurs on the screen
9. User control granted to learner
10. Computer-Managed Instruction employed
11. Feedback used appropriately
12. Records stored on magnetic devices for future retrieval
13. Content designed to be altered
14. Random generation used
15. Packaging designed for component parts
16. Teacher's Manual and Student Manual provided
17. Technical design used:
    Quick response time
    Quick loading time

---

[2] Vicki L. Blum Cohen. "Criteria for the Evaluation of Microcomputer Courseware", *Educational Technology*, 23, 1, January 1983, pages 9-14.

The following list of twenty-five items is the "Courseware Evaluation" of this guide:

1. *The content is Accurate.*
2. *The content has educational value.*
3. *The content is free of race, ethnic, and sex stereotypes.*
4. *The purpose of the package is well defined.*
5. *The package achieves its defined purpose.*
6. *Presentation of content is clear and logical.*
7. *The level of difficulty is appropriate for the target audience.*
8. *The Graphics/sound/color are used for appropriate instructional reasons.*
9. *Use of the package is motivational.*
10. *The package effectively challenges student creativity.*
11. *Feedback on student responses is effectively employed.*
12. *The learner controls the rate and sequence of presentation and review.*
13. *Instruction is integrated with previous student experiences.*
14. *Learning is generalizable to an appropriate range of situations.*
15. *User support materials are comprehensive.*
16. *The user support materials are effective.*
17. *Information displays are effective.*
18. *Intended users can easily and independently operate the program.*
19. *Teachers can easily employ the package.*
20. *The program appropriately uses relevant computer capabilities.*
21. *The program is reliable in normal use.*
22. *Evaluator Recommendation.*
23. *Describe the major strengths of the package.*
24. *Describe the major weaknesses of the package.*
25. *Describe the potential use of the package in classroom settings.*

Figure 1.

Many teachers also mistakenly shun the real requirement that our instructional programs and operations should be, more or less, goal-/objective-oriented in the guidance of learning, perhaps through the advocacy of philosophy expressed in Seymour Papert's <u>Mindstorms</u>, or because of the misinterpretation of this. In any case, a serious computer-using teacher's concern is briefly expressed in "Letters to the Editor", by Brochmann (1984). One might further ask how many of us understand the philosophy in such a way as to translate it into computer implementable terms beyond "Turtle LOGO".

Letter to the Editor

This is a very exciting time to be a teacher. I don't mean the "excitement" generated by our recent differences of opinion with the crew in Victoria. I mean the excitement of *Mindstorms*. More and more teachers are paying homage to Guru Papert and his philosophy of Logo. Great stuff this. Turtles will replace chalk. Recursion is our passport to the future.

I really don't think we understand what's going on at all. Precisely what does "doing Logo" accomplish anyhow?

I enthusiastically endorse the notion that student-directed exploration is a powerful learning mechanism. I marvel at the potential of microworlds...but I am troubled by the fact that I can't seem to identify what definable learning objectives are to be achieved. It is easy to scoff at "the curriculum". But darn it, if we are supposed to be teachers, it follows that we should have a reasonably clear idea of what it is that we are teaching. With Logo I don't think we do.

I suspect that when we have access to the benefits of hindsight we will realize that in 1983 and 1984 we were galloping down some paths that ultimately turned out to lead no place in particular.

But I do believe that computers offer possibilities for learning through exploration of, yes, microworlds. The trick lies in creating microworlds with properties more closely related to the real world.

Harold Brochmann

B. Need for Theory-Based Thinking and Research on CAL

Many conferences and workshops on computer uses in education which I have attended seem to conclude with a loud call for the development of research or theory based CAL software. It is not difficult to agree with a commonly held view that most educational courseware is poorly conceived and developed. This suggests that the actual and potential power of computer hardware technology is under utilized. It seems likely that our superbly engineered and sophisticated microcomputers are being deployed as "electronic page turners", rather than as intelligent, interactive learning guides.

I believe that an optimal use of the computing power already or shortly available to the educational profession, can be realized best through our systematic thinking about the learning processes of the human information processing system, as well as its interface with the computer information processing system. How many educational professionals, even those who have already contributed to the available courseware market, have exercised their trade skills of instructional and program designs, prior to coding their teaching ideas into computer languages?

In this connection, it would be useful to look at what kind of learning models might be adopted by ordinary classroom teachers in their day-to-day actual

practice. Szabo (1983) made some interesting observations from common experience
with current educational practice and summed up as follows:

> "Current educational systems operate, perhaps unconsciously,
> using a model of the human learning which argues that students
> learn best when they <u>receive</u> information and <u>copy</u> information
> at the <u>same rates</u>, learn <u>competitively</u> from <u>print</u> materials,
> and are <u>reinforced</u> for correct behaviours."

Granting that there may be some exceptions to the above observations, we seem to
have a hard time to disagree with it. As long as the teachers' working model of
human learning remains unchanged and until educational courseware available on
the market improves in quality, I am afraid our expectation of computer uses,
especially CAL, to assume an innovative mission of enhancing education may well
remain a dream.

While thinking about the role that CAL can and should play in present day
educational practice and considering serious economic restraints, my constant
quest has been one of the cost effectiveness questions involving human and
computer resources. Namely, what is it that the computer can do more effectively
and efficiently than human teachers? Today, I am here to share with you my
thoughts about it in pursuit of a reasonable response to the question. Instead
of trying to cover a wide range of issues related to the question, I should like
to focus on how CAL can be implemented to promote learning with understanding,
marking some basic assumptions which should serve as benchmarks for developing
a CAL theory.

C.   Some Basic Assumptions for a CAL Theory

Essentially, the task of the CAL application of the computer is to optimize the
effectiveness and efficiency of communication between two information systems,
one that of the computer and the other human. To this end, we should recognize
the need for different assumptions, to be made in particular about human learners.
First, the learner is an active participant with an incessant craving for self-
respect in his interaction with his environment, especially in a learning
transaction. He is not a passive agent, letting incoming information just pass
through. We have already witnessed the decline of the programmed instruction
technology, ultimately due to behaviorism's failure to admit this assumption.

Second, the learner is a constantly growing individual with a unique history of
individual differences in perceptual and mental abilities, both verbal as well
as non-verbal. Therefore, learners are different in their readiness for new
learning in the cognitive, affective, and psychmotor domains.

Third, the learner learns best when motivated intrinsically, rather than
extrinsically, with the disposition of self control. The educational merit of
intrinsic motivation, as related to learning and instruction, is well argued by
Lepper and Malone (1983).

Fourth, the learner's coding and transformation activities with learning materials
are ultimately individualistic and personal affairs, based on past learning and,
most critically, feedback information.

Learning with understanding, as opposed to reception learning, requires the
active use of three kinds of information on each learning trial: (1) the current
information extracted from a given task, (2) the learner's relevant and existing
knowledge, and (3) the feedback information from each trial outcome, which
reflects conflicts between his current understanding and what is to be understood.
The learner predicts and tests a relation or concept on the basis of the
formation of some alternative hypotheses. When it is confirmed, it enters the
learner's cognitive structure of knowledge. Since it resides in a meaningful
structure, its retention and transfer levels are expected to be very high.

D. Some Benchmarks for CAL Design and Implementation

Earlier, I indicated a set of four benchmark assumptions towards a theory of
learning with understanding, and subsequently specified some aspects of cognitive
learning, useful for the CAL implementation. What are specific and practical
ways in which the ideas can be put into CAL design and implementation? One of
the most important implications for CAL is that the notion of learning with
understanding can be best realized by designing learning programs in an inductive
approach, with an appropriate amount of learning guidance. Some of these ideas
were implemented with positive results by Lee (1983). In a way, the amount of
guidance in concept learning can constitute a program design variable, which can
be manipulated in terms of the four concept learning paradigms. The most
popular in the CAL research literature is the expository method, incorporating
the deductive approach. One prominent example appears to be the instructional
paradigm consistently used by Tennyson and his associates (e.g., Tennyson, Dean,
Christensen, & Park, 1984). The reported effects of such instructional design
variables as the amount of instruction, the sequence of instruction,
instructional display time, and advisement information, may well show up
differently under other than the expository mode of instruction. Of course, the
relative merit of the inductive approach, as compared to the deductive, needs to
be experimentally assessed.

Second, the learner should be recognized as an active participant with a strong
desire to control learning events. This is enhanced by informing him about the
learning goals and objectives and also by delegating some responsibility for
learning management to the learner. The former activates the goal-directed
strategy; the latter determines the degree of learner control. It appears that
the total learner control strategy, as intended, may not be effective and
reliable (Snow, 1981), unless the learner can be assumed to have full-blown
metacognitive ability. An adaptive program- control was found to be more
effective than learner control of management (Tennyson, et al. 1984). A truly
generative, adaptive program-control model needs to be further developed
(McCann, 1981).

Third, the learner's general aptitude, as well as pre-instructional knowledge
and skill, would be restructured as a result of new learning. Thus,
restructuring can be most facilitated when based on prior learning, through
transfer of prior learning retained by new learning. In a way, most new learning
is a transfer of prior learning. Accordingly, new learning will be optimized if
it starts at the limits of the learner's present level of understanding. The
program design may well include relevant pre-instructional tests and their
proper uses.

Fourth, the initial representation of learning materials should be in a form to
facilitate internal representation. For example, either linguistic or
pictorial materials should be made easy for the learner's initial coding. The
level of presentation depends on his developmental competence level and
requires that a careful choice of computer textual or graphic presentation be
made, on the basis of codability, information density, etc.

Fifth, the learner's representational and transformational mental operations can
be made easier through psychologically appropriate and fine-tuned task and
process analyses. Such analyses are almost mandatory for the effective
implementation of not only inductive and deductive mental operations, but also
for maximizing the utility of feedback. A balanced mix of the two, with a view
to enhancing learning with understanding, can be readily implemented in CAL
sessions. Such task analyses would lead to defining specific learning events
which draw specific responses from the learner, ranging from a simple, ready-
made response to open and free responses.

Sixth, the most critically important role that an expert teacher is expected to assume, is to provide useful advice to the learner to the right degree at the right moment. The learning guidance function can be cast in a one-to-one friendly dialogue situation when we develop cost effective ways, in which teaching expertise is incorporated into MYCIN-like expert programs, applicable to various declarative knowledge domains (Clancy, 1979). For the time being, however, we need to work with less than desirable dialogue techniques, given a circumscribed knowledge domain.

Seventh, pacing the units of learning materials should be based on the mastery criterion which each learner attains. The effects of the degree of learning on the acquisition of related or superordinate concepts (units) and the retention of the original learning have been found to be the most powerful and robust variable for optimal retention and transfer. Practice or rehearsal can be couched in different surface contexts to maximize the transfer and the restructuring of prior concepts or schema. It is noteworthy here that the old issue of "mastery learning", debated for sometime in the education research community, appears to be a pacing management issue, given a group learning situation with little guidance function in a real sense. A properly implemented CAL can render such an issue trivial. When the CAL is well implemented, it will certainly educe and enhance the learner's intrinsic motivation, maintaining the learner's sense of challenge, curiosity, control, and striving. A related problem is that of dealing with individual differences, not only in learning rates but also in work schedules. This can be readily taken care of through a CMI aspect of the CAL program.

Finally, our commonly held view about feedback, i.e. that the positive reinforcement delivered immediately after the learner's response is the most effective, needs to be re-examined. This is not true. Unfortunately, the reinforcement, which is a central concept of behavioral psychology, has been viewed by many as equivalent to feedback. A reasonable view is to regard the reinforcement event as having two aspects: one informational and the other motivational. The informational component would have real functional significance as feedback to the learner's information processing activities. Its primary function is to provide the learner with information concerning the correctness or appropriateness of his previous response in the light of the task requirement. It provides an assessment of the degree of conflict between his current understanding and the target understanding. Thus, feedback events may vary in timing (immediate versus delayed), complexity (simple versus elaborate), frequency (frequent versus infrequent), and the like. The multifaceted feedback events can be generated and delivered as intended in the optimal CAL mode.

Postscript

I shall stop listing too many possibilities, for us to think about here, because my preoccupation, as I indicated at the outset, is still with the question: What can be done better or more cost effectively by computers than by human teachers?

While reflecting on my own preoccupation with the broad context of using computer in education, it seems fitting to cite two useful quotes:

> "... too many schools still follow an established recipe for disaster: first, policy makers choose the hardware, then decide on the software (Chorover, 1984)."

> "... the introduction of computers into primary and secondary schools is basically a mistake based on very false assumptions (Weizenbaum, 1984)."

Keeping these two caveats in mind, we cannot avoid a broader question: What do we want to do with the superbly engineered and powerful microcomputer?   I should like to suggest that we return to the pedagogy of good sense.

References

Brochmann, H. (1984). Letter to the Editor. Computer Using Educator, **3**, 6.

Chorover, S.L. (1984). Cautions on computers in education. Byte, **9**, 223-226 (June).

Clancy, W.J. (1979). Tutoring rules for guiding a case method dialogue. International Journal of Man-Machine Studies. **11**, 25-49.

Lee, S.S. (1983). A Learner-based computer instructional system: An Experiment. A paper presented at the 1983 AEDS 21st Annual Convention, Oregon, U.S.A. pp. 185-188.

Lepper, M.R. & Malone, T.W. (1984). Intrinsic motivation and instructional effectiveness in computer-based education. In R.E. Snow & M. J. Farr (Eds), Aptitude, Learning and Instruction: III Conative & Affective Process Analysis, Hillsdale: LEA.

McCann, P.H. (1981). Learning strategies and computer-based instruction. Computer and Education, **5**, 133-137.

Ragsdale, R. (1983). The case against courseware evaluation. A paper presented at the 1983 Annual Conference of Canadian Society for the Study of Education, Vancouver, B.C. Canada. June 5-8, 1983.

Roblyer, M.D. (1983). Toward more effective microcomputer courseware through application of systematic instructional design methods, AEDS Journal, **17**, 23-32.

Sall, M. (1984). A critique of five instructional computer software evaluation forms. Computer Using Educator, **3**, 43-50.

Szabo, M. (1983). Improving computer based learning courseware through application of cognitive science learning theory. A paper presented at the 1983 AEDS 21st Annual Convention, Oregon, U.S.A. pp. 328-338.

Tennyson, R., Christensen, D.L., & Parks, S. (1984). The Minnesota adaptive instructional system: An intelligent CBI system. Journal of Computer-Based Instruction, **11**, 2-13.

Weizenbaum, J. (1984). Another View from MIT. Byte, **9**, p. 225 (June).

Discussion after paper of <u>Wills</u>

<u>Penter</u> opened the discussion by asking What is the basic philosophy of microcomputer use at the elementary level?
<u>Wills</u> replied, that it is to prepare the pupils for modern society. Primarily to help them in learning all subjects, not simply to study computing.

<u>Martin</u> asked the maximum number of hours a teacher could study at university, and <u>Wills</u> replied that a student could study from 55 hours to a maximum of 200 hours in computer courses.

Discussion after the papers of <u>Wibe</u> & <u>Walstad</u>, <u>Kerner</u> and <u>Lee</u>

<u>Christiaen</u> to Wibe & Walstad: Very little has been said about didactics; shouldn't there be more attention paid to this?
<u>Walstad</u> agreed: It is important, but I did not have time to stress that in my paper.
<u>Martin</u> posed a question about Pascal making up 40% of a compulsory course or an optional course. The reply was that it was taught in a course for teachers going to teach informatics as an individual subject.
<u>Wright</u> commented that we should not underestimate the abilities of elementary teachers, noting that many of them are capable of work in Pascal and other higher languages.

Rapporteurs: Dennis Harkins & Birthe Olsen

SESSION 6

Chairman: David Tinsley

INFORMATICS AND TEACHER TRAINING
F.B. Lovis and E.D. Tagg (editors)
Elsevier Science Publishers B.V. (North-Holland)
© IFIP, 1984

JUDGING THE VALUE OF MATERIALS FOR USE WITH MICROCOMPUTERS

R. Lewis,
Institute for Educational Computing,
S. Martin's College,
Lancaster, UK

Various forms of materials used with micro-computers are
discussed. Those which create opportunities for pupils
to engage in various forms of problem solving, assisted
as appropriate by their teachers, are considered in
detail. The evaluation of such materials by developers
and teachers is described and the importance of teacher-
pupil relationship in this context is stressed.

INTRODUCTION

In a paper with such a title it is essential to define the terms being used.
In the context of using micro-computers in schools, this relates specifically
to the role intended for the computer. Whilst classifications are rarely
water-tight, it is possible to identify a number of categories of computer-
related material. These include

A.   materials intended for practice and reinforcement which are usually
      for use by individual pupils;

B.   materials which provide the opportunity for pupils to investigate a
      topic or theme, usually intended for small group use but sometimes
      effective as the basis for a whole class tutorial;

C.   materials through which the pupil (or small group of pupils) raises
      the level of communication possible with the system, in some cases the
      'knowledge' of the system.

The word 'materials' is used to cover software, worksheets, problem sheets and
so on. The selection of these is predominantly in the hands of the teacher,
though pupils can be (should be) allowed to select these learning resources
themselves.

Before concentrating largely on the value of materials which fall into the
second of these categories, a few words should be devoted to the other two.
Materials, often simply programs, in category A are by far the easiest for
teachers to make use of and they can be very popular. The traditional,
largely didactic, lesson goes on as normal and pupils can be directed or
encouraged to spend some time using a program which may be motivating and
rewarding. An important factor, particularly for younger pupils is that, when
using such programs, their attention span is longer than normal though this
may be due to novelty and may wear off eventually.

The essential characteristic of materials in categories B and C, is that the
system (hardware plus software) provides pupils with <u>tools</u> for problem
solving. The system has a minor role to play in terms of assessing what the
pupil does; the system is seen as a laboratory which provides feedback on
pupils' ideas. The dominant methodology is one of <u>teacher assisted learning</u>
with a variety of other resources (including computer hardware and software)

available to the pupil. One of the most important effects of such a
methodology is the change in the relationships which exist between the teacher
and the class and its individual members. As will be considered later, the
nature of these relationships is critical in arriving at criteria on which to
base judgements of the value of the available materials. In contrast to the
use of materials in category A, the appropriate use of category B and C
materials may demand shifts from existing classroom methods. The demands on
teachers who adopt a problem solving approach are considerable. The approach
requires a deep and broad understanding of the topic and of the ways children
perceive the topic, together with conducive personal relationships. These are
all necessary to create a level of self-confidence, firstly in the teacher and
then in the pupils, appropriate to this pedagogic style.

The more challenging the problems tackled by pupils, the more exacting is the
teacher's task. This is particularly the case when pupils arrive at the stage
of selecting their own problems. It is a natural extension of the philosophy
to give pupils this ultimate control but it is far from clear that this
benefits learning. The careful selection of appropriate problems requires a
great deal of skill on the part of the teacher. It must also be recognised
that many pupils feel safer in rather less open-ended situations.

It becomes all too easy for teacher assisted learning to shift towards teacher
directed learning, which is safer. This is particularly true when the pupil
may discover a rather better strategy for solving a problem than that apparent
to the teacher. It takes courage to accept that we learn from our students
and we maybe somewhat loathe to admit it. It is necessary to define the nature
of the problem solving tasks which characterise category C materials. At one
level these are programming tasks. It is common at the moment for these to be
limited due to the limitation of the software tools available to the pupil (as
discussed elsewhere, (Lewis, 1984)). For the future, one may expect to
involve pupils in tasks such as data base design for particular purposes and
to the creation of modest learning systems which fringe on robotics and other
intelligent knowledge based systems. Evaluation is fairly scarce in this area
though it is perhaps the oldest use of computers in education, for example the
work of Dwyer concerning elementary programming (Dwyer, 1971). More recently
evaluation has been undertaken in Cambridge (Johnson and Harding, 1979) and by
Hartley (1984) in the field of model building.

The discussion will now concentrate on Category B materials. The final
judgement of their value will be considered in relation to criteria adopted
during the development process and by serving teachers. Much of this is based
on experiences gained with the Computers in the Curriculum Project at Chelsea
College, London and during in-service training courses in the North West of
England.

DEVELOPMENT CRITERIA

During the development process, criteria are set at each stage. These will be
considered under the headings:

- pedagogic design;
- academic validation;
- technical evaluation;
- classroom trials;
- production, quality control.

As mentioned earlier, the materials being considered are designed to provide
the opportunity for pupils to undertake investigations of various topics. The
way in which pupils are introduced to the study may vary from being quite
open-ended to being rather carefully structured. It is clearly possible to

set pupils the task of simply exploring the behaviour and relationships which are present in the topic under study. On the other hand, many pupils would be aided in their work if they were provided with a framework for their investigation. One way of providing such a framework is to select a series of leading questions or problems. These may be organised as a set of worksheets and may well include activities which do not involve the use of a program. A particular advantage of this design strategy is that individual teachers can change or supplement the worksheets prepared by the authors. This will most certainly lead to a greater level of acceptability, as teachers can orient the work to suit their own teaching style and their own pupils. Clearly, the software design must be such as to provide pupils with the options of easily obtaining outcomes which enable them to solve the problems which have been devised. Again, flexibility is the key to acceptability.

The software associated with this style of material often, but not always, depends upon a model or data set which represents the system being explored. It cannot be stressed too strongly that the validation of this representation is the sole responsibility of the author(s). Whilst other aspects of the material can be evaluated by teacher-users, this is far from true of the sometimes complex models embedded in the software. Recently, a Mathematical Association Working Party strongly criticised the mathematical content of materials produced for primary schools under the auspices of the UK Government's Microelectronics Education Programme. Our primary teachers are working in a demanding area when introducing basic concepts – they could well do without this kind of support from microcomputer materials! The best possible authorities need to be consulted about the models used and when simplifications or assumptions are made, these must be stated explicitly. It is essential that teachers are aware of the basis of the software and appropriate aspects of this must be made known to the pupils as well. The research and consultation required at this stage is difficult and time-consuming: however, short-cuts must be resisted. This may be difficult for a development group as funding agencies or commercial considerations exert pressure for high levels of productivity. Quality must take precedence over quantity.

The same considerations, equally time consuming, are needed with respect to technical evaluation. Software needs to be robust, yet flexible and easy to use. In recent years, as many teachers have become more experienced in applying micro-computers in their classrooms, the demands of the profession have become more exacting. Computer software should be no longer seen as finalised by the author but as a resource which can be tuned to individual needs. Teachers' increased skills include the ability to make changes so long as the original design of the software presents a well organised and documented product. It is not necessary to go into detail about the adequacy of the student-machine interface, or about robustness. These aspects of software should be assumed to have been handled expertly.

The formative evaluation stage, mostly accomplished through classroom trials, is highly significant. It must cover the three aspects already discussed, namely, educational, academic and technical validity. Whilst the author, or those devoted to using computers in their classrooms, may find materials easy to use and successful, other teachers may not find this so. As has been mentioned already, the nature of the teacher-class and pupil relationship will influence the style of material which a teacher finds valuable. From this point of view, it is likely that material written by a group of teachers will be less idiosyncratic, and hence more widely acceptable, than material with only one author. The Project at Chelsea found that the following check-list of questions provided a good basis for obtaining feedback from trials teachers.

"   Students' Printed Material

    S1 Do the questions provide an adequate framework for students'
       activities not involving the program?
    S2 Do the questions provide an adequate framework for students' use
       of the program?
    S3 Is the pre-requisite knowledge of the questions adequately
       covered:
       -   in the printed material itself
       -   by being deducible from the program
       -   otherwise?
    S4 Is the language used appropriate to the age/ability of target
       students?
    S5 Are the illustrations adequate?
    S6 Could the layout be improved?
    S7 Are there particular points of difficulty/confusion?

Teachers' Material - Does this adequately provide:

    T1   a statement of objectives?
    T2   a statement of the level and pre-requisite knowledge?
    T3   a statement of the rationale for the unit, its scope and limitations?
    T4   suggestions re use of material in class, classroom organsation, etc.
    T5   warnings of places likely to give student difficulty?
    T6   warnings about program limitations?
    T7   a statement of the computer model and assumptions made?
    T8   references to other sources, etc?
    T9   hints or comments on questions in the student material?
    T10   suggestions for extensions or increased flexibility?

Program

    P1   What, if any, failures occurred?
    P2   Are there unhelpful/misleading messages?
    P3   Does the program have a structure which makes it easy/convenient to use?
    P4   Are students puzzled by the display or uncertain what is expected of
         them?
    P5   Could the display of information be improved?
    P6   Is essential information lost from the display at any time?
    P7   Do changes in the display happen too quickly or too slowly?
    P8   Was the program used by students or as a class demonstration?

General

 Your free ranging comments on the value of the unit would be valuable.
 Why would you use it again (or not)? Also, it would be valuable to know
 of any data you may have on students' performance linked to their use of
 the material. Anecdotal evidence e.g. students' comments, your own
 observations, are always valuable.   "

Having taken the trouble to ensure that the various stages in development have
been covered thoroughly, it would be unwise to neglect the final, but crucial,
stage of production and quality control of the product. As publishers become
more experienced in handling computer based materials, this task becomes one
of decreasing significance for the developer. However, it was not so many
years ago that non-printed elements had to be supported by development teams
and even now software support/aftercare may still be a responsibility that
should be retained by authors. The problems of quality control are
fortunately being eased as the education market orients itself away from
audio-cassettes!

INFORMATION PROVIDERS

A number of agencies have the task of providing information about computer related materials. These include publishers, distributors, teachers centres, teacher trainers, journals and magazines. At the present time in Britain, it is often difficult or impossible for teachers to obtain inspection copies of material. In this climate the role of the dissemination agencies is crucial and yet the task is a very difficult one. The question to be addressed is:

What information do teachers need in order to be able to make judgements on the value of the material <u>to them</u>?

It is this last phrase which is critical and requires expansion.

It is usual for reviews or evaluation reports to make judgements. More often than not these judgements are based on one individual's view of the material and its perceived value in the classroom. As has been indicated earlier, these perceptions, however well founded, can only be valid in the context of the author's own classroom relationship. Another teacher with another class may find that these judgements are of little value. One arrives at this conclusion if one believes that the value of a classroom resource is first and foremost a function of the teacher-class relationship. However good the design, however sound the structure, a piece of material will only be of value if it suits, supports or promotes human communication in the classroom. This view is equally applicable to materials un-associated with computers.

Naturally, various strategies have been adopted by information providers in the attempts to fulfil their task. A selection should be mentioned.

-     OECD/CERI Project on Computer Sciences in Secondary Education during the mid-1970's. A framework for describing material was devised and comprised the following sections:

  1. <u>Title</u>:
      <u>Source</u>:
      <u>Materials</u>:
      <u>Date of this outline</u>;

  2. <u>Subject and Specific Topic</u>

  3. <u>Educational Aims</u>

  4. <u>Advantages of the use of this material</u>

  5. <u>Pre-requisites on the part of the student</u>

  6. <u>Student involvement</u>

  7. <u>Time of involvement</u>

  8. <u>Computing facilities</u>

  9. <u>Stage of development</u>

  10. <u>Further information</u>

-     CONDUIT (University of Iowa) have review panels in a range of disciplines to whom materials are submitted to be evaluated before acceptance by CONDUIT in their library of materials for distribution and support. A thorough educational review is followed by a stringent technical assessment, the latter quite understandable as the organisation undertakes to maintain the software they distribute. Although somewhat dated, their Authors Guide (CONDUIT, 1978) remains a valuable document today.

-    MUSE (Micro-computer Users in Secondary Education, based in the UK) undertakes the distribution of programs (and sometimes documents) to its members. Its 1982 "Program Assessment Sheet" relates mostly to the software. Of its 50 or so questions, typically graded on a "good/fair/poor" scale, about 40 are concerned with program control, structure and robustness.

-    MicroSIFT (Northwest Regional Laboratory, Oregon) has an ambitious evaluation procedure which covers educational and software content but also considers social appropriateness in terms of ethnic and sex bias.

It is worth noting that the reviews being discussed are not formal evaluation studies such as might be undertaken by an evaluation project. † Often, and this is their strength, they are undertaken by serving teachers. However, this does place constraints on what can be expected. Practising teachers do not have the time, nor the legitimacy, to subject their pupils to special experiments for this purpose. It is not unusual to find shorthand ways of obtaining information.

Perhaps the most appropriate approach to the problem of providing information is to ask the question: What would teachers like to know about a piece of CAL material? This is a question which I have posed to a number of groups of teachers in recent years in two contexts. The first was in relation to a single page summary for inclusion in a file containing a unit of material. Its purpose was to speed up the task of teachers in reviewing the material themselves. The file contains a number of such summary pages and each teacher using the unit is asked to contribute a personal review. The page is kept simple in the hope of encouraging as many contributions as possible. The items on the pro-forma are:

        0.   Title, target pupil, intention
        1.   Initial information
        2.   Teacher support material
        3.   Pupil material
        4.   How the material was used
        5.   Was the intention achieved?
        6.   Pupil motivation
        7.   Problems in use/foreseen
        8.   Would you use it again?
        9.   General comments

The second review framework has arisen from the inclusion of reviews of materials in a new journal †† in the field. An attempt is being made to produce rather more formal reviews than those usually found in magazines and journals without an excessive burden of evaluation being placed on the teacher-reviewers. Another important aspect of this review process is to respond rapidly to newly published materials and yet include the experience of classroom use, not in contrived situations but in the normal pattern in which various topics are taught.

† For a view of strategies for this work reference may be made to Kemmis
    et al (1977) and Strachen (1983).

†† The Journal of Computer Assisted Learning to be published by Blackwell
    Scientific Publications of Oxford.

Such aims are impossible to achieve. The closest approach so far formulated has been to tackle the review in two stages. Based on a reviewer's judgement of the publisher's information and the material itself, a teacher will undertake a short-term preview, where possible involving a few pupils. The preview will be largely factual but will cover issues which are essential to others in their consideration of the materials' possible value.

" PREVIEW

1. Technical block to include statement based on publisher's information and the physical material itself.
   a) title;   b) subject/topic;   c) age range;
   d) publisher/date;   e) originator;   f) extent;
   g) price;   h) copyright status;   g) hardware needs

2. Educational content/mode, stated aims/intentions and pre-requisites (cf. author/publishers statements on range etc.)

3. Ease of use/flexibility   – how easy to get initial flavour
                                        – open/closed style
                                        – ability to select parts of package
                                        – repeated use by pupils

4. Preparation time   – to become fully familiar with the package
                                  – to create (additional) pupil/other material

5. Printed material   – structure, clarity, validity, possible extension
                               – help to teacher in obtaining flavour

6. Software   – amount of text, reading level
                     – screen images
                     – consistency
                     – use of codes/symbols
                     – hardware requirements

7. Other equipment/materials needed

Part of the formative evaluation check-list referred to earlier may act as a guide to items 5 and 6.

For material which comes through the preview process with credit, a second longer process based on classroom experience of the material's use will result in a detailed review. Again a defined framework will be used in order to provide a style which will become familiar to readers and which it is intended will improve the level of communication between reviewer and potential user. The items to be covered in the review are:

" REVIEW

1. Personal experience of classroom context – mode of use.

2. Pupil reaction/interaction – motivation.

3. Pupil time – in preparation;   at the machine;   in follow up.

4. Problems in use.

5. What cognitive experience does the reviewer believe pupils underwent?   "

As reviewer's circumstances, type of school,etc., are bound to flavour both preview and review, a short one-line profile of each reviewer will be contained in the journal. In this way it is hoped that an interpretation of the reviews will be possible for teachers in quite different types of school, something missing from current practice.

CONCLUSIONS

No paper on the value of educational materials for use with micro-computers can be complete without reference to the learners. However, the observations I wish to make on this are rather brief and, as they form key conclusions to the preceding discussion, they are included here.

The emphasis in the paper has been on materials which form resources for learning. The aims of teachers in using such materials may be behavioural, cognitive, or some mixture of the two. Summative evaluation will be rarely appropriate and it is my view that teachers themselves are the only judges of the value of various resources for their pupils. During my time as a teacher of laboratory based science to pupils, I was left in little doubt about the value of the experiments and investigations which my pupils undertook. Some failed to 'work' for the majority of the class, others failed for a portion of the class, others promoted interest, discussion and enquiry. With experience of teaching those pupils, it did not require a formal evaluation study to indicate to me which investigations were valuable for the pupils. One major demand was in preparation time, time to explore the material for myself and be at least reasonably equipped to anticipate difficulties which pupils might encounter. Time is in short supply for most teachers and a priority for developers, disseminators and trainers must be to assist teachers in formulating strategies by which they can make judgements on the value of material in a rapid and reliable way. I am coming to the conclusion that there is no such thing as good or bad material, rather there is material which is of value to a teacher with a certain class and material which has little or no value in that situation. Only one person can make that decision.

REFERENCES

Lewis, R., (1984)   Programming for Teachers (in proceedings of IFIP Working Conference - Teaching Programming) North Holland, Amsterdam

Johnson, D.C. and Harding, R.D., (1979)   University level computing and mathematical problem solving ability. Journal for Research in Mathematics Education $\underline{10}$, 1

Hartley, R.J., (1984) Evaluation of a CAL package for modelling Computer Education $\underline{8}$, 1

Dwyer, T., (1971) Some Principles for the Human Use of Computers in Education,   International Journal of Man-Machine Studies $\underline{3}$,3

Strachen, R.M. (editor), (1983)   Guide to Evaluating Method National Extension College: Cambridge

Kemmis, S., Atkin, R., and Wright, E (1977). How do Students' Learn? Occasional Publication No.5,   Centre for Applied Research in Education, University of East Anglia: Norwich.

CONDUIT (1978) Author's Guide (eds. Peters, J.H. and Johnson, J.W.) University of Iowa.

INFORMATICS AND TEACHER TRAINING
F.B. Lovis and E.D. Tagg (editors)
Elsevier Science Publishers B.V. (North-Holland)
© IFIP, 1984

THE PROFESSIONAL DEVELOPMENT OF TEACHERS

IN COMPUTER EDUCATION WITHIN AUSTRALIA

Judith H. Hammond,
NSW Institute of Technology,
Sydney,   Australia

Kevan Penter,
Education Department,
Perth, Western Australia

The development of computer education in Australia has occurred at different times and in different ways in each State and Territory. As a consequence, there is a variation in the methods and styles of professional development for teachers. In 1983, the Australian government initiated a Federal program to provide an Australia-wide focus on computer education. This paper describes some of the initiatives that are currently being undertaken in two States and which fit the proposals of the Federal government plan for the professional development of teachers.

1. THE AUSTRALIAN SCENE

Australia is a vast country divided into six States and two Territories. Its total land mass covers 7.6 million square kilometres, yet the population is less than 15 million. The largest State is Western Australia covering the western third of the continent with a population of a mere 1.4 million, whilst the smallest State is that of Tasmania (an island off the south east coast of the mainland). The most populous State is New South Wales with approximately 5.4 million people, of whom over 3.3 million live in the city of Sydney. The Territories are the Australian Capital Territory, which includes the national capital city of Canberra, and the Northern Territory, a sparsely populated tropical area in the central north of Australia.

Australia has two extremes in population distribution; on the one hand, large urban populations concentrated mainly in the capitals of each State and Territory and, on the other hand, a mostly rural population scattered over the more hospitable parts of Australia, generally around the coastal fringe. The centre of Australia is largely arid semi-desert, and is virtually unpopulated, except for one town (Alice Springs), isolated farms and a handful of mining communities.

Any national program for training teachers must account for the two extremes - most people being large town and city dwellers and a small but significant minority living in scattered rural communities and isolated areas. This dichotomy must be taken into account even within States and particularly so in the larger States of New South Wales and Western Australia.

2. <u>STATE INITIATIVES IN PROFESSIONAL DEVELOPMENT</u>

This paper describes initiatives taken in the States of Western Australia and New South Wales. The former is one of the earliest states to develop a computer education program, and now prefers to give it the title of informatics education. Although some enthusiastic teachers in New South Wales have been using computers in schools for a number of years, it was not until 1983 that computer education was coordinated officially at a State level.

2.1   <u>WESTERN AUSTRALIA</u>

The population of Western Australia is mainly located in the Perth urban area. Vast areas of the desert interior are unsettled. This pattern has resulted in education having a strong central focus with little devolution of authority. The Education Department of Western Australia administers government-funded education throughout the State. The central model has offered significant advantages in implementing computer education throughout the State system.

An export-oriented economy and proximity to the highly competitive Asian countries, have led successive Western Australian governments to place emphasis on the adoption of advanced technology, thus maintaining international competitiveness. A recent example of the State's emphasis on advanced technology was the successful challenge for the America Cup yachting trophy. The need to adapt successfully to information technology has been reflected in the education system. Since 1977, a major training effort has been underway to provide the teaching force with the skills necessary to utilize information technology.

2.1.1   <u>Who Will Train The Trainers?</u>

Australia, in common with many other countries, has faced a period of restraint in public expenditures. This pressure has weighed heavily on the education system. At the same time, the need to rapidly expand teacher training in the area of information technology has occurred and has taken system authorities by surprise. A way of achieving maximum impact with the limited resources available was required.

The decision was made to adopt a central model for teacher train-ing and set up a State Centre to nurture the "critical mass" of expertise considered necessary. Today this central body coordinates the development of educational computing throughout Western Australia. It has developed as a centre of excellence and has functioned as a "clearing-house" for new ideas. A well-equipped Microcomputer In-service Centre has been set up, catering for large groups of teachers undertaking courses that emphasise practical experience of a "hands-on" nature. This "critical mass" of skilled personnel, some of whom are appointed permanently while others are seconded on a rotational basis, has partially overcome the problem of "training the trainers".

Experience has shown that it is also essential to regularly upgrade the skills of those providing the training. Western Australia has benefited in this way by drawing on the skills of international experts. For example, in 1983 Professor J. Hebenstreit, Chairman of IFIP TC3, was invited to Perth to conduct a series of seminars for key personnel. These seminars proved to be particularly successful in raising overall standards, and in forcing a re-appraisal of entrenched attitudes.

2.1.2   Teacher Training Strategies in Western Australia

In developing strategies for teacher training, the model adopted has been largely based on centrally organised, "face-to-face" courses. Consideration has been given to using various aspects of information technology (particularly television and micro-computer software) to deliver teacher training on a distance education model. A television programme is currently being produced for screening late in 1984, as an introduction for teachers and the community to information technology and its place in education.

As in other Australia states, the most urgent need is to provide training for those already in the teaching service. Over recent years, only a small number of new graduates enter the teaching profession as the rate of growth of the school-age population has slowed down. Most teachers have graduated and achieved professional success without being familiar with information technology. Many confess to bewilderment, even anxiety, in the face of rapid developments in information technology and the pressures applied to place computers in schools.

Courses have been developed to provide teachers, system administrators and educational leaders with an initial introduction to information technology. The structure of teacher training programs permits an individual to commence with a short, introductory experience and then progress through a graduated series of courses as additional competence is acquired. Ultimately, the structure can lead to post-graduate and other degree courses in informatics education.

It has become clear that little can be achieved by classroom teachers, however well they are trained, without the support of the community and those in leadership positions in schools. Thus training courses have been developed to introduce informatics to school principals and to teachers in various specialist roles. Another innovation has been the development of courses for people occupying positions of educational leadership in parent and community organisations.

2.1.3   The Need For Evaluation

The pressures of coping with the ever-expanding demands for informatics teacher training tend to push into the background concerns about the evaluation of the program. As a consequence, an urgent need is now seen for an independent, _formative_ evaluation of the teacher training strategies. Usually, participants are asked to evaluate the success of the course they have just completed. However such evaluations tend to be distorted by the "halo effect" that immediately follows participation in a stimulating experience.

A form of evaluation is required that investigates, over an extended period, teacher behaviour following participation in a training course. Such evaluation should consider, amongst other things, the effectiveness with which classroom objectives are being achieved on a regular basis. For those responsible for the administration of the training, it is all too easy to measure success on the basis of the number of courses conducted, or the number of teachers involved, or even on the basis of the mastery of content objectives by teachers. What really matters is the quality and quantity of learning by students, and teacher training must be a means to that end.

2.2   NEW SOUTH WALES

New South Wales was the first State to be settled in Australia and is approaching its bicentenary in 1988. It has built up a long tradition of centralised government. Whilst Western Australia occupies a third of the land mass of Australia, New South Wales contains a third of the entire population of the country. It is ranked within the top ten cities in the world and is the business and financial centre of Australia. The remainder of the population lives in two industrially-based cities and rural towns and communities with locations ranging from lush pastures and farmlands to desert.

Although the education department has traditionally been strongly centralised, it has recently changed direction and has embraced a regional model. Today, there is a significant movement towards decentralisation. The State government education system is divided into ten regions, with the central administration being based in Sydney. The emphasis is now devolving towards school-based curricula. There are also a large number of non-government schools, including many catholic and other denominational schools providing a diversity of educational styles.

2.2.1.   Coordinating Computer Education

New South Wales is one of the most recent States to coordinate computer education programs into a State-wide program, although computer courses of various kinds have been taught in NSW schools for about ten years. In October, 1982 the State Minister of Education issued a general guideline statement on computers and

computing in education(1).   Then followed a general policy
document, defining the NSW Department of Education's policy in
relation to computer education and set out the department's
priorities. They are focussed in the short term mainly on the
allocation of limited resources.   The priorities are:

> "* Learning about computers will have a greater emphasis than
>   the use of computers as teaching-learning aids.
> * The use of computers as teaching-learning aids will have
>   greater emphasis than their use for administrative
>   purposes and resource management.
> * Activities designed to promote computer awareness for all
>   students will have greater emphasis than more specialised
>   elective courses.
> * Activities designed to increase computer awareness in
>   secondary years 7-9 (ages 12 to 14) currently will have
>   greater emphasis than computer education in either the
>   primary or senior secondary years."

These priorities should be kept in mind when looking at
the planning for, and the types of courses being undertaken, in
the professional development of teachers in NSW. It is intended
that a fully developed Computer Awareness and Computer Studies
syllabus will be available for optional implementation in schools
for 1985 and that all schools will be providing these courses by
1987.   Thus the need for a large number of teachers to become
competent to take these courses assumes top priority.

At the beginning of 1983, the NSW Department of Education set up
a Computer Education Unit (CEU) consisting of an officer-in-
charge, a seconded computer science academic with long experience
in computer education, four seconded teachers and two clerical
staff. The role of the Unit is to act as the State's focal point
for all aspects of computer education within the State school
system.   Amongst its numerous responsibilities, the professional
development of teachers is a high priority.

2.2.2   The Development Of A Professional Development Program

The implementation of the programs planned during the first year
of operation of the CEU commenced in 1984.   Emphasis is being
placed on the continuing education of teachers, as the proposed
computer education curriculum will be taught largely by teachers
already appointed to schools. As in Western Australia, it is
recognised that all pre-service teachers need courses in their
initial training, but the initial emphasis of the CEU
professional development programs in the immediate future is in
the area of in-service training.

The CEU sees its role as an initiator of professional development
programs and as a supporter and coordinator of activities already
being undertaken at both the regional and local school level.
Because computer education is a new area in the curriculum, there
is for the most part a lack of understanding by teachers of
computer and computing and of the NSW Department's aims and

objectives. In-service courses currently being offered in the
State program give guidance to teachers about the content
required in their training sessions and about the aims and
objectives and methods of assessment needed for courses conducted
at the regional and local school level.

The main constraints operating in the development of desired
training courses are:

      *   the large number of teachers with either no previous
         experience, or with minimal knowledge of computing;
      *   the scarcity of trainers with an extensive knowledge of
         computing;
      *   the short period of time available in which to train the
         teachers;
      *   limited funds for training purposes.

The CEU has approached the task of planning the in-service
professional development of teachers in the following way:

1. Identification of needs.
    This resulted in a wide variety of topics being identified,
    ranging from developing a school computer education policy to
    elementary computer operation and the use of databases.

2.   Establishing the target groups for training.
    These included:
        teachers, trainers and regional computer consultants;
        principals - a most important group as their attitude
        toward computer education affects all decisions made in
        the school environment;
        parents - who are interested and involved in school
        activities and often the provider of funds for new
        hardware and software.

3.   Setting priorities.
    Taking account of the above needs, the following priorities
    have been established:

  (a) Writing workshops where the aim is the development of
      courseware and curriculum modules/materials.
      (It should be noted that a highly successful residential
      workshop for 30 participants from all the NSW regions was
      conducted early in 1984 to develop a number of modules on
      topics defined in the identification of needs).

  (b) Field-testing courses using funds available from state in-
      service sources. These are to be based on the workshop
      modules in the areas of:
        The role of the school's computing coordinator;
        Introducing teachers to computers in education;
        Computer education policy for school principals

  (c) Conducting courses, based on workshop modules, requiring
      significant amounts of hardware and therefore

particularly suited to being conducted by the CEU staff.
Typical courses would cover the areas of:
    Educational Software - specification, design,
    development and evaluation
    Local Area Networking and data communications.

2.2.3   Evaluation Of Modules

The development and field-testing of modules is now in progress.
Evaluation of these courses may lead to modification or
introduction of further modules. It is anticipated that the
final modules will be available for regional centres and schools
to conduct their own courses during 1985. The modules are
sufficiently flexible in format that an individual course can be
structured to suit the particular requirements of the group of
trainees.

It should be noted that other professional development programs
are also available. This paper is concerned only with the
Computer Education Unit's coordinated approach, designed to
minimise the "reinventing the wheel" syndrome in the production
of in-service courses.

2.3   PROBLEMS OF TEACHER TRAINING IN COMPUTER EDUCATION

Problems facing those responsible for teacher training in
computer education are no doubt similar in many parts of the
world. The Australian experience has been that major
difficulties arise (but are not confined to) the following areas:

(a)   Rapid Rate of Change

The area of computers and informatics has for the past forty
years been subject to an escalating rate of change. This
applies not only to information technology itself, but
equally to the range and types of hardware, software and
teaching materials utilised in schools. In order to keep up
with these developments, teachers need regular and reliable
access to information about new developments, and the
knowledge and skill to evaluate them in relation to their own
educational strategies. It has been estimated that
teachers should undergo retraining every three to five years
if they are to remain effective. Therefore, opportunities
for regular participation in in-service courses are
essential. The problem of frequent retraining has not yet
been resolved, as resources are currently stretched to the
limit providing for those with no knowledge in the area.

(b)   New Discipline without Established Traditions

It is often noted that the strongest influence on teachers'
pedagogical techniques is the way in which they were
themselves taught in school. This cannot apply in
informatics and computing as the area is a recent arrival in

the curriculum and does not have any tradition. Moreover,
unlike other technological subjects such as chemistry,
physics or mathematics, there is no established base of well-
founded curriculum theory or teaching techniques. Therefore,
it is even more important for computing and informatics
teachers to be equipped with the skills neceesary to create
their own techniques.

(c) Community Pressures and Expectations

In Australia, community awareness of information technology
is growing rapidly. This is leading to a consensus that
computer education must start in primary (elementary) schools
and be strongly supported at all levels thereafter.
Community pressures are reflected in a high demand for places
in computing courses. Finding the necessary trained staff to
support the provision of additional student places is a major
problem. Training of these teachers to an appropriate
standard is a process requiring time. It is well-known that
many students are more knowledgeable about computers than
their teachers. The future public perception of and
confidence in educational institutions is likely to be
significantly influenced by the degree to which these
institutions are seen to be responding successfully to the
challenges of the new technology.

3. THE COMMONWEALTH COMPUTER EDUCATION PROGRAM

The first initiatives toward computer education on a coordinated
national basis occurred at the beginning of 1983, when the
Commonwealth Schools Commission recommended that a program of
computer education should be developed for 1984. It perceived
that computer education in schools was of fundamental importance
to Australia's future. It looked closely at the resources
available to both the State and the non-government school
authorities to undertake a large scale program and came to the
conclusion that Commonwealth initiatives and funding support were
essential.

3.1 THE NATIONAL ADVISORY COMMITTEE

In March 1983, a National Advisory Committee on Computers in
Schools was established. The terms of reference given to the
Committee was to provide an initial report to the Commonwealth
Schools Commission by the end of September, 1983. This report
would provide advice on:

"*   The use of computers in schools as they relate to the
      educational needs of boys and girls enrolled in primary,
      secondary and special schools;
 *   The rationale for a national program, including desirable
      short and long term educational, social and economic
      outcomes;
 *   An implementation plan, and associated guidelines, for the

introduction of a national Schools Computing Program into primary, secondary and special schools, including its integration with State and non-government schools policies and provisions. This plan will include options for the allocations of funds among States and sectors, advice on desirable minimum standards of provision, and on ways of achieving an equitable sharing of resources and services across Australia;

* A plan for generating and supporting discussion and awareness within the community and especially within the school communities of school computing and its applications;

* Evaluation activities relating to computing in schools and to the provision and operation of the proposed national program" (2).

This Committee immediately established working parties to provide it with specialist advice in the areas of –

1. Professional Development
2. Curriculum Development
3. Software/ Courseware
4. Hardware
5. Evaluation
6. Support Services.

The recommendations which emerged from the working party reports totalled fifty-two and were accepted and endorsed by the Commonwealth Schools Commission and the Australian Government with only a few dissensions, notably in relation to recommendations about the choice of hardware.

3.2 RECOMMENDATIONS CONCERNING PROFESSIONAL DEVELOPMENT

In this paper, only recommendations relating to professional development will be discussed.

The view was taken that if the National Computer Education Program was to achieve its objectives, it would be essential that teachers be provided with the time needed to understand computer technology and be able to work through the issues related to integrating the technology into the total curriculum. Hence, professional development has been given the highest priority in the allocation of funds for 1984.

Recommendations for professional development include the following:

"* Particular attention should be paid to the full participation of women teachers, non-mathematics and -science teachers and disadvantaged groups amongst teachers;

* Men and women in professional development activities should reflect their proportion in the teaching service on a State-by-State basis;

* the use of and further development of existing structures for delivering professional development;

*   the implementation of professional development chosen
     from a selection of alternatives, such as long and short
     courses, mobile consultancy teams, school networks, action
     research, audio-visual tutorials, television courses in and
     out of school time and regional, state and national
     conferences;
*   that the central role of the school Principal be recognised
     and reinforced;
*   Tertiary institutions providing pre-service education of
     teachers should include in the courses of all students,
     studies of the application of computers to education.
*   Efforts should be made to identify, to make known and to
     support persons who are able and are prepared to provide
     leadership in schools computing.
*   Teacher associations in all subject areas should be
     encouraged to allocate a segment of their conference
     programmes to the applications of computers in their
     subject area."(3)

3.3   IMPACT OF THE NATIONAL COMPUTER EDUCATION PROGRAM

The National Computer Education Program is just beginning. The
funding for the whole of Australia for the next three years is
$18 million (Australian) or 12 million pounds sterling with the
funds for 1984 being set at $6.2 million (Australian). Many
teachers and pressure groups feel that this amount is not
sufficient to support the work to be done, but the total amount
of funds available is finite. Much planning is being undertaken
to establish the structures and principles and lay the foundation
for the next three years' work at both the State and the Commonwealth level.

The Program has already had a favourable effect on teacher
training in Western Australia and New South Wales. Resources
available from this Program are enabling an expansion of
provisions for teacher training. It has confirmed certain
directions already being followed (for example, the need for
computer literacy for all teachers), and has set new directions
in other areas (for example, the need for increased parent
participation).

It is too soon to measure any concrete results from the Commonwealth Schools Commission's Program. However, one effect is
already apparent. The announcement of the Commonwealth Government's intention to provide funds for computer education has
given rise to much needed discussion and debate in educational
circles about desirable goals and funding priorities. The status
of computer education has been lifted by the announcement of a
national program. Planning for the national program has brought
together for the first time, some of Australia's most able
specialists in computer education. In a country where there are
long distances between major population centres, this has been in
itself a most valuable outcome.

REFERENCES

(1) Hon. R.J. Mulock, N.S.W. Minister of Education, "General Guideline Statement on Computers and Computing in Education", Sydney, 1982.

(2) "Teaching, Learning and Computers", a Report of the National Advisory Committee on Computers in Schools, The Commonwealth Schools Commission, 1983, p. 3

(3) ditto, p. 35

INFORMATICS AND TEACHER TRAINING
F.B. Lovis and E.D. Tagg (editors)
Elsevier Science Publishers B.V. (North-Holland)
© IFIP, 1984

TRAINING EDUCATORS TO USE COMPUTERS IN INSTRUCTION:
THE MECC METHOD

Don Rawitsch and Richard A Pollak,
Minnesota Educational Computing Corporation
St Paul, Minnesota, USA

The Minnesota Educational Computing Corporation (MECC) has been training educators in instructional computing for over a decade. Since 1974, thousands of Minnesota educators have learned to use computers through MECC's efforts, beginning with a focus on timeshare computing and then shifting to the use of microcomputers. MECC's work in this area is unique in the United States in that it is the only example of a statewide training effort in instructional computing supported by state government funding.

This paper will briefly describe MECC's approach to training and the types of training that have been offered.

PHILOSOPHY

MECC's training programs are based on a philosophical notion of how educators can best be taught to use computers. The following are the basic tenets of this philosophy.

(1) Start with what educators know.

Training should lead educators into the use of computers by building on the knowledge with which educators are already comfortable. The computer is a new tool for most educators, but it does represent a teaching medium and educators are familiar with a variety of other media already. Although computing brings with it a host of new jargon, much of computer use can be explained using more familiar language. Computing is a type of activity which educators will often be fitting into curriculum and teaching plans that already exist. This, then, is the place to start, not with totally new technological topics such as computer design, terminology, or programming.

(2) Relate technology to instruction.

The key work in "instructional computing" is "instruction". Training programs should, therefore, include as much information about instruction as about computing's technical side. Topics such as operation of the computer, caring for the computer, and how computers work should be balanced by topics such as computing's place in the curriculum, designing lesson plans for computing activities, and evaluating software applications.

(3) Keep the forest in sight through the trees.

Because computing is new, trainers have much new information to impart. However, faced with an inundation of material, participants might drown in the detail. Training sessions must focus on main points and give participants essential information. Additional detail can be added as they see usefulness of it.

(4)   Computer training means using computers.

Training sessions in computer use must include adequate time for participants
actually to use computers. This hands-on work should put no more than two
people on the same machine so that they get enough chance to do the assigned
tasks. Hands-on activities should be preceded by good instructions and
followed by debriefing led by the trainer.

(5)   Trainers must be teachers.

Instructional computing trainers must understand the environment of their
participants and must serve as models of how to teach effectively. Computer
experts who do not know how to lead groups will not do. Educators who know
computers and are good teachers usually make the best trainers.

TRAINING TOPICS

Training in instructional computing can cover a wide variety of topics.
Following is a list of topics that have formed the basis of MECC training.

(1)   Creating Computing Plans For a School or School District

(2)   Computing's Fit Into The Curriculum

(3)   Locating Sources of Equipment, Materials, and Support Services

(4)   Operation and Care of Equipment and Media

(5)   Operation of Specific Software Applications

(6)   Using Computer Languages For Problem Solving

(7)   Evaluation Equipment, Materials, and Support Services

(8)   Integrating Computing Into Learning Activities

(9)   Computer Programming As a Discipline

(10)   Operation of Computer Utility Software For Personal Use

(11)   Designing Computer Materials

Not all educators need training in all of these areas. Those with planning
responsibilities most need topics (1)-(3). For general classroom use, teachers
need topics (4)-(8). Topics (9)-(11) serve people with more specialized needs.

TYPES OF ACTIVITIES

MECC has chosen to name its training staff "User Service" because assisting
educators in learning to use the equipment and software they obtain requires
a variety of activity beyond presenting formal training sessions. Following is
a list of activities MECC User Services has carried out with and for educators
in support of instructional computing.

(1) Visitations.

Educators feel most comfortable when they can learn about something new in their
own familiar environment. Periodic visits to sites being served allow the
services person to become familiar with the computing environment first hand, to
answer user questions face to face, and most importantly to build trust within
the users. Travel is inherent in user services work.

(2) Informational presentations.

The world of computing changes rapidly and users are always eager to keep up
with it. Beginning users especially have a need to be brought up-to-date with
information about what services are available and how they can be obtained.
Informational presentations to groups of teachers, parents, school administrators,
school boards, and professional groups are a significant part of user services.

(3) Training workshops and classes.

Beyond receiving background information, educators want to acquire specific
knowledge and skills that will help them better utilize the computer in their
work. An important part of user services work is teaching, either through
single session workshops or formalized classes. This type of activity also
requires that formalized training materials be developed.

(4) Meetings for local computing coordinators.

Each site receiving services probably has a key person assigned to coordinate
instructional computing activity there. User services staff not only provide
help to these people, but also expect their advice and cooperative effort in
return. Special meetings should be held periodically with these key facili-
tators so that they have input to larger scale planning efforts.

(5) Newsletters.

Some kinds of information is best distributed in writing. User services staff
will need to publish newsletters of some kind.

(6) Publishing training materials.

Because trainers cannot hope to work with all educators in their local area,
they must depend on local training efforts to take place. It is easiest for
others to do training if the "experts" have already designed a training plan
and set of materials.

AMOUNT OF MECC ACTIVITY

Since the 1974-75 school year, the MECC User Services staff of 7-10 trainers
has carried out hundreds of training activities. The graph below shows
information on the quantity of site visits (plus percentage of the 430 Minnesota
school districts visited), informational presentations, workshops (1-4 hours in
length), and classes (8-16 hours in length). Though the number of classes is
lower than counts in other areas, the reader should keep in mind that each class
is the equivalent of two to five of the other activities. Notice that MECC's
emphasis has shifted in recent years from activities of shorter duration to the
more in-depth training offered through classes.

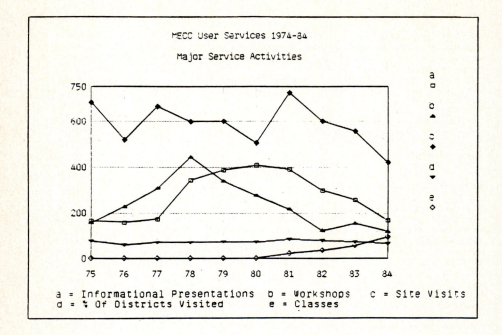

MECC User Services 1974-84

Major Service Activities

a = Informational Presentations   b = Workshops   c = Site Visits
d = % Of Districts Visited   e = Classes

CHARACTERISTICS OF TRAINERS

Effective trainers for instructional computing need a wide variety of skills
and personal attributes. Certainly they should possess characteristics typically
associated with "good" employees": hard working, helpful, pleasant, and so on.
Characteristics needed specifically for this type of training are listed below.

Skills

(1) Teaching Skills.

The amount of time spent making presentations and teaching workshops and classes
demands that the person be expert in organizing, sequencing, and presenting
material in a way that helps people understand and remember it.

(2) Programming skills.

A user services staff person need not be a professional programmer but will need
skills in this area for helping users with programming problems and teaching
sessions on how to program computers.

(3) Curriculum design skills.

The creation of training materials requires a knowledge of how to design and
sequence learning activities, often in written form, so that teachers find them
valuable for classroom use.

(4) Writing skills.

User services staff are called on to do a lot of writing for design of curriculum materials, production of newsletter articles, and correspondence with users. Skills in written communication are highly important for doing these things well.

(5) Problem solving skills.

This type of service might require being "on call" for up to fifty key "customers" and they will never run out of problems for which they need help. Being able to reassure dissatisfied users, plan ways to solve their problems, and do this for many people simultaneously is an indispensable skill for user services staff.

Personal Attributes:

(6) Creativity.

There are always new ways to do things which might be more effective or interesting than the old ways. Whether it is design of materials, teaching a class, or solving problems, creativity will make a person more effective in service users.

(7) Initiative.

Computing is such a new field for so many educators that people supporting instructional computing will never see the end of requests for assistance. A service person must know how to "run his own show" much of the time and respond to user problems promptly.

(8) Diplomacy.

In any newly emerging field different people will have varying ideas on how things should be done. The user services person will probably work for an organization with policies of its own. He must be able to work with people within those policies while making them feel that flexibility exists to meet their needs as often as possible.

(9) Background.

Even a person with all of the above characteristics will have his credibility partially judged by his previous experience. Most valuable will be a background that matches that of those being served. Thus, a person providing user services to elementary and secondary schools will benefit from having once been such a teacher in terms of knowing the demands and politics of that work situation. A user services team would benefit from a mix of backgrounds, including people from different subject area specialities and different "grade" levels (elementary, secondary, and college

MECC Published Training Materials

MECC has published numerous training products to assist local schools and school districts implement their own training. The publications can be purchased from:

> MECC Distribution Centre
> 3490 Lexington Avenue, North
> St Paul, MINNESOTA
> USA   55112

Titles that are currently available include some of the following:

    Computers in Mathematics Curriculum

    Computers in Teaching

    Instructional Computing Presentations

    Using the Computer in the Classroom

    Computing Tools: Spreadsheets

    Computing Tools: Databases

    Computing Tools: Word Processing

    Introduction to LOGO for Teachers

    Introduction to PASCAL for Programming Teachers

    LOGO: Words and Ideas

    Beginning AppleSoft Basic

    Structure Design and Programming

    Writing Support Materials for Instructional Computing

Write to MECC for the complete listing and description of training material. Most training materials are accompanied by computer diskettes.

Discussion

Chairman: J D Tinsley

Rapporteurs: D M Watson
B Samways

The Chairman divided the session into two parts; the first was the paper presented by R J E Lewis.

Penter suggested that we must have summative evaluation to assess courses and asked Lewis how he ranked his check list which contained many independent considerations. Lewis commented that summative evaluation of process is hard, though much easier for content. For the teacher a preview (a first impression), should be followed by a thorough review of classroom practice a year later.

De Kruif stated that in his experience many programs were so bad that teachers can easily waste time just looking at them. Surely there is a need for an evaluation group? Lewis drew attention to the problems that teachers have when they return to school and that some follow up courses are offered.

van Weert asked Lewis if there was a difference between evaluating traditional materials and computing materials. Lewis replied that there was not. van Weert suggested that, as we consider computers in Education, we should perhaps review our methods of evaluating traditional materials. Lewis stated that one gets to know the reviewer and whether or not one generally agrees or disagrees with that person.

Lee suggested that we should look at the design end; i.e. who developed the material, though Lewis pointed out that this could result in everything looking the same, although a combination of the two would be best.

The second presentation was by J Hammond and R Pollak.

Lewis asked Hammond if the exposure to computer materials raised the level of computer literacy; to which she replied that computer awareness needs the use of computer materials and so this must take place. Hardware though is a "way-down-there" part. Penter added that the National Report encourages the use of Utilities (word processors, spreadsheets, databases) and that children enjoy using these.

van Weert commented that Australia was wise in its computer awareness/literacy approach, rather than classroom computer use, though Pollak stated that computer awareness/literacy will go away.

Millin asked if the materials, as they were "free", were appreciated by the users. Hammond pointed out that some courses are paid for and that these were expensive. Her course members included the unemployed, mum + dad + children, doctors, managing directors (on the quiet). The important thing is to get people talking to each other. Discussion is the base whereby change will take place.

Tinsley noted the high costs involved in developing high quality software and that MECC has over seventy people so engaged. Pollak added that their ideas for software came from teachers and that a package takes about nine months to develop and costs about $30,000. Software should be so designed that it can be changed by the teacher over many year's use. Colour, graphics and sound are currently the things that motivate children. In answer to van Weert's question, Pollak felt that as a software producer MECC was now influencing the real world, though this was only a recent development. Currently, we need science programs, for example, that can be used like the pin-ball construction kits.

de Kruif concluded the questioning by returning to the earlier comments about the evaluation of traditional materials. He felt that although they should be the same as for computer materials, this was not the case at present. Lewis stated that when supporting teacher/pupil activity he could see no difference between evaluating Physics experiments and worksheets and History resources with maps and computer databases. The same objectives would apply to both.

SESSION 7

Chairman: Ulrich Bosler

INFORMATICS AND TEACHER TRAINING
F.B. Lovis and E.D. Tagg (editors)
Elsevier Science Publishers B.V. (North-Holland)
© IFIP, 1984

THE SWISS SCHOOL OF INFORMATICS
AS PART OF THE MIGROS CLUB SCHOOL
AND THE PROBLEM OF INTERNAL TEACHER TRAINING

Thomas Steiger

Coordination Office of the Club Schools
Federation of Migros Cooperatives
Zürich, Switzerland

The Migros Club School is the largest adult education
institution in Switzerland. The existing situation in
the educational sector of informatics and the special
organisational structure of Migros have a considerable
influence on the concepts underlying the training of the
course tutors in the framework of the Swiss School of
Informatics. In the last part of this article, an attempt
is made to depict the complex system of the sources of
information which are relevant to the development of the
courses of instruction as well as to the further education
of the course tutors. The whole system is based on the
unity of the staff in those institutions responsible for
development and for teacher training activities. In this
article, the contents of these training activities are
not discussed. Rather, the institutional organisation
of the school, as a factor for the feasibility of teacher
training, is the central subject of this essay.

INFORMATICS IN THE SWISS EDUCATIONAL SYSTEM

We shall only touch briefly here on the educational situation in the sphere of
informatics in Switzerland. It is a fact that only now have the relevant
educational activities become the subject of broader and more specialised
discussions, and the specialists and other interested parties involved are still
a long way from having reached agreement. The educational activities can be
categorised according to the educational aims and, within these, according to
those carrying out the activities.

Hitherto, (and even now), the conventional training of specialists, such as
programmers, analysts and hardware specialists has been, quantitatively speaking
for the main part product-orientated, and, in the sphere of in-service training,
mostly under the direct control of the computer and software suppliers. For a
long time, there has been a state-controlled training course for analyst-
programmers, which is offered by private and semi-private educational
institutions. Further developments in the field of computer training courses
have only very recently been carried out.

Up-to-date profiles of information technologists with their various
specialisations are only just emerging in Switzerland. In the very recent past,
universities and polytechnics have organised appropriate training courses. On
the level of higher professional training, an attempt is being made at the
present moment through state-run crash programmes to overcome the backwardness in

the computer training of professionals from electro-technical or commercial
backgrounds. The scope of these efforts, on a university level, as well as on a
professional training level, will nevertheless be modest for some years to come.

In the area of elementary professional training, the desired integration of
computer studies into the training courses has hardly been realised. These
wheels grind extraordinarily slowly also. Much the same must be said of the
public school system. There is still no consensus as to what extent and with
what priority a subject of computer studies should be introduced into the
different levels in primary and secondary schools. It is left mainly to the
individual efforts of the teachers to determine the extent of these activities.
It is impossible to talk of more than basic steps towards the training of state
teachers.

The adult educational institutions in Switzerland have discovered the existing
gap in the market, but have so far made no attempt to fill this with a systematic
educational programme. In connection with the diffusion of micro-computers, a
situation of chaos associated with false promises concerning the courses offered
has arisen, which is obviously often connected to direct product marketing
interests.

In view of this situation, the Migros Club School, which is the largest adult
education institution in Switzerland, intends to take the initiative and open the
Swiss School of Informatics by offering a wide variety of courses of the highest
quality in response to market demands.

THE SWISS SCHOOL OF INFORMATICS AS PART OF THE MIGROS CLUB SCHOOL

In 1944, Gottlieb Duttweiler, the founder of Migros, created the Club Schools
with a clear socio-political committment. The founding concept was - analogous to
that of the commercial Migros, which is to guarantee the provision of the
population with economically priced goods for their basic needs - the creation of
means of access to cultural products, especially in the educational sector. It
was therefore by no means fortuitous that the Club School was originally planned
as a language school. In accordance with the socio-political committment, the
Club School was never self-sufficient, but was always subsidised by Migros.
Approximately two thirds of the turnover must be recuperated from course fees,
while about a third is derived from the so-called "cultural levy". By its
statutes, Migros is obliged to make half a percent of its turnover available for
cultural purposes.

On this foundation, the Club School has developed strongly. Today, it is by far
the largest adult education institution in Switzerland. In view of its importance
it can be compared with the Volkshochschule in West Germany. In 53 educational
centres, more than 7.3 million hours in 300 different subjects are taught by over
400 full time staff and 4,600 course tutors. Courses are available in all sectors
of adult education : languages, leisure, training and further education.

The above-mentioned situation and the socio-political committment of the Club
Schools have a definite influence on the profile of the Swiss School of
Informatics. The courses should also be offered in economically deprived regions
and should reach all essential target groups. From a quantitative viewpoint, the
most significant target groups will be children and young people, those with an
interest in general knowledge and those who will apply the course at their place
of work. But qualitatively speaking, those participants who wish for a
professional qualification as analyst-programmers or data processing project
leaders are decisively important. Here also, there is an educational bottleneck

in Switzerland, but these people represent in addition a qualitative challenge
for the Club Schools.

For this reason, what is offered constitutes a very broad spectrum which is
structured to correspond to the varied interests of the participants. Great
importance is bound to be attached to the aspect of "thought-training", ie. the
training of those key capacities which extend beyond the purely instrumental
application of computer equipment. The methodological preparation of the course
material takes account of the different target groups.

Just this brief representation of the Swiss School of Informatics and its areas of
operation suffices to make it clear that such a demanding aim can hardly be
achieved without special endeavours in the area of teacher-training. However,
this circumstance is not new for the Club Schools, for surely it is characteristic
of private adult education that it introduces innovations in fields for which
little preparatory work has been done in an existing educational system.

THE PROBLEM OF TEACHER TRAINING

In order to explain our approach to the solution of the problem of availability
of trained specialist teachers, it is necessary to describe the organisational
structure of the Club Schools in more detail.

As a commercial retail trade organisation, Migros is divided into 12 largely
autonomous cooperatives. To each of these organisations an autonomous Club School
is similarly affiliated. Statutorily, the cooperatives, or alternatively, the
Club Schools, are not obliged to work together. Effectively nurtured co-operation
therefore depends to a large extent on a consensus and is the expression of
perceived economical advantages.

**Planning, development and realisation are therefore managed purely from the centre
only in rare cases. As the central servicing office, the Migros Federation of
Cooperatives** has the task of developing concepts and offering central coordination
services. However, it has to sell all its services to the cooperatives, while the
latter are only obliged to accept the offers if better conditions cannot be found
on the free market.

In the case of the Swiss School of Informatics, by request of the regional Club
Schools, the project was developed and made ripe for decision centrally by the
Coordination Office with the assistance of outside specialists. As to the
realisation of the project, a far-reaching agreement was made that the future
regional Schools of Informatics should be run identically, ie. with the same
hardware and the same course materials. For the actual development work a federal
solution adapted to the structure of the organisation was chosen, which, as will
be realised in the course of this article, greatly simplifies the solution of
further education problems.

In all the larger regional educational centres full-time information technologists
have been appointed who make a percentage of their work, which depends on the
stage of development, available for the central development of course materials.
The project management is the task of the Coordination Office, which also
participates actively in the development work.

This arrangement assures two things. Firstly, the professional identification of
the main people responsible for the regional schools is largely guaranteed through
personal participation in the development, as well as through the constant
decision-making process in working conferences. The danger of alienation at the

centre is more or less eliminated. Secondly, the first transfer stage of the
acquired know-how remains institutionalised with the main people responsible in
the regions, which means it is permanently available.

This situation can be represented graphically as follows :

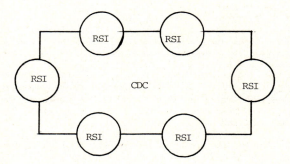

RSI : People responsible for the regional Schools of Informatics
CDC : Central Development Committee

The second transfer stage, which is ultimately decisive for the quality of the
course, namely the transmission of the acquired methods and materials to the
course tutors, is merely supported by this form of organisation, but not
guaranteed. The part-time course tutors have to be enabled to organise the
lessons according to the format developed with the assistance of special,
regionally organised training programmes. For this purpose, the Central
Development Committee works out guidelines for the regional training of course
tutors. This assures the second transfer stage.

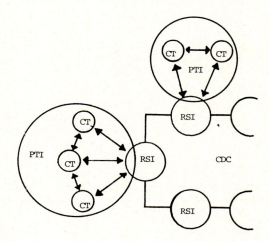

CT : Course tutor
PTI : Permanent regional training institutions

The course tutors teach almost totally outside their regular employment. Apart from the acute problem of financing this training, this basis assures the flow of know-how relevant in professional practice, and of solid course experience, into the tasks of development and revision. On the other hand, the level of training of these course tutors is in some cases very high only in special areas, while the degree of general knowledge is often relatively modest.

Concerning knowledge of teaching in adult education and the methodological organisation of the actual lessons, there is considerable expertise at the Club Schools, which is based on many years of teaching experience. This know-how can be made available on the spot for the setting-up of the school and for the training of the teachers.

A further important input into this system is made through the link with the industrial training centres of the different Migros enterprises and other firms, which want to carry out the training of their personnel under the direction of the Club Schools. By means of these contacts, the economically relevant training needs have to be constantly monitored.

But we have not yet described all the flow of information necessary for the success of the school. In addition, the project has a Supervisory Committee which secures contact with the institutions of the public-legal education system. Besides representatives of the higher educational institutions, such as universities and polytechnics, it includes officials familiar with educational topics. Most important of all, the representatives of the company decision-making committees also sit on this Supervisory Board.

The complete information network in connection with the acquisition and transmission of course material and course methods is represented as follows. The relative size of what is represented is not significant.

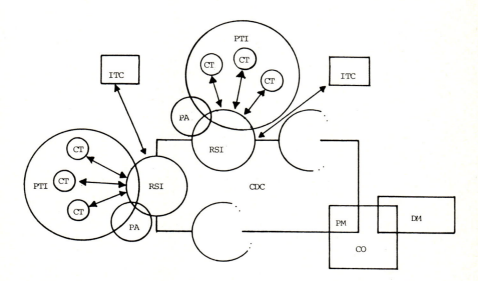

PTI : Field of permanent training institutions
CO : Committee organ : creates the link between the development committees, the
      public-legal institutions, the opinion-leaders and the decision-making
      boards of companies
ITC : Industrial training centres
DM : Decision-maker (Migros)
CT : Course tutor working outside regular employment
PM : Project management
PA : Pedagogical advisers at the Club Schools with many years of experience in
      the field of theory and practice of teaching
RSI : People responsible for the regional Schools of Informatics
CDC : Central Development Committee

As to the quality of the Swiss School of Informatics, the most important role,
besides the course tutors, is played by the regionally responsible information
technologists. They are the ones who bear the burden of the development work as
well as coordinating information between those with different kinds of experience.
Their capability will determine the success of the Swiss School of Informatics.

INFORMATICS AND TEACHER TRAINING
F.B. Lovis and E.D. Tagg (editors)
Elsevier Science Publishers B.V. (North-Holland)
© IFIP, 1984

TEACHER TRAINING IN INFORMATICS IN SWITZERLAND
WITH REALIZATION IN THE CANTON OF GENEVA

Jean-Bernard Roux
Etudes Pédagogiques de l'Enseignement Secondaire
Geneva Switzerland

The Swiss structures resist changes. Because of prestige and
regional rivalries, Switzerland has perhaps missed its turn in
informatics. The first problem to solve was the training of
everybody in informatics. The example of teacher training in
informatics, particularly in the Canton of Geneva, is the
subject of this paper.

INTRODUCTION

To understand the Swiss education system, we must first look at the country itself.
Switzerland is a country of banks, chocolate, watches and cheese. That is the
primary vision strangers have of our country. Today, watch-making, machine-tool,
textile industries are stalled. Some prosperous industries have been caught in
the trap of conservative policy and success. In Swiss industries, there are, in
fact, unbelievable forces of inertia which have to be defeated.

Switzerland is a highly democratic country where decision processes often prevent
the acceptance of new ideas. That is the reason why our country has missed its
turn in informatics. It could have had the technology if it had asserted itself.
Japan is not so far away and its success is based on this raw material.

A number of discoveries and ideas have been produced and have grown up in
Switzerland, but have had to leave the country to be successful. To mention only
informatics, Pascal, the well-known and widespread language, was developed in
Switzerland. However, this language spread only after it became known in the
United States, and we now buy Pascal from the Americans themselves.

However, we must be aware that Switzerland, if it does not export its ideas and
technology, may be susceptible to attempts of colonization. The considerable
delay in acquiring new technological information could be harmful. But now it
seems that education should provide support for this electronic revolution, to
approach it boldly, with efficiency and criticism, to keep our free will and
autonomy. Furthermore, education must assure us an opening and an intellectual
autonomy to allow us to create, produce and export.

EDUCATION AND INFORMATICS [1]

Switzerland is a four language confederation, meaning four different cultures. It
is split into 23 areas called cantons, which stand highly independent towards the
central authority. That is the Helvetic Federalism, the pride of our country.
This system gives each canton great freedom concerning its educational system. A
single common program is hard to achieve.

Informatics, as a way for students to acquire knowledge, would require a deep
transformation of the Swiss educational system, because it would include
obligatorily the mixing of disciplines and the creation of a more and more

autonomous educational system. Swiss people are not convinced in the main that informatics is part of their general culture.

New media are coming. Will we be strong enough to accept these novelties critically and selectively? Knowing where they come from, their structure, and in what context, are uncertainties which we have to learn and resolve.

Switzerland is the most computerized country in the world, but teaching of this type hardly exists. Switzerland has had to call strangers to make up the deficit of people knowledgeable in informatics.

Today, private schools, informatics enterprises, centres of diffusion of informations and editors of software divide the market of teaching in informatics among them. This seems to be promising.

As to the labour market, Swiss firms need many people knowledgeable in informatics. But the person most in demand is the specialist in a non-informatic profession with knowledge of data processing. In that way, a kind of gap is growing between knowledgeable and "an-alphabetic" people.

To fight the trade in education, the telematics power, the expropiation of the market of education by the private sector, the public education try to react by introducing lessons for everybody. Teacher training is, of course, the first priority.

TRAINING IN INFORMATICS IN GENEVA

Since 1960, some experiences in teaching informatics in Geneva, especially facultative lessons, have been gained. The Department of Public Instruction in Geneva has decided to introduce the teaching of informatics to all students (12-20 years old) after 1985. In fact, from 1990, each student in Geneva will have a basic teaching in computer literacy.

Before beginning this experiment, priority was given to the training of teachers. Formerly, teachers were self-taught people. Later, a training was created for teachers who wanted to teach facultative lessons. The introduction of the topic of computer awareness needs more teachers. The number of actual teachers and members of universities is insufficient.

The following table shows the importance of demand (Figure 1) :   [2]

DATE	CONCERNED STUDENTS	Modes of TEACHER TRAINING
since 1969	less than 10%	self-taught
since 1979	10 - 15%	some lessons
from 1985	100%	the subject of the paper

Figure 1
Demand of training

Many estimates were made before introducing new courses. The first estimate made concerned the students (Figure 2) :

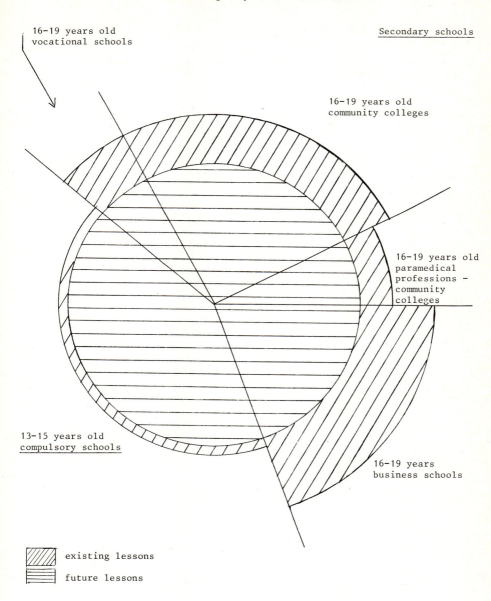

16-19 years old
vocational schools

Secondary schools

16-19 years old
community colleges

16-19 years old
paramedical
professions –
community
colleges

13-15 years old
compulsory schools

16-19 years
business schools

existing lessons

future lessons

Figure 2.

Diagram of student populations, showing consequences for demand of training.

The second important estimate is that concerning teachers. There were, of course, some teachers who had already been taught. But they are not numerous. It is impossible to teach all the teachers in one year because of the small number of teacher trainers. This training will take more than five years and will involve four hundred people.

To fulfil the objectives of computer awareness for the students, new training has been developed. It will be four years long, but teachers will be able to give lessons after two years. The following diagram shows this new concept (Figure 3).

The didactical use of computers has not been forgotten. It remains a primary aim and in this respect, the teachers' training is again important.

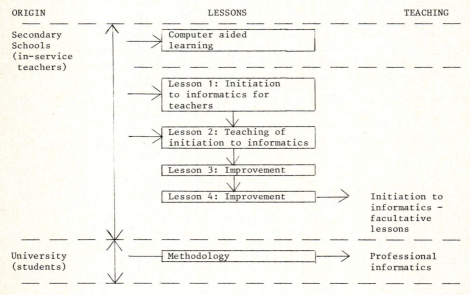

ORIGIN   LESSONS   TEACHING

Secondary Schools (in-service teachers)

Computer aided learning

Lesson 1: Initiation to informatics for teachers

Lesson 2: Teaching of initiation to informatics

Lesson 3: Improvement

Lesson 4: Improvement → Initiation to informatics – facultative lessons

University (students)

Methodology → Professional informatics

Figure 3
New plan for teacher training in Geneva

Here are the details of the objectives of the lessons shown in the diagram: [2]

LESSON 1   (33 weeks, 2 hours per week)

OBJECTIVES

To familiarise with informatics.

To give teachers elements of general culture.

To learn elements of programming.

CONTENTS

Some stages in the computer story – description of computer systems – concept of models, algorithms and flow charts – high level programming languages – comparison of languages – a lot of personal work in the subject – CAL in different subjects (both scientific and literary) – dangers of informatics – visits to installations.

LESSON 2   (33 weeks, 2 hours per week)

OBJECTIVES

To make the teacher capable of giving lessons of familiarisation in informatics, taking into account the basic training of these teachers (literary, scientific, commercial, ...)

CONTENTS

Evolution of a computer system – functions of a microsystem – analysis of a problem problem and concept of the algorithm – concept of information and natural and formal languages – concepts of structured programming – vocational guidance in informatics – concept of **editor** – didactical use of spreadsheets – concept of file system and use of data base management – didactic and practical use of text processing – computer graphics and computer aided design – introduction to data structures – telematics and networks – teletext, social controls and security – informatics and society – use of didactic products – concept of artificial intelligence – authoring languages – new technologies in the firm – concept of operating systems, standardization, human factors, interactivity.

LESSONS 3 AND 4   (66 weeks, 2 hours per week)

OBJECTIVES

To give teachers the necessary knowledge for teaching informatics at a higher level.

CONTENTS not yet defined.

LESSONS: Computer Aided Learning (33 weeks, 2 hours per week)

OBJECTIVES

To train teachers to use computers in their lessons.

REMARKS

Although the content of the present document is centred on informatics as a study object, it would be wrong to conclude that there is no activity in the matter of the didactical use of computers in schools (CAL).

Awareness of informatics is more than the learning of an interdisciplinary tool or a way of thinking. It is relevant to general culture rather than the informatics subject itself.

The essence of the challenge is to teach a great number of our students to be thinking people and not just specialists.

REFERENCES

[1] Informatique – informations no. 18, groupe informatique de l'enseignement secondaire, Genève, December 1983.

[2] Etudes pédagogiques de l'enseignement secondaire, groupe informatique de l'enseignement secondaire, formation en informatique dans l'enseignement secondaire (June 1984).

INFORMATICS AND TEACHER TRAINING
F.B. Lovis and E.D. Tagg (editors)
Elsevier Science Publishers B.V. (North-Holland)
© IFIP, 1984

IN-SERVICE AND PRE-SERVICE TRAINING OF PRIMARY
SCHOOL TEACHERS IN INFORMATION AND COMPUTER
APPLICATION IN EDUCATION

Daniel Millin, Benzion Barta

Ministry of Education and Culture
Jerusalem, ISRAEL

A short overview of computer activities in the Israeli school
system is given - leading to the requirement to provide computer
education to all students at colleges of education and to all
teachers actively employed in schools. A scheme of courses is
presented, followed by a more detailed discussion of courses
intended for primary school teachers. The implementation of some
of these courses is described, followed by conclusions after a
first year of large scale implementation.

KEY WORDS: Teachers-Training, Computer Applications in
            Education, Computer Literacy, Primary-Schools,
            Computer-Education.

INTRODUCTION

Information technology will continue to develop at a rapid pace, while knowledge
and understanding of social and human aspects lag behind.

In order to close the gap, much more interdisciplinary work is necessary. More
spreading of information on computers is required (popularization of interdisciplinary science and application in the literal sense of the word). Analysis of
differences between new technologies in manufacturing and in administrative
sectors will be mutually beneficial. As information technology will become a
growing concern in all nations, with increasing demands for skill, acceptance and
sensible application, agencies of all types - both private and public - will be
faced with the problem of bringing current staff to an adequate level of
competence and keeping up with developments.

These phenomena have a tremendous impact on traditional teaching methods and on
future generations. In the following paper an attempt is made to examine the
possibilities of using micro-computers as a tool for training teachers, who will
have to cope with new technologies and adjust themselves to unknown developments.
It is expected that most of us will have to change our occupations and learn
new concepts and techniques. Thus it seems that new teaching methods using
micro-computers as a tool for developing logical thinking and problem-solving
procedures incorporate a great deal of pedagogical potential for teachers and
students,as well. On the other hand, micro-computers may easily become external
"playing machines", used only by small groups of teachers.

GENERAL TRENDS IN ISRAEL

1. Israel has started last year the planning of a national program for Information
    Technology. The National Committee for Information Technology was appointed
    by the Government and, subsequently, nine subcommittees were formed to deal

with specific areas in which I.T. could and should be encouraged and supported in Israel.

As a result of intensive study and serious consideration, several sub-committees have already submitted their primary recommendations. Three out of nine subcommittees strongly recommend large investments in the field of education and in the development of human resources. The subcommittee for technology recommends a national computer-assisted learning program to be initiated immediately as a joint project of governmental institutions and private industries.

2. The Ministry of Education is giving high priority to the development of the variety of activities related to computer applications in the educational process and their equitable distribution within the educational system. In 1979, the Committee for Computers in the Educational System was created with the purpose of dealing with all aspects of computers in education within the whole range of educational institutions supervised by the Ministry - from Kindergarten up to tertiary education (except universities).

The topics being presently given priority for implementation are as follows:

1. Teachers' training and updating. This topic includes courses on an introduction to computers and their educational applications as described in this paper. It includes also, courses to qualify teachers of Computer Sciences, of professional Computer Applications and of Computer Literacy.

2. Introducing a nation-wide curriculum for teaching Computer Literacy, for the grade span from first grade to 8th grade.

3. Further development and implementation of Drill and Practice in basic skills, mainly in the primary education.

4. Computer-related Vocational Education - development of new curricula for vocations specializing in computers (software and hardware) and updating curricula of most professions, as regarding computer applications specific to each one.

5. Teaching of Computer Science in high-schools as a general science education subject, part of the matriculation examinations.

6. Development and implementation of various approaches of Computer Aided Learning.

All of the topics mentioned are accompanied by adequate research and evaluation. Most of them have to deal with aspects of hardware selection and standardization, courseware and software portability, etc.

COMPUTERS IN SCHOOLS

Many teachers feel that schools have been too quick and too uncritical in adopting computer programs while pushing other valuable educational courses aside, whereas many others believe that only a rapid implementation of computer technology in the educational system will save the school from irrelevant education. It is felt that most educators advocate the immediate introduction of computers into all schools. This is due, to some extent, to the "status appeal" and to the belief that computer studies will considerably improve students' readiness for life. On the other hand, a lot is said about computer literacy. Apparently, it serves more as a slogan or a set of long-term goals than as a clear concept which schools can easily translate into educational objectives.

In effect, without clearly defined educational goals in teachers colleges, where basic skills and knowledge are taught, we may easily "miss the point". For this reason it is vital to clarify our needs and expectations from the "future teachers" who will cope and cooperate with new technologies in computer-literate schools.

Teachers colleges must develop a long view of where they are going. "They need long-term as well as short-term goals along with practical long-range planning that takes into account the time, resources and training needed to put those goals into effect. And they need to step back, slow down, and take the time necessary to change in an orderly way"[1].

Reconsideration of our achievements and expectations is needed, and as soon as possible!

Essentially, the teacher's role in the classroom is changing due to computers and other educational media. Individual differences are constantly increasing. It is felt that, with the aid of computers, students are making better progress and teachers have to use more and more individual instruction. The uniformity of the classroom is disappearing, and a comprehensive knowledge of individual instruction becomes a vital need for every teacher. Thus, computers as a tool for individual instruction (CAI, CMI) may be of great help in schools.

Computer-assisted instruction technique provides teachers with immediate feedback and diagnostic data about their students and enables each student to learn according to his needs and interest. On the other hand, it seems that in the near future students will begin to control computers and express themselves through the programs they create. Computers will be used in each classroom as a tool for gathering relevant data on the one hand and as a playing-tool on the other.

TEACHERS TRAINING

Concerning teachers' training, starting with the school year 1983/84, a compulsory computer introduction course has been implemented in teachers colleges. The main purpose of this 60 hours' course is to enable teachers to know and understand computers in order to function competently in our society.

For this purpose, thirty colleges out of forty-three were equipped with computer centers (6 to 16 units per school). 75% of this expenditure was allocated by the Ministry of Education. About 2000 students took part in these courses, and for next year (1984/85) an increase of about 50% is expected.

Teachers applying for in-service training were offered a variety of computer courses, and more than 1000 of them attended computer classes during the year 1983/84. Most demands were for introductory courses, computer applications in education and computer-assisted learning courses.

As it looks now, there are four main areas of competence to be taught:

a) basic skills and knowledge of computer operation, programming and capabilities

---

(1) D. Watt: Computer Literacy In Educational Computing, March 1984.

b) skills required for using a computer for intelligent use in educational
    administration

c) knowledge about computers - how they work, their applications, capabilities
    and limitations within schools, such as: CAI, CMI, CAD/CAM

d) understanding needed to evaluate the uses of computers as they affect
    individuals and society as a whole.

It is essential to establish suitable programs for future teaching purposes. This
should and can be done only if the teaching objectives are well defined. This is
not an easy task, as we are dealing, within the framework of the teachers
colleges, with a great variety of future teachers: teachers for primary schools,
middle schools and secondary schools. Each population requires a curriculum
designed according to its objectives.

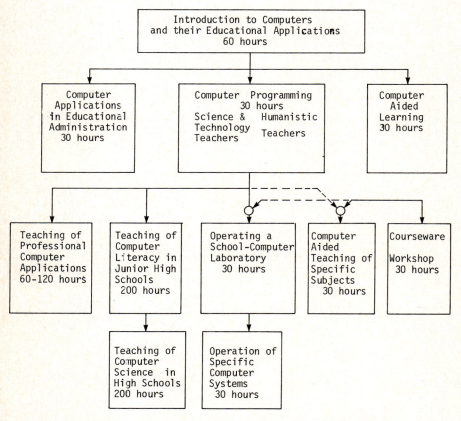

Fig. 1 - The overall scheme of teachers' training and updating courses.

Courses for teachers' training and updating are organized in Israel according to the overall scheme described in Fig. 1. This scheme describes a general approach. The scheme out of which many modules were actually implemented is neither unique nor compulsory, and there are various approaches at different institutions which were implemented experimentally during the last school year.

The course "Introduction to Computers and their Educational Applications" is the most widely delivered. It covers basic concepts of computer structure, operation and programming; an introduction to the world of informatics, telematics, including social aspects; an introduction to computer applications to learning, educational administration and a first experience with computer-aided learning systems. This type of course is delivered (as a compulsory subject) at Colleges training primary school teachers, at Schools of Education at Universities and as updating courses for teachers of primary and secondary schools, for supervisors and managerial staff. The detailed syllabus will vary according to the audience and the institution providing the course. Details about the content of the courses for primary school teachers are given in a separate section of this paper.

Other courses of interest to primary school teachers are:

* Computer Aided Learning - providing a more detailed knowledge of approaches, systems amd methodologies for integrating the use of computers into the teaching-learning process.

* Courseware Workshops - dealing mainly with courseware evaluation, and with first concepts of author-languages and courseware authoring.

* Computer Aided Teaching of Specific Subjects - deals with specific materials and methodology. Taking this course may require a better knowledge of programming (according to the nature of the applications), in which case, the Programming Course may be a pre-requisite.

A teacher completing these courses should be able to integrate effectively the use of computers in his teaching activities - having a loose support from adequate advice and guidance teams set up by the Ministry of Education and/or the courseware production teams. He should also be ready to join courseware authoring teams, after some further study and experience.

* Operating a School Computer Laboratory - provides practical knowledge on equipment and software selection, lab-set-up, operation, scheduling, maintenance.

* Operation of Specific Computer Systems - deals with details of the systems which were installed or selected by the school. This type of course is expected to be provided by the equipment suppliers.

When the Computer is to be used for computer aided learning - which is the case for elementary schools - the course on Computer Aided Learning is to be a second pre-requisite to these last two courses.

A teacher taking these last courses is expected to assume responsibility on the management of school's computer laboratory.

The implementation of the last five courses has been, till now, offered as updating courses, and at a rather limited extent. Many more such courses will be taught in 1985/85. Also, they will be offered as elective subjects at Colleges and Schools of Education.

HOW IT WORKS

At Ben Gurion University in Beer Sheba, four in-service courses were implemented during the last year, with considerable success. Each course included sixty hours, which were taught during twenty meetings.

1. The first course was designed specifically for primary school teachers and offered the following topics:

   - computer structure
   - computer operations
   - micro-computers
   - evaluation (what is a good computer program)
   - the role of computers in education
   - computer assisted learning
   - LOGO
   - word processing
   - creative projects.

   Main objective of this course was to provide teachers with basic knowledge about computers and enable them to consider and evaluate the use of computer packages in schools.

2. The second course included kindergarten instructors, and had the following topics:

   - basic knowledge about computer architecture
   - algorithms
   - how to use software packages
   - LOGO
   - computers applications in everyday life
   - computers and their impact on society.

   General objectives of this curriculum were:

   1. To understand the meaning of computer implementation in schools

   2. To teach a programming language as a tool in problem solving.

   3. To get acquainted with some computer packages related to kindergarten

   4. To develop some skills which will enable instructors to use computers in kindergarten.

3. The third program was prepared to suit the purposes of school administrators. The following subjects were taught in this course:

   - introduction to micro-computers
   - how to buy a micro-computer
   - computer applications in educational administration
   - computer graphics
   - computer assisted learning
   - LOGO, SUPER-PILOT
   - word processing
   - how to evaluate software for school purposes.

   Objectives of this course were similar to the one taught to teachers, with emphasis on administrative aspects of computers applications.

4. Fourth program was offered mainly to inspectors and included the following subjects:

   - computer applications in education
   - data processing
   - information systems
   - LOGO, SUPER-PILOT
   - BASIC
   - computer architecture
   - algorithms and flow-charts
   - evaluation of software packages

As in previous programs, the purpose of this course was to provide the inspectors with basic tools to cope with these new technologies.

It should be stated, that all four courses were highly appreciated by the attendees. As a result of this year's experience the University had to double the number of courses for the coming year 1984/85.

A point of interest may be to mention that each program was independently developed by a member of the University staff, and according to this year's experience a coordinated curriculum will be offered.

Similar results were achieved at Beit-Berl Teachers College, where four different populations of educators took their courses.

1. One group included administrators who attended a sixty hours course. This course was a part of a general updating course, and its objective was to introduce administrators into the "computer world".

2. Students from five different classes took a sixty hours computer-literacy course. No pre-requisites were required and only few students had mathematical background. In spite of that their achievements were quite good and many students required advanced courses for the next year.

3. Teachers who came for inservice training took a 150 hours course. The purpose of this one was to prepare teachers to understand, use and implement computer assisted instructions techniques in their work. Beside that, one half of this course dealt with BASIC programming and problem solving.

4. The fourth group attended a retraining course which included mainly science teachers. This course's objectives were to prepare teachers for teaching computer-literacy in primary and middle schools. One hundred and fifty hours were taught during the first year. Another three hundred hours are required in order to get a formal certificate to teach computer science.

It might be concluded that all the above mentioned courses were offered only for the last year. They represented only a part of the in-service training and training of primary school teachers and administrators. It is felt that there is a great deal of interest among teachers to join this type of courses and it is hoped that within the next four to five years the vast majority of teachers will have at least 60 hours of computer studies.

CONCLUSIONS

1. Teaching basic computer-literacy courses to a variety of students at teachers colleges became an achievable goal.

2. For many students sixty hours course is not enough and there has to be a possibility to proceed with advanced courses.

3. A variety of programs has to be offered. It is essential to teach not only basic computer concepts but also computer applications in education.

4. An on-going support has to be provided for teachers after completing the basic courses.

5. Retraining should become an integral part of all teachers' studies. It is essential to apply experimental learning techniques which will provide effective and creative training. This training process has to be constantly evaluated and updated.

6. Computer training and retraining should be well integrated in the institutions, taking into account educational needs and social environment.

7. Teachers colleges should become guiding and dissemination centers which will provide necessary and updated information about: learning programs, courseware, software and relevant information about computer use in education.

8. Colleges and schools must open widely their computer centers and provide computer access to all students. In the near future, computer libraries, which will lend home computers and programs, will become popular and will enable every student to get acquainted with these new technologies.

Only serious consideration of computer implementation in the educational system and well designed curricula will meet our hopes and expectations.

REFERENCES:

1. Conclusions and Recommendations, "Training for Tomorrow, IFAC/IFIP Conference, Leiden,The Netherlands,June 1983

2. Gizycki R.V., Weiler U. "Consequences of a Broad Introduction of Microprocessors for Educational and Training Policies", The German Federal Ministry of Education and Science, Ref. IIA5, Bonn,October 1979

3. James E.B., "Personal Computing Systems for Research and Development", Computer Centre,Imperial College, London S.W.,January 1981

4. Report of the Subcommittee on Technology, Education and Manpower, Ministry of Telecommunication,Science and Development, February 1984

5. Watt D. "Computer Literacy", Popular Computing, March 1984

INFORMATICS AND TEACHER TRAINING
F.B. Lovis and E.D. Tagg (editors)
Elsevier Science Publishers B.V. (North-Holland)
© IFIP, 1984

INFORMATICS AND TEACHER TRAINING IN HUNGARY

L. VARGA

L. Eötvös University of Budapest, Hungary

The first computers in Hungarian secondary
schools were installed in the middle of the
seventies. On the basis of the experiment
in 1981 the Ministry of Education decided
on a program the aim of which was to install
microcomputers in secondary schools. Now
more than 1000 microcomputers are in the
schools as teaching aids. The universities
play an important role in training teachers
for the use of these computers. In the
paper, courses and experiences about the
training at the Loránd Eötvös University of
Budapest will be discussed.

INTRODUCTION

In spite of the title of my paper, I shall not try to cover the
whole field of teacher training in Hungary, but will concentrate on
the work of the L. Eötvös University of Budapest. The reason of this
is that our university plays an important role in teacher training
for secondary schools in respect of informatics. The Computer
Science Department of the University has been doing this job under
close cooperation between the Pedagogic Institute for Continuation
Courses of Budapest and the University.

To establish the general use of school computers in secondary schools
we decided four years ago to bring microcomputers into teacher
training. We equipped our laboratories with microcomputers using
common financial sources. At present, we have three laboratories
equipped with micros. In the beginning, the microcomputers ABC only
were purchasable for us in Hungary. We got down to work using these
computers. But in 1982 we installed HT-1080Z microcomputers in our
laboratories because this computer has been chosen by the Ministry
of Education as a standard school computer. The computer HT-1080Z
has a Z80 as CPU, 12 KB /ROM/ for a BASIC interpreter, 1.5 KB
/monitor/, 16 KB /RAM/, a cassette recorder and interface.

This four year period of teacher training at the University is
discussed in this paper.

THE THREE-SEMESTER COURSE

Probationer teachers from all natural science subjects have received
training in computing since 1972 at the University. Two contact
hours per week are available for the training. One semester
consists of 14 weeks.

In 1979 the Computer Science Department installed ABC microcomputers. Recently two laboratories with ABC computers and one laboratory with HT-1080Z computers have become available for teacher training. There are seven computers in each laboratory, one for the teacher and six for the students. During the lesson two students work at the same computer.

Students start at the university with different backgrounds in programming. The first semester is devoted to abolishing these differences and bringing the students to the same level in Basic programming. During the first semester they gain sufficient knowledge to write user friendly programs for given mathematical algorithms.

In this course the aim is to use computers as teaching aids, i.e. the students must be able to develop programs for teaching their special subjects. Generally these programs are developed for demonstration and simulation of physical, chemical or biological phenomena.

The training method is the following:

In a lesson the problem to be solved, together with the necessary information, is presented to the students. They develop the program for the next lesson, and at the beginning of the lesson they demonstrate the result. After that the different quality factors of the programs /reliability, understandability, maintainability, and so on/ are discussed and experiences are summarized in order to develop good programming habits. Both the programming methodology and the pedagogical quality of a program are examined.

COURSES IN COMPUTER STUDIES

The courses, based on the above three semester courses, are organized for probationer teachers of mathematics in the 5th-8th semesters of their studies, in order that they may be able to teach computing in secondary schools. For the degree in Computer science they have 8 contact hours per week in each semester. At present, a fixed program in Computer Science is offered by the University for students, so they have no opportunity for choosing courses from an offered set. The fixed program is the following:

Theory of computing is a one semester course with two hours per week. This is an introductory course to the whole field of automata and formal languages. It concentrates on the theoretical bases of programming languages and their compilers.

Programming is a three-semester course with 4 hours per week in each semester. It concentrates on programming methodology using the programming language Pascal. The language structures in other programming languages are also examined. The course attempts to give a general introduction to software tools /operating systems, compilers, and so on/. Experience is given to the students by the use of software tools at the computer PDP 11/40.

The digital technique course aims to present the general principles of computers and to examine the computer architectures by specific reference to microcomputers. Interface devices are available for the standard schools computer so that a microcomputer can be used for controlling simple laboratory experiments. This is a four semester course with two hours per week.

Computer applications is a two semester course with 4 hours per week. This course attempts to give a general introduction to the whole field of computer application. Mainly data bases, information systems and process control problems are discussed. In the greater part of the course the problems of a computerized classroom are examined, and the microcomputer is used as a tool in the complex teaching-learning process. The students develop programs for the different activities of a teacher in the classroom, and for school administrations.

Methodology of computer education is a one semester course with 2 hours per week. Computer education requires a special pedagogical treatment. In this course, pedagogical problems and educational methods for teaching computing in a secondary school are discussed.

THE ONE-YEAR COURSE FOR TEACHERS

This course has been organized for the teachers of secondary schools of the capital by the Pedagogic Institute for Continuation Courses of Budapest since 1979. The teachers are trained by university teachers in microcomputer laboratories of the Computer Science Department at our university. From 1979 about 500 teachers from all the current subjects in Hungarian education received training in this course. The teachers attend the course in addition to all their teaching duties. They have 3 hours per week. In spite of this fact the drop out rate of participants is only a few percent.

The curriculum of this course is like that of the three-semester course organized for the probationer teachers of the University, so the teachers have an opportunity to get in courses in computer studies for the degree in Computer Science. We have decided to organize evening courses for the next academic year.

THE ONE YEAR DIRECTED COURSE

A positive result of the above one-year course is that many teachers have decided to include program systems in their subjects. In order to be able to do this job they have wanted to consult specialists when necessary. In this course the teachers have 3 hours per month when they can consult the university teachers. In a consultation the university teachers offer special books and papers to them and help them to solve their problems in developing a program.

CLOSING REMARKS

At present, more than 1000 microcomputers are installed in the secondary schools. The teachers in these schools have received a minimum of training at a short course. The microcomputers are very popular among the pupils. This situation inspires the teachers to make themselves masters of computing. Our experience shows that many teachers shoulder the courses in addition to their teaching duties. Recently there have been more applicants for our courses than places available for them.

Discussion:

Report on papers by Steiger   (Switzerland, presented by Morel)
                      Roux   (Switzerland)
                      Millin   (Israel)

Discussion of paper by Roux.

Kristel asked how it was that there was so much inertia in Switzerland – why
cannot the country react to the changes required in computer education? Morel
indicated the lack of reaction by quoting the results of a study done in 1966,
which indicated that if changes were not made to the traditional watch making
industry of the country, then Japanese competition would destroy that industry.
Fifteen years later, the Swiss watch making industry was practically destroyed
by Japanese competition. Roux explained that there was little unemployment in
Switzerland and few other social problems: therefore, there was little pressure
to react. Kristel suggested that it was easier to instal computers, than to
change the educational/industrial system. Roux agreed with this point.

Bosler asked how it was possible for a country to become one of the most
computerised in the world without training its own population in informatics.
He argued that it can only be possible if the country imports skilled personel.
Aigner asked if 'Computer Education' was necessary. He argued that industry
needed specific research and development skills, but otherwise general information technology courses were sufficient. Russell pointed out that in any country
the education of young people was an investment in the future. Importing skill
may be a short term remedy, but in the long term education was needed in order
to innovate. Ahlstrom suggested that teacher education was needed before the
mass use of computers in education. Morel replied that teacher training was
slow and expensive, whereas the purchase of hardware was quick and relatively
cheap. van Weert pointed out that changing the formal education system takes a
very long time, due to the inbuilt inertia of state institutions, whereas private
schools such as Migros can change quickly. This may account for the relatively
good record of small private schools in the teaching of informatics. Morel
agreed that Migros had shown the ability to react quickly. Migros also had
more finance available than the state system and need only concentrate on one
small part of the traditional curriculum. However, even with these advantages,
Migros still had problems with teacher training. van Weert suggested that it
was easy to attack the state educational system, because in most cases state
systems do not have a sensible development strategy. Attempts are made to design
a curriculum for up to 30 years into the future. What ought to happen is that
a curriculum be developed which should run for only 4 or 5 years at the most.
After this time it should be evaluated and changed. In informatics it is not
possible to plan further into the future than this. We must allow more
flexibility in state educational systems. Aigner pointed out that curriculum
development was bound to take a long time. Educationalists involved in
informatics were probably not the best people to plan changes in other areas of
the curriculum. However, educationalists in other areas knew very little about
informatics. The first need was for training courses for the teachers of
teachers. Who was going to run such courses? Staff at teacher training colleges
tended not to have the necessary background in informatics.

Discussion on paper by MILLIN/BARTA

van Weert pointed out that both the schemes suggested by Roux and Millin
indicated that teacher training in informatics needed many hours. The system
used in the United Kingdom took only two days and that was too short. Watson
agreed, but pointed out that many professionals working in informatics in the
United Kingdom did not agree with the system. There were many differences
between national and local initiatives, and also between the requirements of
industry (who sponsored the scheme through the Department of Trade and Industry)
and education. Watson also pointed out that any national initiative will be
subjected to many pressures from many areas of society and may well end up
being a poor compromise because of this. Barker suggested that it was not
reasonable to expect teachers to take courses of possibly 200 hours in length,
without some professionals enhancement at the end. Promotion must be allowed
for in any teacher training system. Kristel agreed with this point and
reinforced it by saying that the Dutch government were to initiate, in the years
1986-1990, a system of giving degrees to teachers of informatics. He was sure
that some promotion system was necessary. De Kruif suggested that training new
specialist teachers was very expensive and this may be why there was a call to
integrate the use of computers across the curriculum - it cost less.

Alhstrom asked if there was concern in Israel about the social impact of computers.
Millin replied that social pressure seemed to be asking for informatics to be
taught early. Ahlstrom suggested that at the age of 12 or 13 years students
needed to be told how computers will change society. Morel pointed out that
there was little activity in primary schools. Some children were interested in
computers, but teachers did not know how to use them or the social implications
of informatics.

Wright referred to a previous discussion by pointing out that some universities
in the USA were offering Masters degrees for courses which could take many hours
over two summers to complete. These courses contained some programming element.
Holm suggested that in the present economic climate many teachers were taking
such courses not for promotion but for job security. Kristel pointed out that
job security and promotion were the same thing! Walsted thought that teachers
attending formal extended courses lasting 300/400 hours should be rewarded by
the promotion system, but that shorter informal courses were for personal
development and did not merit promotion. Blakeley informed the group that in
the United Kingdom the British Computer Society had a working party which was
studying a number of diploma/degree courses which did not meet the standards of
the British Computer Society. In the future, teachers of the informatics may
well join professional bodies such as the British Computer Society.

Kristel asked if there was any real connection between education and telecommunication, as there appeared to be in the presentation by Millin. Millin replied
that the real connection was that the same national committee had studied both
aspects of informatics.

Bosler presented some information about informatics in West Germany. It was
based around the following points made by Tinsley:-

                        'Teachers need time.'
The first work in informatics was started 15 years ago in the 17-19 age range.
3-4 years ago a pilot project was started by their being involved in curriculum
development
                        'Students know more than teachers'
This was allowed for by the fact that students were encouraged to select their
own project themes.
A major point in the presentation by Bosler was that:-
'Classical in-service training does not help in the early stages of innovation'.

Watson again raised the question of who trains the teacher trainers. Millin
stated that in Israel, Ben Gurion University in Beer Sheba had taken a leading
role in the training of teachers. There were other teacher training centres
where Government support had helped to encourage the development of software and
support materials. The Ministry of Education also had a department which was
looking into the problem. Koerber indicated that universities in West Germany
were developing teacher training systems by discussion between departments
already involved in teacher training. New ideas are developed and tested on the
students. Broderick stated that in the long term future Informatics will not be
developed by teachers but by government departments. However, in Great Britain,
the Department of Education and Science did not appear to want to do anything.
All was not lost, however, as the Manpower Services Commission had taken over
some of the initiative from the Department of Education and Science. Unfortunately when the Manpower Services Commission take action they do not allow for
teacher training. They have done some good work with private educational centres,
which reinforces a point made previously. Christiaen stated that in Belgium
there was a conflict between specialists who are interested in industrial
development and those who are interested in educational development. In his
opinion, there was not enough emphasis on educational development.

Rapporteurs: Erna Scholtes
Colin Watkins

CLOSING SESSION

REPORT ON DISCUSSION GROUPS

IN THE FIRST ROUND OF DISCUSSIONS THE FOLLOWING QUESTIONS WERE DISCUSSED:

1 Main Themes

    1.1 Informatics Literacy for all Teachers
        Question 1: Should an individual teacher be "more" informatics-
                  literate than an individual citizen; and if so, in what
                  respect and how is this literacy to be attained?

    1.2 Teacher Training for Teachers of Informatics
        Question 2: Teacher training courses in informatics normally
                  include such topics as:
                  programming, machine architecture, etc.
                  Should some or all of the following topics also be
                  included?
                        Social implications
                        Systems analysis
                        Design of (educational) information systems
                        Design of educational software

    1.3 Computer Aided Learning, e.g. Simulation
        Question 3: Should the learner always be in command of the computer
                  and learn through discovery (as advocated by LOGO
                  adherents)?
        Question 4: Will software for computer aided learning be ready-made
                  with a content that cannot be altered, or will it be
                  ready-made "content free" (software)?

    1.4 The Computer as the Tutor/Teacher

    1.5 The Computer's Place in the Management of Learning
        Question 5: Will economic reasons (e.g. machines are cheaper to
                  operate than people) force computers into the
                  educational system as tutor/teachers; if so, how will
                  the teaching be organized and managed?

2 Broad Issues

    2.1 Methodologies of Implementation
        Question 6: Should implementation activities be directed towards
                  the involvement of teachers in their own changing
                  classroom situations and should training strategies
                  follow a pattern of discovery, involvement, self
                  confidence and creativity?

As a result of the first round of discussions, some answers to the questions
posed were formulated and new questions/issues raised.

Discussion Group 1 answered Question 1 as follows:
    Yes: to attain this literacy _more_ managers of resources/learning in
    school are needed, more critical evaluation and awareness of
    possibilities is needed and there is a further need to talk to experts.
    There is _no more need_ of programming skills.

Discussion Group 3 replied to Question 3 thus:
    The answer to this question depends on the students' aim:
    – problem solving
    – having other microworlds
    – assessment to identify weaknesses in students' understanding
    – enhancement of creativity

Discussion Group 4 had the following conclusions with regard to Question 4:

–   The question poses a false dichotomy. There will probably be a
    continuum from software which is "in the can" and allows the teacher
    no flexibility, through to that which offers the teacher considerable
    opportunity for tailoring the interaction to suit his/her classes.
    There needs to be a mix between utilities and traditional CAL.

–   The answer to the question will in part depend upon the assumptions
    that are implicit in the relationship between teachers and students.
    Effective use of computer aided learning will probably demand a less
    formal relationship than has often been the case in the past.

–   Bearing in mind the considerable effort and cost involved in
    producing good software, the balance needs to be in the direction of
    "content free" utilities, which enable the classroom teacher to have
    influence and control over the package ("fine tuning"). Such
    utilities offer two advantages:

    (i)   they can be used more than once; perhaps for a variety of tasks,
          classes and subjects:

    (ii) teachers are more inclined to adopt material when they feel
          involved in its creation.

–   The translation of courseware from one national (spoken) language to
    another poses additional problems. Cultural and linguistic
    differences are most likely to be overcome when software becomes
    sufficiently open-ended to allow teachers to stamp their own
    personality on the package.

In the first round of discussions, questions/issues were formulated for the
second round of discussions. These question/issues were:

1. Deschooling: will it come about?

2. Will the use of computers indeed change the curriculum and the role of
    the teacher?

    2.1 Can we change one facet only of education whilst holding everything
         else constant, or are we really talking about a fundamental change
         in education?
    2.2 If the role of traditional education has been to diminish
         creativity and teach conformity as the mover of the child through
         the system, what will happen if children are put in control of
         their learning environment?
    2.3 Should we need adapt the aims of education to informatics or adapt
         informatics to the aims of education?

A balance needs to be found between changes to the school curriculum, which are <u>forced</u> by advances in information technology and the adoption of information technology only when it serves the needs of the existing curriculum. How do we find that balance?

2.4 How far will the use of computers in education allow examining to take place outside the conventional classroom? What effect would this have on the role of the teacher?

2.5 Does the use of LOGO require more or less involvement with the computer on the part of the teacher? More or less classroom skills? And in a broader perspective: which skills and which tasks will engage the teacher of tomorrow?

2.6 How can education help to develop creative brain power, rather than stereotyped thinking?

3 What strategy is to be pursued in order to produce high—quality software?

3.1 Who should create courseware materials — teachers, software designers, or multi—skilled teams?

3.2 If a team approach is adopted, is it necessary/possible that the balance of control on the team should lie with teachers?

3.3 Are the needs of education so specific that dedicated utility packages are necessary, for example, a spreadsheet package designed specifically for education? Can we use a commercial utility package and simply mask off the parts that are too complex or confusing for students?

3.4 (Related to 2.3)
Will the software drive changes in the curriculum, or will existing curriculum objectives determine the way in which we develop and use software?

3.5 Given the marketing strategies of the computer/software manufacturers and service companies, can we avoid the commercialization of education?

4 Teacher Training for Teachers of Informatics

Some important objectives for teacher training are:
To achieve some understanding of the social, economic, technical and organizational implications of information technology, in order to increase long range understanding of a fast changing high technology society.

The methodology (didactics) of informatics is to be included in teacher training; some part at least of the methodology teaching has to be project—oriented; it is also considered necessary to teach the teacher courses with the same methodology as used in the classroom. This offers teachers the opportunity to reflect on the methodology.

Teachers of informatics have two roles in school: that of an educator and of an adviser and inspirer: teacher training should

therefore provide the teacher with the ability to manage complexity
and to select appropriate methods in view of their roles.
The content of teacher training courses should be dictated by the
need for the teachers to adapt to changing information technology.
This implies the teaching of concepts that are as invariant as
possible.

5 The majority of the school population will end up as users of computing
and Information Technology Systems rather than being involved in their
creation.

What is necessary for this majority group to know? What is necessary for
their teachers to know?

How should the knowledge be incorporated into the curriculum?

In the second round of discussions newly formed discussion groups produced
reactions to these questions/issues.

These reactions formed the input to the discussions in the plenary
discussion session.

Reactions to Question 1:

There is less need for formal education that forces pupils to learn in a
synchronized way.

The general answer is 'yes': there will be deschooling.

Reactions to Question 2:

We must not destroy the confidence of our teachers by rapid change. There
are many changes taking place and we should reinforce open learning by
introducing change with support.

Perhaps the role of the teacher will change only if the teacher trainer
changes his role.

The computer offers opportunities for new types of curricula and methods,
but these have to be taken.

Reactions to Question 3:

The creation of courseware materials should be done by a small team of
multi-skilled people, including an educational psychologist and media-
designer.

In this production, teachers should play a significant role in the early
stages of development and the final evaluation. The production should
include a field test in schools.

Dedicated utility packages are needed for all children. The packages should
be approached from a didactical point of view. Technology, in and out of
school, influences the curriculum and changes the efficiency of teaching.
It might change the philosophy of the curriculum.

One should be aware of commercial influence (e.g. free gifts).

Educational administrators should recognize the force to be dealt with.

Reactions to Question 4:

There should be at least one specialist teacher of informatics in every school. All other teachers should have an awareness of informatics and some of these should be able to teach informatics to an awareness level.

The preparation of such a teaching force is by pre-service as well as in-service training. The subject is substantial and this should be reflected in the amount of time given to an in-service course. One year full time (or its equivalent) is reasonable.

The specialist teacher should engage in some school based in-service training of his/her colleagues.

Reactions to Question 5:

Everyone is an indirect user and some are direct users.

Everyone needs skills/understanding/attitudes with regard to:
Social Implications
Employment
Control (power)
Roles and Relations
Fear
etc.

Technical Implications
Garbage in/Garbage out (validation)
Input/Process/Output Cycle
Man/machine interface
etc.

REPORT ON PLENARY SESSION (Thursday 4.00)

The following plenary session addressed four main issues, de-schooling, technology-driven change, software development issues and teacher trainer problems.

Differing views were expressed by Bosler and Penter on what was meant by de-schooling. Aigner suggested that it might mean more opportunities for few and fewer opportunities for many; there could be more time for social education and self-directed learning, since fewer trained people would be needed in the future. Watson emphasised the shift to ongoing education for all members of society, including teachers.

There was agreement that change is inevitable. Bosler used the analogy of a school of fish following a leader as long as the gap between the school and the leader was not too great. Wills agreed that change needs to be slow, with much support provided for teachers. Social implications (Johansen) and the placing of short-run problems in perspective were mentioned (Bollerslev, Kristjansdottir and Tinsley).Technology is not of itself going to change where we are going (Lee) although it may bring about our goals more efficiently. Tinsley warned against the danger of pre-occupation with technology when teachers were facing other problems such as job security and pupil discipline.

Content-free software would enable the teacher, rather than the software producers, to decide what is taught (Bollerslev); it would also make economic sense (van Weert) and provide students with real-life experience, although some education specific packages would be needed (Raymont). Watson suggested that teachers would not be able to use content-free software without some structured materials to provide a context for their lessons. Tinsley pointed out the dangers of focussing technological emphasis strictly on the curriculum, rather than looking at other areas of development, such as management software.

Many aspects of the problems faced by teacher trainers were touched upon. Bollerslev's suggestion for workshops to produce computer based courseware for use in teacher education raised some doubts that this was feasible on an international level (Raymont) because of cultural differences, although Kristjansdottir felt that small nations especially could benefit from such a workshop. Other resources mentioned were literature produced by world conferences (Tinsley) and sources outside education (commercial organisations); trainers should also be capable of creating their own opportunities for professional development (Hammond).

Models of development do not have to be top-down (Bosler), they can be bottom-up, starting in the classroom (Barker) and even the cascade model is susceptible to recursion with feedback at all levels (Russell). Millin felt that the computer was making us face the deeper issues of teacher attitudes and roles in the classroom. Changing these is likely to be dependent on trainers themselves adopting new roles (Bollerslev), since teachers tend to teach in the way they themselves are taught (Lee), perhaps being influenced most strongly by their own school education (Aigner), which may work against innovation. Positive approaches were suggested by some participants. Trainers should not only use good techniques, for example, guided discovery, but should couple this with a discussion of the accompanying theory (Bollerslev). Bosler mentioned the Stanford 'teaching by laymen' project and Wright pointed out the existence of research which showed that teachers can learn new techniques by practising them with their peers. Finally, Tinsley emphasised the importance of refreshment of the trainers, especially by giving them the opportunity of working in the classroom with innovative teachers.

Barry Blakeley
Dianne Martin

CLOSING ADDRESS

J.D. TINSLEY

At the beginning of the conference, I spoke of the need to retain a healthy criticism of the enthusiast, whose preoccupation with computer systems can mask an appreciation of where those systems can made a real contribution to the educational process. Your discussions and comments have shown how aware we have become of such dangers.

In comparing the variety across the world of organisational arrangements for teacher education, it has been important to focus back on the needs of the individual teacher, who needs time to come to terms with new technology. Your concentration on the best examples of current practice has helped to identify the essential components of all such activity.

We have questioned the quality of educational software and considered the methods of evaluation necessary to prevent new generations of teachers and learners from exposure to the inept. Your pooled experience has shown how important it is to set out our objectives and establish a monitoring system, before embarking on expensive development programmes.

We have tried to set the computer revolution in the historical context of educational development and attempted to determine whether we are seeing a passing phase or a paradigm shift. Your different experiences have given us all a clearer perspective, which will benefit our current work and assist with our future plans.

For me, a phrase will remain long after the rhetoric has lost its impact. In considering questions of definition we talked about "content free" software. This describes a system whereby teachers can create a learning scheme for any discipline, using the computer as a tool like a book or a chalk board. In future perhaps, we should plan to organise "content free" conferences! You have shown by your good fellowship and common understanding that education thrives through personal contact. We must never allow ourselves so to automate the learning process that human interaction is lost. I wish you well for the future and a safe journey home!

CLOSING SESSION

Rapporteurs: R Morel
                E Vincent

The Chairman asked a number of participants who had submitted written comments to speak to them.

Kristel said the conference had covered a wide spectrum, with good results. A future conference might well deal with a small number of fundamental issues, to be discussed in depth.

Kristel also suggested that attention be paid to the proposal for the development of algorithmic application environments, to assist in the teaching of problem solving as an alternative to the use of programming languages.

Raymont stressed that the subject of teacher training must not be dropped. The present conference had largely catalogued existing experience. A way forward would be a conference to consider in depth those areas which had presently been shown to be difficult.

Kristjansdottir was grateful for the number of questions raised during the conference.

Harkins emphasised the importance of facing up to the questions posed by technology and change, difficult though they may be, and exploring ways of answering them.

Penter commented on the excellent spread of people invited, the superb organisation of sessions, his appreciation of those participants who were speaking English not as their first language, and the opportunity to question one's narrow national perspectives and values.

LIST OF PARTICIPANTS

Ahlstrom, K-G
Gravorsgatan 12
58266 LINKOPING
Sweden

Aigner, Helmut
Bundesministerium fur Unterricht und Kunst
Minoritenplatz 5
A1014 VIENNA
Austria

Barker, Peter
Centre for Computer Education
Moray House College of Education
Holyrood Road
EDINBURGH
EH8 8AQ
Scotland

Blakeley, Barry
61 Park Avenue North
LONDON
N8 7RS
UK

Bollerslev, Peter
Rojlevangen 40
2630 TAASTRUP
Denmark

Bosler, Ulrich
IPN
Olshausenstrasse 40/60
D 2300 KIEL
FRG

Camerero, Ernesto Garcia
Moratin 48
MADRID - 14
Spain

Christiaen, Hubert
Katholieke Universiteit Leuven
Kandidatuurcentrum
Celestijnenlaan 200A
B-3030 HEVERLEE
Belgium

Fothergill,Richard
Microelectronics Education Programme
Cheviot House
Coach Lane Campus
NEWCASTLE-UPON-TYNE
NE7 7XA
UK

Friedman, Margaret
Rand Afrikaans University
Department of Computer Science
Auckland Park
JOHANNESBURG
S Africa

Gorny, Peter
Universitat Oldenburg
Postfach 2503
D2900 OLDENBURG
FRG

Hammond, Judith
School of Computing Sciences
New South Wales Institute   of   Technology
PO   Box   123
BROADWAY
New   South   Wales
Australia

Hansen, Kim Foss
Sondergaardsvej   58
DK   3500 Vaerloese
Denmark

Harkins, Dennis
2349 E Vine Street
HATFIELD
PA 19440
USA

Hellawell, David
City of Birmingham Polytechnic
Westbourne Road
BIRMINGHAM
B15 3TN
UK

Holm, Povl
Kildevej 16 B
DK 3300 Frederiksvaerk
Denmark

Johansen, Lars Runo
Skyttenstraede 3
3000 HELSINGOR
Denmark

Johnson, David C
Centre for Science and Mathematics Education
Chelsea College
Bridges Place
LONDON
SW6 4HR
UK

Jones, Ann
Micros in Schools Project
Open "niversity
Walton Hall
MILTON KEYNES
MK7 6AA
UK

Kerner, Immo
Paedagogische Hochschule Dresden
Sektion Mathematik
Wigardstrasse 17
8060 DRESDEN
GDR

Koerber, Bernhard
Freie Universitat Berlin
Z17 SE3
Habelschwerdter Allee 45
D-1000 BERLIN 33
FRG

Kristel, Theo
Sektie Wiskunde en Informatica
NLO Interstudie
Postbus 30011
6503 HN NIJMEGEN
The Netherlands

Kristjansdottir, Anna
Vesturgata 34
101 REYKJAVIK
Iceland

Kruif, Bert de
Centrum voor Onderwijs en Informatietechnologie
Postbus 217
7500 AE ENSCHEDE
Netherlands

Lee, Seeong-Soo
Education Research Service & Computing
University of British Columbia
VANCOUVER
BC V6T 1Z5
Canada

Lewis, Robert
7 Meadowside
LANCASTER
LA1 3AQ
UK

Lovis, Frank
Faculty of Mathematics
The Open University
Walton Hall
MILTON KEYNES
MK7 6AA
UK

Martin, Dianne
Dept. of Electrical Engineering & Computer Science
The George Washington University
WASHINGTON DC 20052
USA

Meisalo, Veijo
Dept. of Teacher Education
University of Helsinki
Ratakatu 2
SF- 00120 HELSINKI 12
Finland

Metrovich, Tom
University of Witwatersrand
Computer-assisted Arithmetic Project
1 Jan Smuts Avenue
Braansfontein 2001
JOHANNESBURG
South Africa

Millin, Daniel
7 Qarqum Street
RAMAT-HSHARON 47247
Israel

Morel, Raymond
CCEES
Case Postale 172
1211 GENEVE 3
Switzerland

Nicholov, Rumen
c/o Professor Todor Boyanov
Centre of Mathematics
Acad Bonchev str bl.8
1113 SOFIA
Bulgaria

Noordhoek-van Leuveren, Margriet
Jan Evertsenstraat 128
1056 EJ AMSTERDAM
Netherlands

O'Shea, Tim
Micros in Schools Project
The Open ''niversity
Walton Hall
MILTON KEYNES
MK7 6AA
UK

Olsen, Birthe
Skovvej 14 B
2750 BALLERUP
Denmark

Penkov, Boyan
Centre of Mathematics
P O Box 373
SOFIA 1090
Bulgaria

Penter, Kevan
Schools Computing Branch
Education Department
150 Royal Street
EAST PERTH
Western Australia 6000

Petursson, Yngvi
Dalsel 15
109 REHKJAVIK
Iceland

Pollak, Richard
Minnesota Educational Computing Consortium
3490 Lexington Avenue North
ST PAUL
MN 55112
USA

Preece, Jenny
Micros in Schools Project
The Open ''niversity
Walton Hall
MILTON KEYNES
MK7 6AA
UK

Puddephat, Michael
Birmingham Polytechnic
Westbourne Road
BIRMINGHAM
B15 3TN
UK

Raymont, Patrick
National Computing Centre
Oxford Road
MANCHESTER
M1 7ED
UK

Reeve, Tim
Education Office
Margaret Street
BIRMINGHAM
B3 3BU
UK

Roux, Jean-Bernard
2 quai Ernest-Ansermet
CH - 1205 GENEVE
Switzerland

Russell, Philip
Microelectronics Education Programme
4 Coleshill Terrace
LLANELLI
Dyfed
SA15 3DB
UK

Salomon, Inge-Lise
Dirchsvej 34 st
DK 2300 COPENHAGEN S
Denmark

Samways, Brian
Birmingham Educational Computing Centre
Bordesley Centre
Stratford Road
BIRMINGHAM
B11 1AR
UK

Scholtes, Erna
Burg Patijnlaan 1268
2585 CJ DEN HAAG
Netherlands

Solms, Sebastian von
Rand Afrikaans University
Department of Computer Science
PO Box 524
JOHANNESBURG
S Africa

Steiger, Thomas
Coordination Office of the Club Schools
Federation of Migros Cooperations
ZÜRICH
Switzerland

Suvilinna, Anja
Koivuviita 4 B
SF-02130 ESPOO 13
Finland

Tagg, Donovan
1 Newmarket Avenue
LANCASTER
LA1 4NG
UK

Taylor, Robert
Teachers College
Columbia University
NEW YORK
NY 10027
USA

Tinsley, David
Education Office
Margaret Street
BIRMINGHAM
CB3 3BU
UK

Turnbull,John
National Computing Centre
Oxford Road
MANCHESTER
M1 7ED
UK

Varga, Laszlo
University of L Eotvos
Department of Mathematics
H-1084 BUDAPEST
Hungary

Vincent, Eric
Faculty of Education
University of Birmingham
PO Box 363
BIRMINGHAM
B15 2TT
UK

Walker, David
Scottish Microelectronics Development Programme
Dowanhill
74 Victoria Crescent Road
GLASGOW
G12 9JN
Scotland

Walstad, Jon
0 Dordihaugen 1
7300 ORKANGER
Norway

Watkins, Colin
Birmingham Educational Computing Centre
Bordesley Centre
Stratford Road
BIRMINGHAM
B11 1AR
UK

Watson, Deryn
Educational Computing Section
Chelsea College
552 Kings Road
Chelsea
LONDON
SW10
UK

Weert,Tom van
Stichting Lerarenopleiding "Ubbo Emmius"
PO Box 2056
9704 CB GRONINGEN
The Netherlands

Wibe, Jan
Nyheimsvn 22A
7058 JAKOBSLI
Norway

Wills, Russel
Dundee College of Education
Gardyne Road
Brougty Ferry
DUNDEE
DD5 1NY
Scotland

Wright, June
Centre for Young Children
College of Education
University of Maryland
COLLEGE PARK
MD 20742
USA